JOURNAL FOR THE STUDY OF THE NEW TESTAMENT
SUPPLEMENT SERIES
47

Executive Editor, Supplement Series
David Hill

Publishing Editor
David E. Orton

JSOT Press
Sheffield

JAMES and
the Q SAYINGS
of JESUS

Patrick J. Hartin

Journal for the Study of the New Testament
Supplement Series 47

Copyright © 1991 Sheffield Academic Press

Published by JSOT Press
JSOT Press is an imprint of
Sheffield Academic Press Ltd
The University of Sheffield
343 Fulwood Road
Sheffield S10 3BP
England

Printed on acid-free paper in Great Britain
by Billing & Sons Ltd
Worcester

British Library Cataloguing in Publication Data

Hartin, Patrick J.
    James and the "Q" sayings of Jesus.
    1. Bible. N.T.—Historicity. Literary sources
    I. Title   II. Series
    225.66

    ISBN 1-85075-267-2
    ISSN 0143-5108

CONTENTS

Preface   7
Abbreviations   9

PART I: JAMES AND WISDOM

Chapter 1
LIGHT ON THE EPISTLE OF JAMES   12
  1. The Scope of the Investigation   12
  2. Divergent Approaches on the Literary Character
    of the Epistle of James   14
  3. The Composition of the Epistle of James   23
  4. The Wisdom Context of James   35

Chapter 2
THE ROLE OF WISDOM IN JAMES AND Q: PARAENETICAL ADVICE   44
  1. The Approach Adopted to Q   45
  2. The Wisdom Genre of Q   52
  3. The Wisdom Character of James and Q:
    Practical Advice and Form of Expression   59

Chapter 3
THE NATURE OF WISDOM IN JAMES   81
  1. Faith, Steadfastness and Wisdom: Pericopae B and C (1.2-8)   81
  2. Belief in Jesus, the Lord of Glory and the
    Wisdom of God: Pericope G (2.1-13)   89
  3. The Wisdom from Above: Pericope J (3.13-18)   97
  4. The Significance of This Investigation   113

Chapter 4
THE PERSONIFICATION OF WISDOM IN Q   116
  1. Wisdom's Role of Doom (Lk. 11.49-51; Mt. 23.34-36)   116
  2. Wisdom's Children and Wisdom in the Market Place
    (Lk. 7.31-35; Mt. 11.16-19)   122
  3. Jerusalem Killing the Prophets (Lk. 13.34-35; Mt. 23.37-39)   126
  4. Thanksgiving and Revelation (Lk. 10.21-22; Mt. 11.25-27)   128
  5. Greater than the Wisdom of Solomon (Lk. 11.31; Mt. 12.42)   131
  6. The Development of the Personification of Wisdom
    in the Jesus Traditions   132
  7. James and Q: Reflection on the Nature of Wisdom   134

PART II: TEXTUAL RELATIONS BETWEEN JAMES
AND THE JESUS TRADITION

Chapter 5
JAMES AND THE SERMON ON THE MOUNT/PLAIN:
  A COMPARATIVE EXAMINATION   140
  1. Chart of Correspondences between James
     and the Synoptic Tradition   141
  2. James and the Q Sermon on the Mount/Plain   144

Chapter 6
JAMES AND THE JESUS TRADITIONS: A COMPARATIVE
  EXAMINATION OF SOME FURTHER SPECIFIC TEXTS   173
  1. James and Further Contact with Q   173
  2. James and Further Contact with the
     Matthean Community Traditions   187
  3. James and Contact with the Gospel of Luke   192
  4. More General Parallels between James and the
     Jesus Tradition   195

Chapter 7
THE WISDOM THEME OF PERFECTION IN JAMES
  AND THE JESUS TRADITIONS   199
  1. The Call to Perfection (Jas 1.4; Mt. 5.48)   199
  2. Perfection and the Law of Love   207
  3. Perfection Comes through the Gift of God's Wisdom   210
  4. The Ethical Lifestyle of the One Seeking Perfection   214
  5. Conclusion   215

PART III: RECONSTRUCTION

Chapter 8
A VISION OF THE EMERGENCE OF JAMES WITHIN THE
  EARLY CHRISTIAN COMMUNITY   220
  1. The Q Community   220
  2. The Matthean Community   227
  3. The Epistle of James in the Context of the
     Early Christian Communities   233
  4. The Results of this Study   240

Appendixes   245
Bibliography   247
Index of Ancient References   256
Index of Authors   265

This work undertakes an investigation into the relationship of the Epistle of James to the traditions of early Christianity, namely the wisdom tradition and the Jesus tradition known as the Q source.

Part I investigates the relationship of James and Q to the wisdom tradition. A compositional analysis of the epistle reveals the role and importance that wisdom plays within the epistle. Wisdom plays an equally important part within the Q tradition and it is judged to be an important connecting link between James and Q. *Part II* examines the relationship of James to the Jesus tradition of the Q source. The chief concern will be a textual investigation of possible connections between James and the various Jesus traditions. *Part III* presents the results of the above investigation by situating James within the context of the world of early Christianity and relates the epistle to the development of the concept of wisdom in early Christianity.

As a consequence of the examination light will be shed on some of the more perplexing and disputed issues related to the epistle. The aim is to re-instate James to the position that it should hold as an important witness to the faith of the early Christian community and to the influence the teachings of Jesus exercise on it.

This work was originally submitted as a thesis for a Doctor of Theology degree in the New Testament at the University of South Africa (Pretoria) in 1988. It was entitled *James: A New Testament Wisdom Writing and its Relationship to Q*. I wish to thank the University of South Africa for granting permission to publish my thesis in this revised form. Above all I wish to express my gratitude to Dr David Hill for his help and encouragement in adapting the style and presentation from that of a formal treatise to that of a readable book. Thanks too are expressed to my thesis promoter, Professor Isak du Plessis, of the University of South Africa, for the guidance he gave me throughout the whole project.

Finally, I should like to thank my typist, Celia McKay, for the painstaking way in which she undertook the task. To all who have encouraged and challenged me over the years I wish to express my gratitude.

Patrick J. Hartin
University of South Africa, Pretoria
April 1990

ABBREVIATIONS

BEThL	*Bibliotheca Ephemeridum Theologicarum Lovaniensium*
BiTod	*Bible Today*
BT	*Bible Translator*
BJRL	*Bulletin of the John Rylands Library*
BZ	*Biblische Zeitschrift*
CBQ	*Catholic Biblical Quarterly*
ET	*Expository Times*
EThL	*Ephemerides Theologicae Lovanienses*
ETR	*Etudes Théologiques et Religieuses*
EvQ	*Evangelical Quarterly*
EvTh	*Evangelische Theologie*
Exp.	*Expositor*
GOTR	*Greek Orthodox Theological Review*
HR	*History of Religions*
HThR	*Harvard Theological Review*
Interp.	*Interpretation*
IThQ	*Irish Theological Quarterly*
JAAR	*Journal of the American Academy of Religion*
JAOS	*Journal of the American Oriental Society*
JBC	*Jerome Biblical Commentary*
JBL	*Journal of Biblical Literature*
JETS	*Journal of the Evangelical Theological Society*
JR	*Journal of Religion*
JRT	*Journal of Religious Thought*
JTC	*Journal for Theology and the Church*
JTS	*Journal of Theological Studies*
JTSA	*Journal of Theology for Southern Africa*
LTP	*Laval Théologique et Philosophique*
NJDTh	*Neue Jahrbücher für Deutsche Theologie*
NT	*Novum Testamentum*
NTS	*New Testament Studies*

RestQ	*Restoration Quarterly*
RExp	*Review and Expositor*
RHR	*Revue de l'Histoire des Religions*
RHT	*Revue d'Histoire des Textes*
RThPh	*Revue de Théologie et de Philosophie*
RTK	*Roczniki Teologiczno-kanoniczne*
ScEc	*Sciences Ecclésiastiques*
SJTh	*Scottish Journal of Theology*
ST	*Studia Theologica*
SWJT	*Southwestern Journal of Theology*
TDNT	*Theological Dictionary of the New Testament*
Theol.	*Theology*
ThEv	*Theologia Evangelica*
ThGl	*Theologie und Glaube*
ThLBl	*Theologisches Literaturblatt*
ThLZ	*Theologische Literaturzeitung*
ThZ	*Theologische Zeitschrift*
TS	*Theological Studies*
TynB	*Tyndale Bulletin*
USQR	*Union Seminary Quarterly Review*
ZNW	*Zeitschrift für die neutestamentliche Wissenschaft und die Kunde der älteren Kirche*
ZThK	*Zeitschrift für Theologie und Kirche*

PART I

JAMES AND WISDOM

Chapter 1

LIGHT ON THE EPISTLE OF JAMES

1. *The Scope of the Investigation*

The Epistle of James is an enigmatic writing. It has provoked divergent attitudes on practically every question raised concerning it. Basic issues of introduction, such as authorship, date of writing and even literary form, have not been solved with complete unanimity. Attitudes among scholars have ranged from assigning to the letter the position of being the earliest writing of the New Testament to that of being the latest, appearing long after the writings of Paul.

This investigation does not aim at examining *per se* these questions of introduction, but, as a result of the direction undertaken, light will be thrown on these puzzling questions. This study, instead, aims at situating the Epistle of James within the thought and traditions of early Christianity. Consequently, two important relationships form the focus of consideration. First, since a compositional analysis of this writing shows that wisdom plays an essential role throughout, the investigation sets out to examine James[1] as a wisdom writing. Seen in this way James accords with that ancient Jewish literary form of wisdom writing which provided a bridge between the Old and New Testaments.

Secondly, in situating James within the context of early Christianity, its relationship to the Q-source needs to be carefully examined. Since Q has strong wisdom tendencies and themes, wisdom provides the initial key for interpreting both James and Q and establishing a connection between them.

---

1. Through this monograph 'James' will refer either to the Epistle of James or to the author without intending to accept a particular person as the author.

James's connection with wisdom and Q has been the subject of different studies undertaken especially over the course of the last few decades.[1] To my mind, however, a completely satisfactory picture has not emerged. An all-inclusive picture of James is needed whereby it is firmly situated in the context of the early church and shown to belong to that wisdom trajectory which extends from the Old Testament wisdom writings through the intertestamental period to the Q source and culminates in the Gospel of Thomas and other Gnostic writings. With this wisdom trajectory as a backdrop one must try to situate or pinpoint exactly where James belongs. This has not yet been satisfactorily proposed. For example, although Hoppe[2] has undertaken a useful investigation, among other things, of the wisdom themes in James and has made an inquiry into its connection with the Jesus tradition, he does not really try to pinpoint the exact relationship of James to Q or to Matthew. Another weakness of most of the investigations into the relationship between James and wisdom has been their failure to observe the role which wisdom plays within the very structure of James. This is an essential point for investigation: it is through an examination of the structure of James that the major themes and purpose of the writing emerge.

A picture of James unfolds which shows the writing to be at the very heart of the wisdom tradition. At the same time the exact relationship of James to Q and the early Christian traditions will be investigated. James stands out not as a writing on the periphery of the New Testament, but as one at the very centre. In line with the wisdom tradition extending from the Old Testament through into the New, James differs from Old Testament wisdom in that the New Testament faith has also exercised a decisive influence on it.

1. Such as R. Hoppe, *Der theologische Hintergrund des Jakobusbriefes* (Würzburg: Echter, 1977); and C.N. Dillman, 'A Study of Some Theological and Literary Comparisons of the Gospel of Matthew and the Epistle of James' (PhD thesis, University of Edinburgh, 1978).

2. Hoppe, *Der theologische Hintergrund des Jakobusbriefes.*

2. *Divergent Approaches on the Literary Character of the Epistle of James*

A number of important scholars stand out as having influenced very significantly the study of this epistle, as will be seen below.

2.1 *A much-neglected writing*

Among the writings of the New Testament the Epistle of James has tended to receive the least attention. This has been its fate from the very beginning: it was only universally accepted as part of the Christian canon in the fourth century AD.[1] Disinterest and distrust of this writing started again at the time of the Protestant Reformation. Luther judged the epistle harshly. In the Preface to the New Testament of 1522 he writes:

> In a word St. John's Gospel and his first epistle, St. Paul's epistles, especially Romans, Galatians, and Ephesians, and St. Peter's first epistle are the books that show you Christ and teach you all that is necessary and salvatory for you to know, even if you were never to see or hear any other book or doctrine. Therefore St. James' epistle is really an epistle of straw, compared to these others, for it has nothing of the nature of the gospel about it.[2]

Because it did set forth God's Law, Luther attributed some value to the epistle.[3] His main objection, however, came from his view that it was opposed to Paul's doctrine of justification by faith alone, which he considered to be of central importance.[4] A further argument against this writing was based on the absence of any mention in it of the central Christian teaching of the suffering and death of Jesus.[5] In printing the Bible, Luther put James together with Jude, Hebrews and Revelation at the end. He showed his disdain for it further by

---

1. F. Mussner, *Der Jakobusbrief: Auslegung* (4th edn, Freiburg: Herder, 1981), 42.
2. M. Luther, *Luther's Works: Word and Sacrament* I (vol. 35, ed. E.T. Backmann; Philadelphia: Fortress, 1960), 362.
3. *Ibid.*, 395.
4. *Ibid.*, 396.
5. *Ibid.*

giving no numbers to it in his table of contents.[1] In his special preface to the Epistle of James, Luther concluded his arguments:

> In a word, he wanted to guard against those who relied on faith without works, but was unequal to the task. He tries to accomplish by harping on the law what the apostles accomplish by stimulating people to love. Therefore I cannot include him among the chief books, though I would not prevent anyone from including or extolling him as he pleases, for there are otherwise many good sayings in him.[2]

This negative assessment had far reaching consequences on the attitudes of biblical scholars to James. This influence has lasted right up to the present century.[3]

2.2 A pre-Christian document

Two influential works appeared at the end of the last century by Massebieau[4] and Spitta.[5] Originally produced independently, they came to the same conclusions. They located the origin of the Epistle of James in a Jewish *Grundschrift* and saw the references to Jesus Christ as later Christian insertions.

The first reference to Jesus Christ occurs in the opening verse Ἰάκωβος θεοῦ καὶ κυρίου Ἰησοῦ Χριστοῦ δοῦλος. Massiebieau bracketed Ἰησοῦ Χριστοῦ, while Spitta bracketed

---

1. *Ibid.*, 394 n. 43.

2. *Ibid.*, 397.

3. The authority of Luther in this regard far outstripped the influence of Calvin who adopted a much more positive approach to this writing. J. Calvin (*Commentaries on the Catholic Epistles* [trans. & ed. J. Owen; Grand Rapids: Eerdmans, 1959], 276) could find no reason for rejecting it in the way in which Luther did. Instead, Calvin actually assigned great value to the Epistle of James. He focused attention on the practical teaching which had a relevance for everyday existence. This relevance applied to almost every aspect of the Christian life (Calvin, *Commentaries*, 276-77). Despite Calvin's positive assessment, as well as the insight he had with regard to James's emphasis on the Law of God, it was Luther's attitude to James which was to predominate in the history of the Church.

4. L. Massebieau, 'L'Épître de Jacques est-elle l'œuvre d'un chrétien?' *RHR* 32 (1895), 249-83.

5. F. Spitta, 'Der Brief des Jakobus', in his *Zur Geschichte und Litteratur des Urchristentums* (Göttingen: Vandenhoeck & Ruprecht, 1896), II, 1-239.

the whole expression καὶ κυρίου Ἰησοῦ Χριστοῦ making the
sentence read simply θεοῦ δοῦλος, which appears in Tit. 1.1.[1]
In the second reference to Jesus Christ, μὴ ἐν προσωποληψίαις
ἔχετε τὴν πίστιν τοῦ κυρίου (ἡμῶν Ἰησοῦ Χριστοῦ) τῆς δόξης
(2.1), Mayor[2] points out that if the words in brackets were
omitted, the sentence would read easily, but with the insertion
of the words it becomes very difficult to understand clearly.
Examination and argument over these two verses proves
nothing conclusively. Christian interpolation can only be
proved from an examination of the whole epistle. If an attempt
was being made to 'christianize' a Jewish document, would it
be limited to two simple insertions—surely it would be appar-
ent elsewhere as well? But, this is not the case.[3] The strongest
argument against this view is the numerous echoes that
appear throughout James of the other New Testament writings, especially the Gospels. More attention will be devoted to
this in later chapters.

Although this view of Massebieau and Spitta did not gain
much support, Meyer revived the concept of an original Jewish document in his 1930 thesis *Das Rätsel des Jacobusbriefes*.[4]
Meyer argued that the Epistle of James was originally a Jewish writing similar to the *Testaments of the Twelve Patriarchs*. It based itself on Genesis 49 as its example where Jacob
addressed his twelve sons in the diaspora and gave them his
blessing. James has written in this genre of an address to the
twelve tribes in the dispersion.[5] Originally a Jewish document,
this *Grundschrift* was later christianized. This editing has
made it difficult to unravel the original Jewish document.[6]
Meyer's emphasis on interpreting James from a Jewish background is most valuable. I think his position in trying to con-
nect James with the wisdom tradition is very important. For

1. J.B. Mayor, *The Epistle of St. James: The Greek Text with Introduction, Notes, Comments and Further Studies in the Epistle of James*
(3rd edn; Grand Rapids: Zondervan, [1913] 1954), cxciv.
2. *Ibid.*, cxciii.
3. *Ibid.*, cxcv.
4. A. Meyer, *Das Rätsel des Jacobusbriefes* (Giessen: Töpelmann,
1930).
5. *Ibid.*, 176.
6. *Ibid.*, 167.

him the Epistle of James lies closer to the wisdom tradition than to Greek thought.[1]

Meyer's identification of James, however, with a Jewish letter to the twelve tribes, along the lines of the *Testaments of the Twelve Patriarchs*, appears extremely forced. His attempt to identify the onomastic allegorical references made to the sons of Jacob is very tendentious and somewhat farfetched. In addition, the argument for Christian insertions or changes really does not withstand a careful examination of the writing, because so many echoes of the Christian Gospel, particularly the teaching of Jesus, appear through the letter.

Meyer's thesis has not received much support from scholars. An interesting exercise was the attempt made by Easton[2] to endorse it. In doing so he pointed out as well the weaknesses in this view. One major failing was the attempt to identify the allusions to Jacob's sons. He argued rightly that if it had been originally a Jewish document, as Meyer defined it, the allusions to the Twelve Patriarchs should shine through more forcefully than was in fact the case.[3] Easton limited the thesis of Meyer to that of the opening and closing sections of the epistle where according to him the Jewish letter of Jacob was still preserved. While Easton began with the intention of supporting the thesis of Meyer, in fact he ended up by accepting what Meyer[4] opposed, namely that James was to be understood as a Greek diatribe more than Jewish paraenesis.

2.3 *Greek influence on James*

2.3.1 *J.H. Ropes*[5] published his commentary on James largely as an attempt to correct the thesis advocated by Massebieau and Spitta. He tried to support the contention that James could only be understood stylistically from the standpoint of the Greek diatribe. Instead of postulating a Jewish document that

1. *Ibid.*, 168.
2. B.S. Easton, 'The Epistle of James: Introduction and Exegesis', in *The Interpreter's Bible in Twelve Volumes* (ed. G. Buttrick; New York: Abingdon, 1957), 10.
3. *Ibid.*, 11.
4. Meyer, *Das Rätsel des Jacobusbriefes*, 168.
5. J. Ropes, *A Critical and Exegetical Commentary on the Epistle of St. James* (Edinburgh: T. & T. Clark, 1916).

was christianized, Ropes argued for a thoroughly Christian writing right from the beginning. This document, according to Ropes,[1] had used the literary form of the Greek diatribe and was written after AD 70 to Greek speaking Jewish Christians in Palestine. Essentially the diatribe is a special form of the Hellenistic popular moral address. As such it had been in evidence since the time of Socrates, but was popularized by Diogenes in the fourth century BC and by Bion of Borysthenes (around 280 BC) who was viewed for many centuries as the founder of the style.[2] In the course of the Roman Empire it became a real art form in which people were assiduously trained. The Stoics used this form and style to great effect. Characteristic of the Greek diatribe, according to Ropes,[3] is a somewhat broken dialogue in which a person faces questioning.

In an extensive examination of the epistle Ropes[4] gives innumerable examples of expressions which correspond to the style and vocabulary of the Greek diatribe. An examination of the examples given reveals that he is trying to force James into a straightjacket, namely that of the diatribe. Ropes appears to operate with a presupposition which he sets out in order to justify an examination of the epistle. There is a methodological fallacy in this: instead of allowing the epistle to speak for itself, James is viewed through the tinted glasses of the presupposition that the Greek diatribe style is operative throughout. The conclusion to which Ropes comes is that James is not a letter nor an epistle, but a 'literary tract'.[5]

Although Ropes is arguing for literary dependence and is not discussing the conceptual or thought aspect, he sees James as having a close affinity with the Jewish wisdom writings.[6] But, with regard to the way or mode in which this thought is expressed, the Greek diatribe, in his opinion, serves to provide the source for James.[7]

1. *Ibid.*, 48.
2. *Ibid.*, 10.
3. *Ibid.*, 12.
4. *Ibid.*, 13.
5. *Ibid.*, 6.
6. *Ibid.*, 16.
7. *Ibid.*, 17.

2.3.2 *M. Dibelius*[1] attempts to build on the work of Ropes, but
endeavours to take his study along a new direction. He issues a
warning about identifying James totally with the Greek diatribe: 'Consequently, despite the stylistic kinship, James cannot
be classified without further ado as a diatribe'.[2] At the same
time Dibelius considers it impossible to view James as an
actual letter because 'there are also no *epistolary remarks* of
any sort'.[3] Instead, he characterizes James as paraenesis,
which he defines as a joining together of isolated sayings which
deal with ethical conduct.

> By paraenesis we mean a text which strings together admoni-
> tions of general ethical content. Paraenetic sayings ordinarily
> address themselves to a specific (though perhaps fictional) audi-
> ence, or at least appear in the form of a command or summons.
> It is this factor which differentiates them from the *gnomolo-
> gium*, which is merely a collection of maxims.[4]

Prime examples of Christian paraenesis (besides James) are
Hebrews 13, the *Epistle of Barnabas*, as well as the *Didache*.
Connected to this category are undoubtedly the sayings of
Jesus, especially the Q source. The interest in paraenetical
material was delivered in the first instance from the example
of Judaism in its missionary activities in the diaspora where it
provided much-needed ethical instruction for the new proselytes.[5] This type of instruction had its roots in the long and
important tradition of wisdom teaching in Judaism which
preoccupied itself with the art of living. According to Dibelius
this paraenesis emerged when the wisdom literature no
longer expressed itself in poetry but in prose.[6] The author of
James was not influenced directly by Greek writings. Instead,
the influence of the diatribe came via Judaism. In this way
Dibelius accepts a part of Ropes's thesis, but limits the signifi-

1. M. Dibelius, *James: A Commentary on the Epistle of James* (trans.
from the German *Der Brief des Jakobus*, 11th rev. edn prepared by H.
Greeven [1964], English trans. M.A. Williams, ed. H. Koester for
Hermeneia; Philadelphia: Fortress, 1975).
2. *Ibid.*, 38.
3. *Ibid.*
4. *Ibid.*, 3.
5. *Ibid.*, 4.
6. *Ibid.*

cance of the Greek diatribe to an indirect influence through Jewish writings.

Dibelius sees evidence of the characteristic features of paraenetical literature throughout James.[1] First, the letter is decidedly eclectic, being ready to use as its source all types of material, not limiting itself to one particular source. A second observable feature is the lack of continuity: no unity of thought or content can be traced in this writing. Instead catchwords are used to establish a connection between the separate sections. Finally, the various moral exhortations do not arise out of any specific situation or context. In fact one is not able to establish the *Sitz im Leben* for the admonitions.

Ever since its first appearance in 1921 Dibelius's commentary has had an influence on studies of James. In fact it is probably true to say that it has had more influence and has been more widely read than any other commentary on James. The views advanced by Dibelius have, in many instances, tended to be accepted without much challenge.

One serious problem is that Dibelius tends to see paraenesis arising in isolation from the *Sitz im Leben* of the community. He wishes to maintain its generally orientated character. Recent investigations into the nature of paraenesis have tended to call this into question. In the supplementary volume of the *Interpreter's Dictionary of the Bible*, Schroeder[2] draws attention to four important life-settings out of which the New Testament paraenesis emerged: (a) The setting in Jesus' life; (b) the oral tradition of the early Church applying the significance of the life and teaching of Jesus to their circumstances; (c) apostolic instructions arising from problems of particular churches and (d) opinions given in reply to specific circumstances.

With this in mind it is important to investigate the origin of the paraenesis of James. The need and life situation of the community provide a clear starting-point. The importance

1. *Ibid.*, 5.
2. D. Schroeder, 'Paraenesis', in *The Interpreter's Dictionary of the Bible: Supplementary Volume* (ed. K. Crim; Nashville: Abingdon, 1976), 643.

given to advice on relations between rich and poor indicates the need for direction in this area owing to the difficulties caused by these divisions within the community. Further, more importance needs to be given to the suggestion that the origin of the paraenesis in James lies in sayings of Jesus himself.

That paraenesis can be traced back to Jewish wisdom literature is a very important insight. Dibelius has corrected the rather one-sided view of Ropes who tried to emphasize the direct Greek stylistic influence upon James. What was essentially an aspect of Jewish wisdom literature was adapted to a Christian milieu. As Dibelius observes: 'The situation would be sufficiently explained by the fact that James, as a Christian teacher, had to pass on moral admonitions to the communities, and that a part of these admonitions had originated in Jewish paraenesis used for the instruction of proselytes'.[1] In the New Testament paraenesis is an essential part of Christian wisdom literature, which has its roots in the Jewish wisdom tradition.

2.4 *A Jewish–Christian document*

What has emerged so far is that James is not simply a Jewish document that has been christianized, but is a Christian writing first and foremost. At the same time the investigations of Ropes and Dibelius and our assessment of them have shown that James is more understandable if it is viewed as part of the Jewish wisdom tradition of which paraenesis was an essential part. In saying this, one is not maintaining that it is a Jewish document, but that the author of this epistle expresses the Christian message in a way which corresponds to the Jewish wisdom tradition. Jesus himself used Jewish wisdom and paraenesis to express his message, and the Epistle of James clearly continues this tradition.

The Jewish element in the method of James's instruction has been emphasized more emphatically by other studies. For example, Carrington states that 'in James we are in a rabbinic school of the type of Ecclesiasticus transfigured by the *torah* of

---

1. Dibelius, *James*, 26.

the Sermon on the Mount'.[1] James is presented as holding the position of an important teacher within his own school. In this way James again resembles the Jewish wisdom tradition. At the same time much of the style of address in James conforms to the method of speaking of the prophets of Israel. In this connection Wifstrand has made an important contribution by drawing attention to the style of apostrophe in James and seeing its connection to that of the prophetic oracles.[2] A further connection with the prophets and wisdom literature is evidenced by the concern shown in Jas 1.27 for widows and orphans. It is a particular concern of the prophets (Mal. 3.5) to have a care for widows and orphans, and this concern also emerges often in the wisdom tradition (Job 29.12-13 and Sir. 4.10).

Fundamentally a Christian writing, the Epistle of James uses the style of Jewish wisdom literature as well as the prophetic tradition to convey its message of moral exhortation and instruction. In stressing these Jewish roots one is not by any means denying its Christian heritage. It merely emphasizes that it is a writing emanating from a Jewish-Christian environment: written by a Jewish Christian for a Jewish-Christian community. At the same time its roots also lie in the very teaching of Jesus, as is borne out by the very large number of echoes of Jesus' teaching. This clearly emerges from a study of the comparison of James to the Q document.

James is the Jewish-Christian document par excellence of the New Testament. It is Jewish-Christian in that it expresses the combined message of Jesus Christ through the Jewish tradition of wisdom, the prophets and their style of expression. It is also Jewish-Christian in that it is written by a Jewish-Christian for Jewish-Christian readers. Viewed in this light the beauty and richness of the Epistle emerge. This study will attempt to allow these two aspects to emerge more fully by showing James as a Christian wisdom writing as well as drawing out its connection with Q and the teachings of Jesus

---

1. P. Carrington, *The Primitive Christian Catechism: A Study in the Epistles* (Cambridge: Cambridge University Press, 1940), 28.
2. A. Wifstrand, 'Stylistic Problems in the Epistles of James and Peter', *ST* 1 (1948), 177.

Christ. All too often in the past this richness of the Epistle of James has failed to emerge, because scholars have been too intent on approaching James from an exclusive and one-sided position. James is not a writing to which the expression *either... or* applies. Rather the expression *not only... but also* helps to unravel and clarify the range of its richness.

3. *The Composition of the Epistle of James*

By composition I understand how the writing holds together. Every writing has a composition of its own and an understanding of this composition enables one to come to a clearer interpretation. As this study is concerned largely with an interpretation of the Epistle of James as a whole, as well as with an investigation of selected passages, it is essential to spell out the approach and attitude adopted towards its composition. Almost every commentary or book on the Epistle of James presents its own division or outline. One can in fact note a twofold attitude towards the outline of James. First, there are those who deny any form of preconceived plan in the epistle. The approach of Dibelius to this epistle is very much along these lines.[1] He sees no continuity of thought running through the letter at all.

Secondly, there are those who have tried to discover some form of overall unity in the writing. An example of such an all-encompassing plan is that of Shepherd who divides the epistle into 'eight homiletic-didactic discourses',[2] each being built around a saying or macarism, which the author has used to suit his theme. Many attractive divisions or outlines have been presented, like that of Shepherd. Unfortunately, none of these has been able to win any measure of agreement, because of the very subjective nature of most of them.

An examination of the structure of this writing does provide a key to unlock and understand the composition of James. The method of discourse analysis is a useful way of gaining an insight into the text through the attempt to discover the deeper

1. Dibelius, *James*, 6.
2. M. Shepherd, 'The Epistle of James and the Gospel of Matthew', *JBL* 75 (1956), 41-42.

structure behind the text.[1] Attention will be given to the results of this analysis to illustrate two points: the epistolary nature of James as well as the main themes of this writing, with the wisdom perspective emerging as essential to both. This approach enables one to unlock the composition of James and at the same time avoids the charge of subjectivism.

3.1 *The epistolary composition of James*

Funk observed that 'relatively little has been achieved in establishing the form and structure of the early Christian letter'.[2] This is a very negative assessment and is perhaps unfair to the number of studies that have appeared sporadically during the course of this century. Complete unanimity has not been achieved concerning the form and structure of the Christian letter. Nevertheless, contributions have been made to enable one to appreciate its form and structure. Roberts has given a good overview of the studies made into the form and structure of the letter over the course of the centuries.[3] His survey shows that it is mainly in the epistles of Paul that these studies have tended to operate. The most noteworthy investigations were undertaken in the early decades of this century by Exler[4] and Schubert.[5]

1. As a method of approach for translating and interpreting the Bible, discourse analysis gained great support in the 1970s among South African New Testament scholars such as J.P. Louw ('Discourse Analysis and the Greek New Testament', *BT* 24 [1973], 101-18), and A.B. du Toit ('The Significance of Discourse Analysis for New Testament Interpretation and Translation', *Neotestamentica* 8 [1974], 54-79). A discourse analysis of the Epistle of James can be found in my thesis (P. Hartin, 'James: A New Testament Wisdom Writing and its Relationship to Q' [DTh thesis, University of South Africa, 1988]). Appendix 1 and 2 contain the important results of this analysis.

2. R.W. Funk, 'The Form and Structure of II and III John', *JBL* 86 (1967), 424.

3. J.H. Roberts, 'Transitional Techniques to the Letter Body in the Corpus Paulinum', in *A South African Perspective on the New Testament: Essays by South African New Testament Scholars Presented to Bruce Manning Metzger during his Visit to South Africa in 1985* (ed. J.H. Petzer & P.J. Hartin; Leiden: Brill, 1986), 187-88.

4. F.X.J. Exler, *The Form of the Ancient Greek Letter: A Study in Greek Epistolography* (Washington: Catholic University of America, 1923).

The structure of the Hellenistic letter, which Paul adapted so successfully for his communication to the churches, is generally seen to comprise four major elements:

(a) Opening formula, incorporating the names of the sender, addressees and a word of greeting;
(b) Thanksgiving formula;
(c) Body of the letter;
(d) Final greetings.[1]

Using this structure and applying it to writings other than those of Paul led some scholars to conclude that writings such as James and 1 John lack the form of a letter or epistle. Dibelius rejected the epistolary genre of James on precisely these grounds, namely that the fourfold elements of a Hellenistic–Pauline letter could not be demonstrated.[2] This judgment is too restrictive. The error is that a too fixed and rigid concept of the structure of a Hellenistic letter is being used. As so often in New Testament studies the approach of Paul is used as the only normative approach. In fact, the structure of a Hellenistic letter was a much richer feature than is generally acknowledged because of the limitations placed upon it by restricting the consideration to the writings of Paul. A very interesting and important contribution to the understanding of the form of a letter is an article by Francis on the opening and closing paragraphs of James and 1 John.[3] In what follows attention will be given to the findings of this article.

3.1.1 *The opening formula (Jas 1.1)*
An examination of the opening verse shows that it confirms very accurately to the normal structure of the Hellenistic-Roman letter of that period. The name of the sender and those to whom the letter is addressed are clearly stated at the beginning. The simple infinitive χαίρειν expresses the greetings normally accompanying any letter of that period. All these are

5. P. Schubert, *Form and Function of the Pauline Thanksgivings* (Berlin: Töpelmann, 1939).
1. J.A. Fitzmyer, 'New Testament Epistles', *JBC* 2 (1970), 224-25.
2. Dibelius, *James*, 2.
3. F. Francis, 'The Form and Function of the Opening and Closing Paragraphs of James and 1 John', *ZNW* 61 (1970), 110-26.

basic features evident in the style of letter writing of that era. James goes even further to illustrate his dependence upon this formal structure by forging a bond between this opening formula and the pericope which follows. This bond is established by means of the similar words χαίρειν (v. 1) and χαράν (v. 2). This remains faithful to the method of the Hellenistic-Roman letter in uniting the two pericopae in some way.[1] James has shown that he has used the opening formula in a manner characteristic of the Hellenistic-Roman letter.

3.1.2 *Introductory formulae expressing themes of the epistle (Jas 1.2-27)*

Here James diverges radically from the hitherto acknowledged form of the Pauline letter. A *thanksgiving* section normally occurs between the opening formula and the body of the letter.[2] The rigid application of this form has often led to the rejection of writings without a thanksgiving section as not being letters. Consequently, the literary form of James as a letter has been challenged because the rest of ch. 1 is not an explicit thanksgiving formula in the manner expressed in Paul's writings. Recently, however, this negative assessment of James has been questioned.

A noteworthy re-examination of the form and structure of the Hellenistic letter has shown that a striking feature of such letters is their tendency to restate the theme.[3] They do this by using a double opening formula involving blessing (μακάριος) and thanksgiving (εὐλογητός) or some similarly related concepts or words. This double use of introductory formulae is also in use in the writings of Paul.[4] In Ephesians, for example, the opening greeting (1.1-2) is followed first by a blessing, which is invoked in 1.3-14 (εὐλογητός..., 'Blessed be the God...') and then by another opening formula of thanksgiving in 1.15-17 (εὐχαριστῶν..., 'giving thanks...').[5] Roberts has also demonstrated that the thanksgiving is not the only distinctive feature preceding the body in Paul's letters. He lists four other distinc-

---

1. Dibelius, *James*, 68.
2. Fitzmyer, *New Testament Epistles*, 224-25.
3. Francis, *Form and Function*, 111.
4. *Ibid.*, 113.
5. *Ibid.*

tive ways in which the body is preceded.[1] Even within the writings of Paul a number of possibilities existed and were used. To operate with the schema given by Fitzmyer in a very rigid way gives a false picture. The studies of Francis and Roberts have shown that μακάριος formulae were often used in conjunction with another formula indicating some form of thanksgiving. Consequently, by using μακάριος formulae in place of thanksgiving formulae, James still operates with an acceptable form of letter writing. As Francis argues:

> In summary, the formal parity and occasional equation of the μακάριος and εὐλογητός formulas and the tendency to use the μακάριος formula parallel with other expressions for thanksgiving and rejoicing confirm the convertibility of the epistolary use of μακάριος in James and the epistolary εὐλογητός in other letters.[2]

What is of special importance with these twofold introductory expressions is that they are used to present the major themes of the epistle. The second expression does not simply repeat the first thought—it presents it in a parallel fashion but carries the thought further in a new direction.[3] In the Epistle of James these twofold introductory expressions are clearly in evidence. The first formula appears in 1.2-11 (introduced by Πᾶσαν χαρὰν ἡγήσασθε, 'Count it all joy'), while the second formula occurs in 1.12-27 (introduced by μακάριος, 'Blessed'). Each paragraph is closely balanced with regard to the other— each comprises three parts which Francis classified in this way:

testing/steadfastness	(1.2-4, 12-18)
wisdom-words/reproaching	(1.5-8, 19-21)
rich–poor/doers	(1.9-11, 22-25)[4]

One of the weaknesses in the presentation by Francis is the attempt to reach identity between the two opening paragraphs. This forces the situation and does not remain faithful

1. Roberts, *Transitional Techniques*, 191.
2. Francis, *Form and Function*, 115-16.
3. *Ibid.*, 117.
4. *Ibid.*, 118.

to his original proposition that the second paragraph did not simply reiterate the first, but actually added new elements to it.

An examination of the compositional relationship among the pericopae (see Appendix B) shows the various themes that emerge in the two sections. In the first, containing the introductory formula of joy, three important themes occur in pericopae B, C and D, namely

Theme one	Testing of faith produces steadfastness (pericope B)
Theme two	Wisdom (pericope C)
Theme three	Rich and poor (pericope D)

In the second introductory formula of blessedness two major themes have emerged:

Theme one	Endurance through trial (pericope E)
Theme two	Sayings on hearing the word, anger and speech (pericope F)

The themes announced in these pericopae B-F become the central topics of the entire letter. From pericope F two themes are developed in the body of the letter, the theme of hearing the word and the theme of speech. Consequently, the outline of the two paragraphs could be expressed in this manner:

1.2-11 Joy	Testing (E); Wisdom (D); Rich and poor (A)
1.12-27 Blessedness	Testing (E); Speech (C); Righteousness of God and human anger (F); Doers of the word (B)

The theme of testing (E) is one that occurs in both introductory paragraphs. Having been repeated twice, it is not considered in the body itself, but is treated in the concluding section of the epistle. The elements appearing in the sections indicated as (A) (B) (C) (D) are the central features and themes of the entire letter. Theme (F) on the righteousness of God and human anger appears in the body of the epistle in the focus given to wisdom. These major themes structure the epistle, not in a haphazard, but in a very balanced way.

3.1.3 *The body of the epistle*

The major themes announced in the introductory paragraphs now become the centre of attention. Four themes appearing in these two introductory paragraphs are taken up again:

    (A) Rich and poor
    (B) Hearers and doers of the word
    (C) Speech
    (D) Wisdom

These four themes are each discussed on two occasions. They are structured in a parallel way so that the theme of wisdom lies at the very centre of the consideration:

    (A) Rich and poor
    (B) Doers of the word
    (C) Speech
    (D) Wisdom
    (D) Wisdom
    (C) Speech
    (B) Doers of the word
    (A) Rich and poor

At the same time a connection is made to a theme announced in pericope F on anger. The righteousness of God is not communicated to those who show anger towards others (1.20). This theme is reflected in the wisdom consideration that occupies pericopae J and K.

A summary of the structure of the introductory formulae and the body of the epistle can be tabulated (Table 1). This analysis shows the author to be preoccupied with four themes in the body of the epistle, namely, rich and poor, doers of the word, speech and wisdom.

The theme (A), dealing with the rich and the poor, includes the whole discussion. The last theme to be mentioned in the first introductory section on joy (1.9-11) is the first to be taken up in the body of the epistle (2.1-13). It is also the last theme to be discussed in the body of the epistle (5.1-6). In this way it includes the whole discussion, embracing all the other themes and appearing as the most immediate and pressing of all the themes. One could deduce that it concerns a practical problem or situation of the readers where the rich are lording it over

Table 1. The Structure of the Epistle

SECTION 1: OPENING FORMULA (1.1)
Pericope A (1.1) Opening address

SECTION 2: INTRODUCTORY FORMULAE (1.2-27)
Part one (1.2-11) Introductory formula: joy

Pericope B	(1.2-4)	Testing–Steadfastness	(E)
Pericope C	(1.5-8)	Wisdom	(D)
Pericope D	(1.9-11)	Rich–Poor	(A)

Part two (1.12-27) Introductory formula: blessedness

Pericope E	(1.12-18)	Testing–Steadfastness	(E)
Pericope F	(1.19-27)	Sayings on:	
(i)	(1.20-21)	Anger	(F)
(ii)	(1.22-25)	Doers of the word	(B)
(iii)	(1.26-27)	Bridling tongue	(C)

SECTION 3: BODY OF THE EPISTLE (2.1–5.6)

Pericope G	(2.1-13)	Partiality: Rich and Poor	(A)
Pericope H	(2.14-26)	Doers of the word/	
		Faith and works	(B)
Pericope I	(3.1-12)	Speech and tongue	(C)
Pericope J	(3.13-18)	Wisdom from above	(D)
Pericope K	(4.1-10)	Advice from a wise man	
		(art of living happily)	(D) D C B A
Pericope L	(4.11-12)	To speak evil	(C)
Pericope M	(4.13-17)	Doers of what is right	(B)
Pericope N	(5.1-6)	Arrogance of the rich	(A)

the poor in the community. The view that this epistle has no
immediacy or is not speaking to a particular situation is consequently wrong. The author is concerned about the situation of
the rich vis-à-vis the poor and he wishes to give them some
exhortation.

The second major theme (B) is the relationship of faith and
action. The parallel passages where it is discussed are 2.14-26
and 4.13-17. They have taken up the theme which was introduced as part of pericope F in 1.22-25. The Christian must be a
doer of the word. By means of carefully chosen examples the
author brings out his teaching very forcefully.

The theme of speech and the power of the tongue is the third
major theme (C). It appeared already in pericope F where it

was introduced under the theme of bridling the tongue (1.26-27). Again it is discussed in the body of the epistle in a parallel way in 3.1-12 and 4.11-12. Here the author shows himself true to the tradition of wisdom literature with its reflection on the power of speech and the evils perpetrated by the tongue.

The heart of the parallel structures which have been created is that of the theme of wisdom (D). It occurred first in the introductory section under the formula of joy in 1.5-8. In the body it appears in 3.13-18 and 4.1-10. These are immediately parallel to each other and form the very heart of the epistle. The very core of its exhortations concern the wise and understanding. At the same time the theme of the righteousness of God, which is communicated to those who show anger to another (theme F), is also reflected here in both aspects of wisdom (D).

Only one theme appearing in the introductory section is not taken up again in the body of the epistle, namely the theme of testing and steadfastness. There are two reasons for this. First, since it is the only one of the introductory themes to be repeated twice, its parallel treatment has already been given in the introductory section where it begins each of the introductory formulae (1.2-4 and 1.12-18). The theme does appear again in the conclusion to the epistle where the call to steadfastness and patience is introduced in 5.7-11. In this way an *inclusio* is made between the introductory formulae and the concluding discussion by means of this theme of steadfastness.

This analysis has revealed the essential features and themes of the epistle. It has also highlighted the essential core of the whole writing. James is a carefully planned work: well thought out and very artistic, but at the same time simply constructed. To a large extent the insight of Francis with regard to the form and function of the opening double theme enabled one to unlock this composition. Yet, Francis was unable to proceed this far, because of his narrow concept of unifying the two introductory themes. The division that he presented turned out to be simply another division, among many others, which was only loosely connected to the introductory passages announcing the theme.

Through this analysis the literary nature of this writing as an epistle has been harmonized with the examination which comes from an analysis of its structure. Each complements the other and together they give a deeper insight into the composition of this writing. This analysis adds weight to the contention that James is a New Testament wisdom writing: the concept of wisdom is at the heart of this epistle.

3.1.4 *The conclusion to the epistle*

It has been argued that it is wrong to take the example of Paul and use it as the only paradigm in a very rigid way. This applies equally to the conclusion of James. It differs noticeably from the customary nature of Paul's endings from which the final greetings and blessing, so characteristic of the writings of Paul, are missing. Francis argues that the absence of a closing formula of greetings and blessing was an option open to a writer:

> To begin with, attention must be called to the fact that many Hellenistic letters, both private (*P. Tebt.* 34, I BC) and public (*P. Tebt.* 29, II BC), both secondary (*Ant.* 8, 50-54; 1 Macc. 10.25ff.) and primary (*P. Tebt.* 34), both early (*P. Tebt.* 29) and late (*P. Oxy.* 1071, V AD)—many Hellenistic letters of all types have no closing formulas whatsoever; they just stop... This does occur in other letters with a double opening statement (*Ant.* 8, 50-54; 1 Macc. 10.25ff.).[1]

An examination of Jas 5.7-20 shows how it can be seen to be an appropriate epistolary ending.

James 5.7-11: Exhortation to patience. The centre of interest in this pericope is an exhortation to patience until the coming of the Lord. Eschatological themes are evident at the end of many of the New Testament letters such as 1 Cor. 16.22; 1 Thess. 5.23; 1 Pet. 5.1; 2 Pet. 3.12-14; Jude 18 and 21.[2] James is easily inserted into this tradition. Within this eschatological context references are made to themes stated previously in the opening paragraphs, such as strife (Jas 5.9 refers back to 1.19) and patient endurance (Jas 5.10 refers back to 1.12). The compositional analysis drew attention to the theme of exhortation to patience, which is a link with the theme expressed in the

---

1. *Ibid.*, 125.
2. *Ibid.*, 124 n. 47.

introductory formulae on testing and steadfastness. This was the only theme repeated twice in the introductory section (pericope B [1.2-4] and pericope E [1.12-18]), yet was not referred to in the body of the epistle. As a theme it includes the entire epistle, appearing both at the beginning and the end.

James 5.12: The oath. Πρὸ πάντων introduces this section. Exler has shown how this phrase, as a closing formula, is connected to a wish for a person's health.[1] An oath formula is quite a frequent occurrence at the end of Hellenistic letters.[2] This shows that Jas 5.12 accords well with the style of the Hellenistic letter.

James 5.13-20: Prayer and the bringing back of a sinner. This section comprises two pericopae. Their main theme is prayer for the needs of another. Such an ending is also evident in 1 Jn 5.14-21 and Jude 17-25 where prayer is offered for another to turn from evil. These concluding statements occur in a context dealing with eschatology. All three letters bear witness to a common approach in concluding a letter. This is surely indicative of a procedure customary at that time.

Jas 5.13-20 is not an isolated, independent passage. It takes up themes prominent in the opening of the epistle. For example, Jas 1.16 issues a warning to the readers not to be deceived, whereas 5.19 refers to those who have fallen astray and have been deceived. Above all the theme of prayer forms a suitable conclusion to the entire epistle because it establishes an *inclusio* with the opening. Since it started with a reference to prayer (1.5), it is fitting that it is brought to an end on a similar note. The harmony achieved between the introductory formulae and the conclusion establishes a firm *inclusio*. This can be represented in the following way:

---

1. Exler, *Form of the Ancient Greek Letter*, 114.
2. *Ibid.*, 127-32.

SECTION 2: INTRODUCTORY FORMULAE EXPRESSING THEMES
(1.2-27)

Part one	(1.2-11)	Introductory formula: joy
Pericope B	(1.2-4)	Testing–steadfastness ————————
Pericope C	(1.5-8)	Wisdom (and Prayer) ————————
Pericope D	(1.9-11)	Rich and poor

SECTION 4: CONCLUSION (5.7-20)

Pericope O	(5.7-11)	Exhortation to patience under trials
Pericope P	(5.12)	The oath
Pericope Q	(5.13-18)	Prayer and a concern
Pericope R	(5.19-20)	for others ————————

3.2 *The importance of wisdom in this structure*
This analysis has shown that the composition of the Epistle of
James conforms to the pattern of other Christian letters
(including Jude and 1 Jn) as well as to the art of letter writing
in Hellenistic times. Its opening formulae, the development of
its themes throughout the body, and the conclusion show that
it is an epistle from beginning to end. Francis supports this
view very well when he says:

> In summary, scholarship must reassess the literary character
> of the epistles James and 1 John in the light of what would
> appear to be carefully styled opening thematic statements, a rec-
> ognizable epistolary close, and the rather substantial literary-
> thematic coherence of the epistles as a whole. James and 1 John
> may be understood as epistles from start to finish—secondary
> letters in form and in literary treatment of their subject matter.[1]

I have argued that the nature of the Epistle of James conforms
both to that of an epistle as well as to that of a wisdom writing.
Its composition revolves around the central theme of wisdom,
and all the other themes focus on giving practical wisdom
advice. More attention will be devoted to the wisdom thrust of
this writing through an examination of the nature of wisdom.
James appears as *the* New Testament wisdom writing.

---

1. Francis, *Form and Function*, 126.

4. *The Wisdom Context of James*

Before undertaking an in-depth examination of the nature and characteristics of wisdom in James, its wisdom heritage will be examined. Attention will be given only to aspects which have a bearing on an understanding of the epistle and the world of wisdom which is the immediate context behind it.

4.1 *Some important aspects of Hebrew wisdom thought*

The wisdom tradition is in evidence throughout the religious life of Israel; consequently, it is not surprising that all parts of the Old Testament bear witness to traits of wisdom thinking. McKenzie has rightly made an important distinction between wisdom as wisdom literature and wisdom as an approach to reality.[1] In the latter sense wisdom thinking is evident in Israelite thought from the very earliest stages.

Only when Israel's sages returned from exile did they produce a literature which reflected their particular traditions and ways of thinking. To give a faithful reflection of Hebrew wisdom thinking, attention will be focused not only on the three canonical wisdom books of Job, Qoheleth and Proverbs, but also on the two deutero-canonical books of Ben Sirach and the Wisdom of Solomon which continue the wisdom tradition in the same mould.

Two aspects of wisdom dominate attention throughout the wisdom thinking of the Hebrew writings, namely the ethical way of life demanded by wisdom and the personification of wisdom itself. The Epistle of James must be viewed against this two-sided concern of wisdom reflection in order to situate it in this perspective.

4.1.1 *Wisdom and ethics*

The aim of all wisdom literature, in particular the books of Proverbs, Qoheleth, and Ben Sirach, is to provide instruction for the art of living, or the mastery of life itself. The ethical teaching of the wisdom writings aims at the correct ordering of life so that one can live happily under the sovereignty of God. The life that they advocate is not a life led independently of

1. J.L. McKenzie, 'Reflections on Wisdom', *JBL* 86 (1967), 1-9.

God, but is in the context of God's sovereignty. A brief overview
of the major Hebrew wisdom writings demonstrates the rich
heritage of the wisdom tradition. As a wisdom writing James
can only be fully appreciated and understood against this
background.

(a) The Book of Proverbs aims at training in the art of living.
Knowledge was never presented in isolation from the context
of one's life. In the quest for knowledge the underlying aim
was to furnish a person with a means to attain the goal of
leading a happy and successful life. Knowledge is never an end
in itself, but the means to that end.[1] For the Israelites this present life was lived in one of two ways: wisely or foolishly. Both
these categories were based upon ethical considerations for
they both implied a specific lifestyle.

Fundamental to the Israelite idea of wisdom is that it is able
to be taught. The task of a parent is above all to instruct the son
in the art of leading a successful life.[2] 'Hear, my son, your
father's instruction, and reject not your mother's teaching'
(Prov. 1.8).[3] Advice was also willingly sought from people who
had already acquired a reputation and prestige in a certain
field. Such would be the royal counsellors whose advice must
be followed or rejected.

The aim of instruction and discipline was to train one in the
art of living. This training brought with it self-control. In this
regard one theme that is emphasized and which is one of the
more difficult areas to master is the control of the tongue. The
tongue has the twofold power of both healing and destroying.
'A worthless person, a wicked man, goes about with crooked
speech' (Prov. 6.12). The correct control of the tongue also
meant that one learned the ability to remain silent when one
could hurt another by saying something. Gossip and all other
misuse of the tongue worked to bring destruction and to

---

1. J.L. Crenshaw, *Old Testament Wisdom: an Introduction* (Atlanta:
John Knox, 1981), 80.

2. R.B.Y. Scott, *The Way of Wisdom in the Old Testament* (New York:
Macmillan, 1971), 49.

3. Unless otherwise indicated throughout this monograph the
English translation of the text of the Old Testament is that of the
Revised Standard Version (1952), while that of the New Testament is
from the 2nd edn of the RSV (1971).

undermine society itself. So universal was the evil that one saying almost equates talkativeness and sin: 'When words are many, transgression is not lacking, but he who restrains his lips is prudent' (Prov. 10.19).

(b) The Books of Job and Qoheleth differ greatly from the approach of Proverbs in that they present a rebellion against the traditional wisdom views. The Book of Job is living proof of the divergent tendencies within the Jewish wisdom movement. The question with which this writing battles is: 'Why should a good man suffer?' At the heart of this question is the problem of retribution advocated by and presumed in the book of Proverbs. Experience has belied the traditional wisdom insight that the good man prospers in this life, while the evil man experiences punishment. 'The fathers have eaten sour grapes, and the children's teeth are set on edge' (Ezek. 18.2) was a familiar expression of this principle of retribution. Job's difficulty comes from the fact that he does not understand the why behind his suffering. The only one who can answer that question for him is God. Yet, God remains consistently hidden.

In this sense Job's search for an answer to his problem becomes a quest for the divine presence, which alone can provide him with a solution to his situation.

Just as Job reacted against traditional wisdom, so too Qoheleth rebels against this traditional wisdom, but in a different way. Qoheleth speaks out against the principle of divine retribution, but this time the attack is more thoroughgoing than was the case with Job. Qoheleth has become intensely critical of the wisdom movement. As Murphy comments: 'The tendency was to put the Lord into a straightjacket tailored by human insights'.[1] This was the problem experienced in traditional wisdom: God was no longer free because the principles that people had elaborated in their wisdom demanded that God operate in a particular way. In effect Qoheleth champions a God who is free and independent.

(c) The Book of Ben Sirach fits into the tradition of wisdom writing represented by the Book of Proverbs. It seems best to describe the aim of Ben Sirach as to present not just the art of living, but more specifically the art of surviving in this world.

---

1. R.E. Murphy, 'Ecclesiastes (Qoheleth)', *JBC* 1 (1970), 535.

Some of these themes are especially characteristic of the treatment contained in the Epistle of James such as that of speech, and the relationship of rich and poor.

4.1.2 *The personification of wisdom*
To solve the difficulty of how one can assign the quality of truth to knowledge derived from the realm of human wisdom the personification of the figure of wisdom took place. This figure dwells in their midst and communicates the gift of wisdom to the wise. The personification of wisdom underwent a development through the course of Hebrew reflection on wisdom. This is seen particularly in the writings of Proverbs, Ben Sirach and Wisdom.

(a) The Book of Proverbs introduces some ideas which are completely novel. When the threat of polytheism had largely removed itself, the post-exilic period saw the development of wisdom along the lines of the personification of wisdom. A golden thread begins which develops until it reaches its final culmination in the person of Jesus Christ in the New Testament. Wisdom is present at the beginning when God created the world (Prov. 8.22ff.). By means of this picture the wise men taught that God, instead of hiding wisdom at the beginning of creation, has in fact made it possible to acquire wisdom. The twofold tendency here is well expressed, namely the desire on the part of humanity to find wisdom and on the other hand the willingness of wisdom to be found.[1] Human effort and abilities are given their rightful position: they must always be seen within the framework and context of God's wisdom (Prov. 8.34-36). With the introduction of the picture of personified wisdom a high-point in the reflection of the wise is reached. Wisdom is not simply a human endeavour and striving: instead it falls within the framework of God's communication of wisdom to all who see her.

(b) Ben Sirach also takes up, and, in his own way, gives the personification of wisdom a new emphasis and direction. In the opening chapter, Ben Sirach took over the thoughts of Proverbs 8 and applied them specifically to humanity in so far as God has granted them wisdom as his gift. Whereas for

---

1. Crenshaw, *Old Testament Wisdom*, 99.

Proverbs the fear of the Lord was seen as the beginning of knowledge (Prov. 1.7), here it becomes the beginning of wisdom (Sir. 1.14). Fundamental to his outlook is the view that all wisdom finds its origin in God who gives it freely to humanity.

In ch. 24 the whole teaching on wisdom comes together, incorporating as well a development of all previous reflection on wisdom. In as much as all created things issued forth from God's word, so too did wisdom arise 'from the mouth of the Most High' (24.3). Ben Sirach does not present wisdom as a person distinct from God, but the personification of wisdom here certainly gave the impetus to this tendency. Wisdom presents herself as an intermediary in the work of creation, assisting God in this task. Wisdom does not simply see her task as being exercised at the creation (as was the case with the Book of Proverbs). This task is made concrete in the very nation of Israel. To them Wisdom issues an invitation to share in the true wisdom that she alone can offer. These words are reminiscent of the words which Jesus Christ was later to use during his invitation to his followers to follow him (Sir. 24.19 = Mt. 11.28; Sir. 24.21 = Mt. 5.6).

(c) The Book of Wisdom[1] brings a number of strands of wisdom thought to their logical fulfilment. From being present at

---

1. Although belonging to the wisdom tradition, the Wisdom of Solomon (referred to for simplicity sake as 'the Book of Wisdom') differs in many ways from the previous works in this tradition. It was the last of the wisdom writings to be written, dating from somewhere during the course of the first century BC. (For a detailed discussion of the various dates proposed, see M. Hadas, 'The Wisdom of Solomon', in *The Interpreter's Dictionary of the Bible* [ed. G. Buttrick; New York: Abingdon, 1962], vol. 4, 861-63.) It was also the only wisdom writing to have been composed in Greek (and not in Hebrew) (Scott, *The Way of Wisdom*, 212). Despite being written in Greek, the author, who is well versed in Greek philosophic thought, is also at home in his Hebraic thought which betrays his religious background. This work was written for the large Jewish community resident in Alexandria in Egypt. Although the Book of Wisdom fits into the line of the tradition of Proverbs and Ben Sirach, this writing also shows some marked differences. Whereas Proverbs and Ben Sirach were written with potential students in mind and their teaching is communicated predominantly in the form of a treatise, the Book of Wisdom's reader-audience is much wider than simply pupils; it embraces both a Jewish and Gentile readership.

the creation (Proverbs), present in Judaism at the time of the Law (Ben Sirach), Wisdom now exercises a cosmic function in which she clearly takes on all the attributes of the divinity.[1] With regard to the other stream of wisdom thought evident in Proverbs and Ben Sirach, namely that of moral instruction, the book of Wisdom also gave a new dimension and insight. The notion of immortality saw the human person as being eternal and attaining recompense, not simply in this world, but in the world to come.

4.2 *The legacy of wisdom*
Wisdom's legacy can be viewed from two perspectives. First, with regard to Israel itself and its own thought: then secondly, looking outward from itself one can see the legacy it has left to the New Testament.

4.2.1 *Wisdom legacy within the faith of Israel*
Brueggemann[2] has viewed the function of Israel's wisdom thought as offering a much-needed corrective to traditional Yahwistic thought. The concentration is no longer on what the past said, but upon the present. How does humanity view things today? The Yahwistic picture of God's control of the world and history is opened up by wisdom thought to give a new direction. Through the personification of wisdom, God is revealed through creation itself. Experience becomes a means by which one can encounter the divine. The value of this

---

1. Scholarly opinion divides on the issue of whether the author remains on the level of personification, or whether he has developed it further by hypostatizing wisdom (i.e. making wisdom out to be a distinct person). J.C. Rylaarsdam (*Revelation in Jewish Wisdom Literature* [Midway reprint; Chicago: University of Chicago Press [1946, 1974], 91) expresses the lack of agreement in this way: 'It is difficult to define these agencies (Divine Word, the Law, the Spirit, and the Divine Wisdom) precisely; there is, for example, no agreement on when such an intermediary may be described as a hypostasis; but, whatever the definition, their express function is to serve as a bridge to span the gap between heaven and earth'. When all judgments are examined, it seems hard to uphold the notion of hypostatization if only because of the fact that it would be extremely difficult to harmonize it with the Jewish faith in only one God.
2. W. Brueggemann, *In Man We Trust: the Neglected Side of Biblical Faith* (Richmond: John Knox, 1972), 115.

meant that everyone was able to make contact with the divine through reflection upon reality itself.

In another direction Israel's wise men placed a corrective on the past by introducing a certain sober scepticism into Israelite thought with the Books of Job and Qoheleth. Here traditional beliefs form the subject of scrutiny. Although they show the loopholes very evident in the traditional statements of belief, such as the principle of retribution, they do not really offer any positive solution to the problem raised. In doing so they do not undermine the faith, but instead they show that faith and doubt do go hand in hand and are two compatible bedfellows. The individual has to live in this world with doubts unresolved, but these doubts find their meaning against the great backdrop of the incomprehensibility of the divine mystery.

Fundamental to the whole wisdom attitude to reality is the conviction that the world is meaningful. Although even Qoheleth time and again repeats the conviction that the individual is unable to discover the secret underlying all things (Qoh. 3.11; 7.14; 8.17; 11.5), there is never a degeneration into frustration and despair or irrationality. The attraction that wisdom had lay in her ability to give something to those who follow. Through the reflection and experience which they handed on over the course of the centuries, the wise men had been able to obtain meaningful insight into human nature and to outline a path to follow in order to cope successfully with life. These wisdom writings mirror the wise man's understanding of reality.

4.2.2 *Wisdom legacy inherited by the New Testament traditions*

As a tradition, wisdom occupies an important place throughout Israel's history of thought. Although its climax was reached in the composition of a corpus of literature, wisdom had its roots far back in the centuries of the past. The wisdom tradition did not end with Jewish wisdom writings. It is precisely this wisdom tradition which forges a bridge between the Old and the New Testaments. Jesus uses the vocabulary and literary tools of the wise to convey his message. In this way Jesus fits into the tradition of the wisdom teacher. In his speeches Jesus makes use of Hebrew parallelism (Mk 4.22), while his parables are extended proverbs, using the Old Testament device of the mashal (Mt. 6.19-21). More important is the fact that Jesus makes use of the thought and message of the wisdom teacher. He takes over the inheritance of the Old Testament and makes it his own, expanding it and giving it an entirely new direction. Further attention will be given to this later when the role that wisdom plays in the Q source is examined.

Among the New Testament traditions Paul and John made use of wisdom thought and each developed a specific wisdom Christology of his own. But, of all the New Testament writings, the Epistle of James shows the clearest affinity to the wisdom tradition. It appears as a handbook of wisdom teachings. An initial examination of James reveals the extent of the influence of the wisdom writings upon this epistle. A detailed survey of similarities between James and this wisdom tradition is given by Mayor.[1] Most of these similarities provided by Mayor are parallels, similarities or even echoes of the tradition. Yet, the vast number of these similarities point to the awareness James had of this body of literature. It is especially in the writings of Proverbs, Qoheleth, Ben Sirach and the Book of Wisdom that the similarities proliferate.

Among the more noteworthy similarities the following are to be observed. From the Book of Proverbs the most striking is the direct quotation made in Jas 4.6 of Prov. 3.34, 'Toward the scorners he is scornful, but to the humble he shows favour'. A noteworthy parallel is found in Jas 4.13-16 to Prov. 27.1: 'Do not boast about tomorrow, for you do not know what a day may bring forth'. Also Jas 1.19 shows a parallel reference to Prov. 17.27: 'He who restrains his words has knowledge, and he who has a cool spirit is a man of understanding'. The writing to which James makes the most allusions is the Book of Ben Sirach. Both writings show a tendency to consider common themes. Ropes has drawn attention to these common themes: 'the dangers proceeding from the tongue (Ecclus 19.6-12; 20.5-8; 18-20; 22.27; 28.13-26; 35[32].7-9), wisdom as the gift of God (1.1-10), prayer with a divided heart (1.27), pride (10.7-18), the uncertainty of life (10.10; 11.16, 17), blaming

---

1. Mayor, *The Epistle of St. James*, cxiii-cxviii.

God (15.11-20), man as made in God's image and ruling over the beasts (17.3f.), the eclipse of the sun and changes of the moon (17.31; 27.11)'.[1] Finally, a few parallels occur between James and the Book of Wisdom: life compared to a mist which soon disappears (Wis. 2.4; Jas 4.14); the connection made between wisdom and perfection (Wis. 9.6; Jas 1.5), the persecution of the righteous and the poor (Wis. 2.10-20; Jas 5.6).

Although one is not trying to demonstrate the direct dependence of James upon one or other of these writings, these associations do point to the detailed knowledge James has of the Hebrew wisdom tradition. This initial examination of the relationship of James to the wisdom heritage will be developed in more detail later. This chapter has shown that from a compositional viewpoint wisdom is indeed the key to understand this writing. The following chapters will investigate the nature of this wisdom thought in James and its method of expression.

1. Ropes, *The Epistle of St. James*, 19.

Chapter 2

THE ROLE OF WISDOM IN JAMES AND Q:
PARAENETICAL ADVICE

The wisdom writings of the Old Testament and the intertestamental period considered wisdom from two perspectives.
First, a decidedly practical dimension was given to wisdom
which presented the ethical demands of a specific lifestyle.
Secondly, wisdom was approached from a more reflective
viewpoint whereby the very nature of wisdom was personified.
These two strands run like golden threads throughout these
writings.

Both aspects also make their appearance in the Epistle of
James as well as in the Q source. Although firmly rooted in the
Hebrew wisdom tradition, James is far more than a mere
continuation of this wisdom trajectory. As argued in the
opening chapter, James is neither a Jewish writing, nor a
writing that was subsequently christianized; but is a fully
fledged Christian writing. A comparison of James with the Q
tradition demonstrates the strength of this Christian dimension of James which emerges even more forcefully from a
comparison of their wisdom dimensions.

1. *The Approach Adopted to Q*[1]

Q is still a much discussed topic in New Testament scholarly circles today,[2] but the hypothesis[3] concerning Q is command-

1. The term Q denotes that material, common to Matthew and Luke, which lies behind these two Gospels and which developed into a unity or document or source. It is variously referred to as the 'Q document', the 'Q source', or simply as Q. Throughout this study the term Q will be used for the sake of simplicity.

2. During the last two decades there has been a considerably renewed interest in the study of Q. Important investigations have been made by W.D. Davies, *The Setting of the Sermon on the Mount* (Cambridge: Cambridge University Press, 1964); H.E. Tödt, *The Son of Man in the Synoptic Tradition* (Philadelphia: Westminster, 1965); O.H. Steck, *Israel und das gewaltsame Geschick der Propheten: Untersuchungen zur Überlieferung des deuteronomistischen Geschichtsbildes im Alten Testament, Spätjudentum und Urchristentum* (Neukirchen-Vluyn: Neukirchener Verlag, 1967); P.D. Meyer, 'The Community of Q' (PhD thesis, University of Iowa, 1967); D. Lührmann, *Die Redaktion der Logienquelle: Anhang: Zur weiteren Überlieferung der Logienquelle* (Neukirchen-Vluyn: Neukirchener Verlag, 1969); W.A. Beardslee, 'The Wisdom Tradition and the Synoptic Gospels', *JAAR* 35 (1967), 231-40; and *Literary Criticism of the New Testament: Guides to Biblical Scholarship* (Philadelphia: Fortress, 1969); P. Hoffmann, *Studien zur Theologie der Logienquelle* (Münster: Aschendorff, 1972); F. Christ, *Jesus Sophia: Die Sophia-Christologie bei den Synoptikern* (Zurich: Zwingli Verlag, 1970); H.C. Kee, *Jesus in History: An Approach to the Study of the Gospels* (New York: Harcourt, Brace & World, 1970); M.J. Suggs, *Wisdom, Christology, and Law in Matthew's Gospel* (Cambridge, MA: Harvard University Press, 1970); J.M. Robinson, 'Logoi Sophon: on the Gattung of Q', *Trajectories through Early Christianity* (ed. J.M. Robinson & H. Koester; Philadelphia: Fortress, 1971), 71-113; S. Schulz, *Q: Die Spruchquelle der Evangelisten* (Zurich: Theologischer Verlag, 1972); R.A. Edwards, *A Theology of Q: Eschatology, Prophecy and Wisdom* (Philadelphia: Fortress, 1976); A. Polag, *Die Christologie der Logienquelle* (Neukirchen-Vluyn: Neukirchener Verlag, 1977); A.D. Jacobson, 'Wisdom Christology in Q' (PhD thesis, Claremont Graduate School, 1978); and 'The Literary Unity of Q', *JBL* 101 (1982), 365-89; J.S. Kloppenborg, 'Wisdom Christology in Q', *LTP* 34 (1978), 129-47; 'The Literary Genre of the Synoptic Sayings Source' (PhD thesis, University of St Michael's College, Toronto School of Theology, 1984); 'Tradition and Redaction in the Synoptic Sayings Source', *CBQ* 46 (1984), 34-62; 'The Formation of Q and Antique Instructional Genres', *JBL* 105 (1986), 443-62; and *The Formation of Q: Trajectories in Ancient Wisdom Collections* (Studies in Antiquity and Christianity; Philadelphia: Fortress, 1987).

3. Jacobson (*The Literary Unity of Q*, 370) rightly notes that the hypothesis of the two source theory arose, not from the desire to construct a
hypothesis, but because 'most scholars felt direct copying of Matthew
by Luke or vice versa was unlikely'. In more recent times objections
have been voiced against this two-source theory. The two main opponents have been W.R. Farmer (*The Synoptic Problem: A Critical Analysis* [New York: Macmillan, 1964]) and A.M. Farrar ('On Dispensing
with Q', *Studies in the Gospels: Essays in Memory of R.H. Lightfoot*
[ed. D.E. Nineham; Oxford: Blackwell, 1967], 55-88) who have tended to
attract a number of supporters. Farmer has in essence reaccepted
what was termed the Griesbach hypothesis. In this view Matthew was
judged to be the first Gospel and as such was the source for both Luke
and Mark. In fact this view envisaged different occasions of direct
copying: Luke copied Matthew, while Mark copied from both Matthew
and Luke. In an excellent article which surveys the position with
regard to the two-source theory, J.A. Fitzmyer ('The Priority of Mark
and the "Q" Source in Luke', *Perspective* [Pittsburgh Theological Sem-
inary] 11 [1970], 131-70) shows how the weight of argument leans very
heavily against the view of Farmer, who wishes to uphold Luke's
dependence on Matthew. On the other hand, there are three major
reasons in support of the two-source theory. These three arguments
are all expressed in a similar way in Fitzmyer ('The Priority of Mark
and the 'Q' Source in Luke', 150), W.G. Kümmel (*Introduction to the
New Testament* [London: SCM, 1975], 64-76), and H. Biggs ('The Q
Debate since 1955', *Themelios* 6/2 [1980/81], 18), and to my mind they
establish the two-source theory as the most comprehensive hypothesis
to date. The three arguments are:

(a) The numerous verbal agreements between Matthew and Luke:
They are so close that they demand a common written source.
Fitzmyer ('The Priority of Mark and the 'Q' Source in Luke', 151) gives
a rather detailed chart to illustrate this. Kümmel (*Introduction to the
New Testament*, 65) surveys the same material and reaches a similar
conclusion: '...the common vocabulary in all sections which come
under consideration is over fifty percent, which can hardly be
accounted for by simple oral tradition'.

(b) The order in which the material common to Luke and Matthew
appears. This betrays a common sequence and is very well investigated
and illustrated by V. Taylor in a number of articles ('The Order of Q',
JTS ns 4 [1953], 27-31; and 'The Original Order of Q', *New Testament
Essays: Studies in Memory of T.W. Manson, 1893–1958* [ed. A.J. Higgins; Manchester: Manchester University Press, 1959], 246-69). What
is so striking is the amount of agreement, not so much with the order
as a whole, but rather with the order of the individual sermons in
Matthew when compared to Luke. In one of his first articles on this
topic, Taylor ('The Order of Q', 29-30) illustrated this agreement by
means of seven columns: the first column was that of the Lucan material in sequence; cols. 2-6 comprised the material common to Matthew

ing a greater respect and carries more weight than any of its rival theories to date. After surveying the literature on and the developments in the synoptic problem in recent years, Fitzmyer[1] argues for the two source theory for two reasons. Firstly, there is the argument from authority in that the majority of twentieth-century scholars have embraced the hypothesis of Q as a solution to the synoptic problem. This is a fact of observation. Secondly, because of its usefulness, Q has paved the way for further investigations into the synoptic Gospels from the perspective of form criticism and *Redaktionsgeschichte*. To this I would add that the Q source helps one to understand the development and transmission of the sayings of Jesus from the time of the historical Jesus through to their emergence in the synoptic Gospels. The hypothesis of Q also contributes to a better understanding of the development of other New Testament writings which show a closeness of proximity to the sayings of Jesus. The task of this and further chapters will be to illustrate the significance of Q for the Epistle of James. This means that Q has relevance and significance

arranged according to the great Matthean sermons; col. 7 included the material in the rest of Matthew. Although he further refined his argument in later articles (especially in 'The Original Order of Q') the thrust of the argument remains the same. Fitzmyer ('The Priority of Mark and the "Q" Source in Luke', 152) shows how forceful Taylor's argument is when he concludes: 'At times this argument from the order of the Double Tradition material has been impugned, but I have so far uncovered no real attempt to cope with or refute the Taylor presentation of it'.

(c) The existence of doublets and double traditions. One can define doublets as accounts of the same event or saying which occur twice in either Matthew or Luke; while double traditions are accounts appearing twice in both Matthew and Luke. 'The conclusion drawn from this phenomenon is that Matthew and Luke have retained in their Gospels the double accounts of the same event or saying as they inherited them independently from Mark and from Q' (Fitzmyer, 'The Priority of Mark and the "Q" Source in Luke', 152-53).

From the above three arguments appearing in a similar way in Fitzmyer, Kümmel and Biggs, the conclusion drawn is that Matthew and Luke, in composing their Gospels, must have used a second source in addition to that of Mark. This source is the so-called Q source which must have been a written source in Greek to account for the above arguments of dependence.

1. Fitzmyer, 'The Priority of Mark and the "Q" Source in Luke', 133.

not only for the synoptic tradition, but also for other traditions such as that of James.

On the basis of the researches that have been made in more recent times[1] into the written nature of Q, one may propose the following general development of the Q document as a written source:

(a) Its origin lies in the proclamation of itinerant wandering prophets[2] who based themselves upon the sayings of Jesus which they handed on in accordance with his commission to go out and proclaim the imminence of the kingdom.

(b) Their proclamation developed into sermons which functioned as instructions. Kloppenborg[3] states that 'compositional analysis suggests that the formative component of Q consisted of several "speeches"': Q 6.20b-49 (without 6.23c); 9.57-62; 10.2-11, 16; 11.2-4, 9-13; 12.2-7, 11-12; and 12.22b-31, 33-34'.

(c) One might see these sermons developing into blocks of Q material, as Bauckham argues.[4] The most famous one of all would be the Sermon on the Mount/Plain where Q material had been preformed into a unity prior to its incorporation into the Q source. In order to demonstrate any connections between material outside the synoptic tradition and Q one must examine whether the connections are with certain blocks of Q tradition, or whether they extend throughout the whole of Q.[5] This is a very important observation. Contact between James and Q cannot be established if it is limited to only one major block of Q material: it must run throughout the

---

1. Studies such as those of A. Polag (*Die Christologie der Logienquelle;* and *Fragmenta Q: Textheft zur Logienquelle* [Neukirchen-Vluyn: Neukirchener Verlag, 1979]); Jacobson ('Wisdom Christology in Q'); R. Bauckham ('The Study of Gospel Traditions outside the Canonical Gospels: Problems and Prospects', *Gospel Perspectives: The Jesus Tradition outside the Gospels,* vol. 5 [ed. D. Wenham; Sheffield: JSOT, 1985], 369-419); P.H. Davids ('James and Jesus', in Wenham, *Gospel Perspectives*, vol. 5, 63-84); and Kloppenborg ('The Formation of Q and Antique Instructional Genres'; and *The Formation of Q: Trajectories in Ancient Wisdom Collections*).
2. I. Havener, *Q: The Sayings of Jesus: with a Reconstruction of Q by Athanasius Polag* (Wilmington: Michael Glazier, 1987), 42.
3. Kloppenborg, 'The Formation of Q and Antique Instructional Genres', 456.
4. Bauckham, 'The Study of Gospel Traditions', 378.
5. *Ibid.*, 379.

whole of Q. If such contact can be shown between James and Q, then strong support emerges for the existence of the Q hypothesis from traditions outside the synoptic Gospels.[1]

(d) Kloppenborg has also drawn attention to a threefold development of the written form of Q. From the already formed material he sees the development proceeding in this way:

> I have argued above that the formative component in Q consisted of a group of six 'wisdom speeches' which were hortatory in nature... This stratum was subsequently expanded by the addition of groups of sayings, many framed as chriae, which adopted a critical and polemical stance with respect to Israel. The most recent addition to Q seems to have been the temptation story, added in order to provide an aetiology and legitimation for Q's radical ethic, but introducing at the same time a biographical dimension into the collection.[2]

(e) Polag had opted for a simpler view of the development whereby the isolated sayings were brought together into smaller groups of sayings which became part of the first redaction of Q. In his reconstruction[3] Q comprises eleven blocks of material and this conclusion is in essential agreement with the idea that Q can be divided into major blocks of material.

(f) Q is not to be viewed as static, but as undergoing further development within the communities where it had taken root, namely within the communities of Matthew and Luke, where it produced Q^{Mt} and Q^{Lk}.

In examining the possible relationship of James to Q, the above developments in the construction of Q must be kept in mind. The question basically is: to which stage in the development of Q does James show possible connections? In order to

---

1. As Bauckham argues: 'Nevertheless, it seems to me that the independent parallels to Q material are of considerable importance to the question of the existence and nature of Q, which is regularly discussed as though only the synoptic Gospels were relevant evidence. Independent parallels to Q material... could help to substantiate the Q hypothesis in its broadest and least dogmatic form...' ('The Study of the Gospel Traditions', 379).

2. Kloppenborg, *The Formation of Q: Trajectories in Ancient Wisdom Collections*, 317.

3. Polag, *Fragmenta Q*, 23-26.

investigate James's relationship to Q one has to operate with a reconstructed text of Q. Over the decades various reconstructions of Q have been made;[1] but that of Polag[2] is probably the most valuable to have been presented to date. His proposed text comprises eleven sections:

(A)   Introduction
(B)   Sermon on the Mount
(C)   John the Baptist
(D)   Mission of the disciples
(E)   On prayer
(F)   Controversies

1. J. Moffatt (*An Introduction to the Literature of the New Testament* [Edinburgh; T. & T. Clark, 3rd rev. edn, (1918) 1961], 194-206) gave a list of no less than sixteen reconstructions of Q and no two of them were identical. Although there is disagreement as regards exact wording, in general one can say that agreement occurs with those passages which belong to the double tradition common to Matthew and Luke (F. Neirynck, 'Q', *The Interpreter's Dictionary of the Bible: Supplementary Volume* [ed. K. Crim; Nashville: Abingdon, 1976], 715). Consequently, the extent of the reconstruction of Q will be limited to those passages in the narrower sense which belong to the double tradition. In more recent times a number of reconstructions of portions of Q have been offered. See J.M. Robinson ('The Sermon on the Mount/ Plain: Work Sheets for the Reconstruction of Q', *Society of Biblical Literature 1983 Seminar Papers* [ed. K.H. Richards; Chico: Scholars, 1983], 451) for a brief list of reconstructions made recently in connection with the Sermon on the Mount/Plain. At present research into reconstructing the text of Q is continuing in the Society of Biblical Literature Seminar on Q. Under the chairmanship of Robinson this seminar is endeavouring to reconstruct the Greek text of Q in a meticulous way. It is his intention to produce a technical commentary on Q (Havener, *Q: The Sayings of Jesus,* 12). A particular focus of attention has been the Sermon on the Mount.

2. Polag, *Fragmenta Q,* 23-26. This reconstruction of Q by Polag is of great importance because it is one of the most recent reconstructions of the Greek text to date. Not all of Polag's reconstructions have been accepted with unanimity—especially some of his decisions to regard passages found only in Matthew or in Luke as belonging to Q material. The translation of these blocks of the material of Q given here is that of Havener (*Q: The Sayings of Jesus,* 117-22) who has translated the text of Polag into English. Attention will be given to this reconstruction by Polag because 'it is the only recent attempt to reproduce Q's text in its original Greek that has been published (Havener, *Q: The Sayings of Jesus,* 12).

(G) On acknowledgment
(H) On proper concerns
(I) Parables
(K)[1] On the responsibility of disciples
(L) On judgment

In essence Neirynck,[2] Edwards[3] and Vassiliadis[4] are in agreement with this list. In examining the relationship of James to Q, I shall use this reconstruction of Polag. This does not mean that I endorse his view of the development of Q, nor do I accept every one of his conclusions uncritically. It will be used simply as a starting-point for the comparison between James and Q. In addition it appears that Luke remains more faithful to the original order of Q.[5] The method of referring to Q will also be that adopted by the SBL Q consultation whereby Q texts are referred to by their Lucan position.[6]

1. Note that Polag avoids using the letter (J) in his reconstruction and passes from (I) to (K) immediately in the sequence. This discrepancy is avoided by Havener in his translation of Polag's text (*Q: The Sayings of Jesus*, 121).
2. F. Neirynck, 'Q', *The Interpreter's Dictionary of the Bible. Supplementary Volume*, 715.
3. Edwards, *A Theology of Q*, xi-xiii.
4. P. Vassiliadis, 'The Nature and Extent of the Q-Document', *NT* 20 (1978), 72.
5. The fidelity of Luke to the original order of Q has become the almost unanimously accepted viewpoint. Taylor ('The Order of Q'; and 'The Original Order of Q') has investigated the matter in depth. He arrived at the following conclusion: 'The investigation has confirmed the view that Luke has preserved the order of Q and has followed it with great fidelity' ('The Original Order of Q', 266). Fitzmyer ('The Priority of Mark and the "Q" Source in Luke', 154) surveys the recent state of scholarship on this issue and arrives at the conclusion: 'A common understanding of Q maintains that Luke presents substantially the original order of Q, while the more original wording is found in Matthew, since Luke has undoubtedly modified Q stylistically as he has done Mark'.
6. See Robinson ('The Sermon on the Mount/Plain', 451) and Kloppenborg ('The Formation of Q and Antique Instructional Genres', 443). For example, 'Q 7.35 = Mt. 11.19//Lk 7.35. This should not, however, be taken to imply that the Lucan wording is necessarily that of Q or that the Lucan location of the text is in all cases to be preferred' (Kloppenborg, 'The Formation', 443). It is simply an easy way of refer-

Once the relationship between James and Q has been established, the question will be pursued as to how James has utilized these sayings. In other words it will be our task to see how James inserts these sayings into his writing and what function they serve within it. But, for the present, the task is to investigate the relationship between James and Q and to see how this relationship is to be established. A starting-point occurs in their respective approaches to wisdom.

2. *The Wisdom Genre of Q*

One of the distinguishing features of both James and Q is the wisdom nature of both documents. Of all the connections that can be shown between James and Q undoubtedly this dimension of wisdom shows the most noticeable similarities. If Q is taken as a document in its own right, it demonstrates a literary unity. Jacobson, in his discussion on the literary unity of Q, quotes Thrall and Hibbard in defining what is understood by a literary unity: 'The concept that a literary work shall have in it some organizing principle in relation to which all its parts are related so that, viewed in the light of this principle, the work is an organic whole'.[1] It is the search for this unifying principle which has been behind the more recent studies on Q[2] and which it will be our concern to examine here.

---

ring to Q based upon the observation that in general Luke tends to preserve the order of Q better than Matthew.

1. Jacobson ('The Literary Unity of Q', 372) who quotes W.F. Thrall & A. Hibbard (*A Handbook to Literature* [rev. edn by C.H. Holman; New York: Odyssey, 1962], 500).

2. One thing the majority of scholars have agreed upon is that the literary genre of Q is not that of a Gospel, as that is known in Mark and the other Gospels. The main reason for this lies in the total absence from Q of the Passion and Resurrection themes. At the same time what narratives there are in Q serve the function of introducing the sayings. It is in these two fundamental ways that Q distances itself from the Gospel genre. Some scholars, using the distinction between kerygma and didache, claimed that because Q lacked a Passion account it could not be associated with the kerygma: instead it was assumed to have a purely didactic role, namely to give instructions to Christians in their religious and moral life (Kümmel, *Introduction to the New Testament*, 71). But this clear-cut distinction between

The article by James M. Robinson on Q, entitled 'Logoi Sophon: on the Gattung of Q', is without doubt a work of tremendous significance.[1] I intend to examine this article in

kerygma and didache is too simplistic. Further precision emerges from the redaction critical studies done on Q.

M. Dibelius (*From Tradition to Gospel* [Greenwood: Attic, 1971], 243-49) argued that the Q material was the result of the Church's efforts to supply a handbook of ethical or moral material for the use of those who had already become members of the believing community. This view rests on the position that Paul's kerygma of death–resurrection was the basis of all Christian theology. This was simply not the case, as Tödt has shown through his presentation of the Son of man christology.

Form critical examination of the synoptic Gospels led to an emphasis on the oral stages of the transmission of the gospel material. 'Form criticism was concerned to move beyond the preceding generation's focus on literary units, and shifted attention to the smaller, oral units of tradition' (Robinson, 'Logoi Sophon', 71). For this reason not much attention was paid by the form critics to the genre of the sayings collection (Robinson, 'Logoi Sophon', 71-72; Edwards, *A Theology of Q*, 14). In focusing attention on the smaller units, the form critics tended to discredit the work of the final collectors of these smaller units. Dibelius (*From Tradition to Gospel*, 59) referred to the evangelists simply as 'collectors' of units of tradition. Bultmann (*The History of the Synoptic Tradition* [rev. edn, Oxford: Basil Blackwell, 1972], 332) maintained that Mark had no real control over his own material—he was simply the first editor putting together the tradition which had already crystallized.

In more recent times a number of studies have been devoted to Q in which attention has been given to a redactional critical examination of Q. Works by Davies (*The Setting of the Sermon on the Mount*); Tödt (*The Son of Man in the Synoptic Tradition*); Lührmann (*Die Redaktion der Logienquelle*); Hoffmann (*Studien zur Theologie der Logienquelle*); Schulz (*Q: Die Spruchquelle der Evangelisten*); and Polag (*Die Christologie der Logienquelle*) have contributed much towards understanding the development of Q and the themes and influences at work in its redaction(s). What emerges quite evidently from these redactional critical studies is that certain themes and motifs are in evidence, but are they as obvious or as important as the various authors maintain? The real solution lies in identifying the literary genre of Q, for this helps to put all the material into a specific framework with a definite direction and purpose in mind.

1. Robinson, 'Logoi Sophon'. The first draft of this paper appeared as early as 15 February 1964 when it 'was read at the meeting of the Western Section of the Society of Biblical Literature in Berkeley, California' ('Logoi Sophon', 71).

depth, because I consider it to be one of the more significant
articles to appear on Q in more recent times. Robinson intends
to show how 'a sayings of the Lord' trajectory extended from
the earliest times right through to the second century, to the
Gospel of Thomas and the *Pistis Sophia*. The key to Robinson's
whole approach lies in the attention that Bultmann[1] gave to
the affinity between the sayings of the Lord and wisdom sayings. While Bultmann did not pursue this connection in Q, he
did draw out the christological implications of the identification of Jesus and wisdom in the Fourth Gospel, particularly in
the prologue. Robinson used these insights of Bultmann to
undertake an in-depth examination of the Q source.[2]

1. Bultmann, *The History of the Synoptic Tradition*, 69.
    2. As Robinson ('Logoi Sophon', 73-74) states: 'This essay, then, seeks
to confirm, clarify, and carry further Bultmann's association of *logia*
and *meshalim* under the concept of 'wisdom teacher', by working out a
name for the gattung [*sic*] of Q, 'λόγοι σοφῶν', 'sayings of the sages', or
'words of the wise' as a reflection in the sources themselves of the tendency constitutive of the gattung to which Q belongs'.
    I should like to briefly to draw attention to the main aspects of Robin-
son's thought. According to him the reference to the sayings of the
Lord as logia comes from the writings of Papias, who calls his study on
the Gospels an 'Interpretation of the Lord's Logia' ('Logoi Sophon', 74,
where Robinson quotes Eusebius, *HE* 3.39.1). In referring to the Gospel
of Matthew he speaks of the 'logia' which some commentators have
connected with Q. Although this designation of the sayings of the Lord
as logia initially became the accepted designation, Robinson ('Logoi
Sophon', 75) contends that the word *logoi* would be the more accepted
terminology. An examination of the Oxyrhynchus and Nag Hammadi
texts and fragments indicates that the titles appended to the end of a
writing are generally secondary, whereas the initial titles appear to be
the more original. An examination of the *Gospel of Thomas* shows this
very clearly. The term *Gospel* appears solely at the end, while the term
λόγοι appears both at the beginning and frequently throughout the
whole work: 'Whoever finds the explanation of these words will not
taste death' (Saying 1). 'If you become disciples to me and hear my
words...' (Saying 19). Consequently, the term λόγοι is used at the very
beginning to refer to the contents of the whole work: 'These are *the
secret words* which the Living Jesus spoke...' (A. Guillaumont *et al.*,
*The Gospel according to Thomas: Coptic Text Established and Trans-
lated* [San Francisco: Harper & Row, 1959], 3-13). The *Gospel of
Thomas*, then, belongs to the Gattung of sayings (*logoi*) and not to that
of Gospel.
    All the synoptic Gospels make use of formulae related to collections
of sayings (λόγοι): Matthew's five books or discourses are in fact collec-

Robinson presented a very challenging perception of the development of Q within the wider framework of the literary genre, namely that of a Gattung called λόγοι σοφῶν. This Gattung was evident in the Hebrew writings, particularly the wisdom books such as Proverbs and Ecclesiastes. In fact a better title for the Book of Proverbs would be that of λόγοι σοφῶν. Even outside of Israel, in Mesopotamia and Egypt, there is evidence of such a Gattung of λόγοι σοφῶν.

I would endorse the view that the genre of Q is analogous to that genre of 'sayings of the wise'. At the same time more

tions of sayings (λόγοι); Luke uses quotation formulae to refer to Jesus' λόγοι; and even Mark seems to bear witness to the use of some collection of sayings. 'From Mark's point of view Mark 4 is then a collection, not of parables, but rather of riddles, allegories, secret sayings. Between the parable of the sower and the two concluding parables of the seed growing secretly and of the mustard seed (4.26-29, 30-32), Mark inserts a series of sayings (4.21-25)' ('Logoi Sophon', 92-93). Behind the Gospels stand collections of the sayings of Jesus such as the Q source. Originally the term λόγοι would be found in the sayings themselves; but with time it would tend to become a term which the redactor would use to characterize the writing. The final outcome of the sayings tradition was twofold: first, the canonical Gospels tended to replace the oral transmissions of the sayings-Gattung in orthodox Christianity. Secondly, within Gnosticism the sayings-Gattung tended to develop into a dialogue of the Risen Jesus with his followers ('Logoi Sophon', 103).

The Gattung of sayings is not a novel invention of Christianity as was the case with the Gattung of Gospel, but is clearly in evidence in the Hebrew writings, in particular in the wisdom literature. The book of Proverbs takes its title from the heading of a few of the collections within the book, namely 1.1–9.18; 10.1–22.16 and 25.1–29.27. However, there are other collections in this book bearing a different title, namely 'the words of. . .'; for example, 'the words of Agur son of Jakeh' (30.1); 'the words of Lemuel, king of Massa' (31.1); and 'the words of the wise' (22.17). In the LXX this reference to 'the words of the wise' becomes λόγοι σοφῶν.

Many of Jesus' sayings undoubtedly had wisdom connotations and their handing on would naturally tend to absorb other wisdom sayings into this Gattung. As Robinson ('Logoi Sophon', 112) notes: 'The addition of further wisdom sayings would be facilitated within the gattung (sic), whose proclivities were to be more concerned with the validity or "truth" of the sayings incorporated than with their human authorship or "authenticity"'. In effect, then, the Gattung of sayings as applied to the sayings of Jesus became a Gattung of sayings of the wise (λόγοι σοφῶν), as was the case in the wisdom tradition of the Old Testament.

credibility must be attributed to these sayings as representing *sayings of Jesus* which aim at transmitting his message and explaining it in wisdom terms against the background of the whole wisdom trajectory of the Hebrew writings. Q is not to be seen in isolation as the only tradition handing on the sayings of Jesus. It would be one amongst others. In fact when Q was written down, the sayings continued in an oral form alongside Q.

Robinson's contention that the sayings Gattung continued in a twofold direction is logical and very attractive. On the one hand they were codified in the scriptures, particularly in the synoptic Gospels accepted by the orthodox Church; on the other hand they developed further by being incorporated and transformed into the Gnostic perspective. Those who have objected to these proposals of Robinson have not really raised any serious objections. Instead, they show a misunderstanding of his presentation.

For example, Devisch[1] finds it untenable. His argument is largely based on the fact that the connection between Q and *Thomas* cannot be maintained. His view that *Thomas* contains no christology[2] is somewhat debatable. He criticizes Robinson for thinking that elements of Gnosticism could be traceable in Q[3] whereas in fact what Robinson maintains is that the tendency of the genre itself is gnosticizing.[4] This particular aspect of Robinson's presentation is most unfortunate and has received the most objections.[5] It is noteworthy that the only example that can be found of a work with a clearly Gnostic tendency is that of the *Gospel of Thomas*, which is the end product of the whole trajectory. But, to argue backwards and to say that the gnosticizing tendency of the genre was always there cannot be demonstrated. It is true that Q tends to suggest a relationship on the part of the speaker of wisdom and 'wise

1. M. Devisch, 'Le Document Q, source de Matthieu: problématique actuelle', in *L'Évangile selon Matthieu: rédaction et théologie* (ed. M. Didier; Gembloux: J. Duculot, 1972), 71-98.

2. *Ibid.*, 85.

3. *Ibid.*, 82.

4. Robinson, 'Logoi Sophon', 112-13.

5. Kloppenborg, 'The Formation of Q and Antique Instructional Genres', 444.

words' with wisdom herself, but this in itself does not mean that there always was a gnosticizing tendency within Q. I would argue that this gnosticizing tendency developed later in the trajectory after the incorporation of Q into the canonical Gospels. It is the *Gospel of Thomas* which illustrates the movement that developed after Q within the λόγοι σοφῶν Gattung towards the presentation of Jesus as the Gnostic revealer. It is *the content* which has developed along Gnostic lines, whereas *the form* has remained the same.[1]

Kümmel also adopts a view opposed to that of Robinson. He maintains: 'But from this it follows that the Gospel of Thomas is undoubtedly not a later form of the same literary genre as Q, but is a later, wholly different stage in the development of the tradition of the words of Jesus'.[2] He goes so far as to assert that 'the Gospel of Thomas can teach us nothing about the origin and literary character of Q...'[3] Kümmel's argument is based on a too monolithic conception of early Christian thought when he argues that the *Gospel of Thomas* has taken over some of the sayings from the synoptic Gospels and has recast them in a Gnostic mould. I think that it is far more logical to assume that over the course of the decades following the death and resurrection of Jesus many responses were made to Jesus. The collection of sayings of Jesus in Q does not represent the only collection nor the total collection that was made. It is too simplistic a view, in the case of Kümmel, to see *Thomas* simply taking some sayings from the Gospels and transforming them. More probably the sayings traditions seen in Q (which was codified in the Gospels) *and* those existing alongside Q and the Gospels formed the source for the development which saw its culmination in the Gnostic perspective of the *Gospel of Thomas.*

It is true, as Kümmel argues, that 'the *Gospel of Thomas* presupposes the transformation of Jesus into the role of a Gnostic revealer', but when he says that it 'shows in this way that it is a literary form of a later period'[4] he has revealed a

---

1. Biggs, 'The Q Debate since 1955', 26-27.
2. Kümmel, *Introduction to the New Testament*, 75-76.
3. *Ibid.*, 76.
4. *Ibid.*

confusion between content and form. The content has been transformed, but the form, namely that of λόγοι σοφῶν, is the same as has been in existence since the time of the wisdom sayings of the Book of Proverbs. Robinson has considered genre not as some static entity, but as something that develops and changes over the course of time, and that is an important consideration. This is evident with the Q source: its content is different from that of the wisdom sayings of the Old Testament, but its form is that of the wisdom sayings. In utilizing the form of sayings of the wise, one must not distort the perspective. They remain sayings of Jesus which aim at handing on his teachings in a wisdom framework. Kloppenborg[1] assesses the insight of Robinson very well when he says:

> Whether or not Robinson is correct in ascribing a specifically gnosticizing tendency to the genre he is surely right in pointing to the theological influence of a genre conception. That Q represents Jesus as a speaker of wisdom rather than as an actant in narratives describing the healings or other miraculous deeds, that Q makes no attempt to situate itself temporally in respect of the Easter events, and that it does not rely upon a narrative structure with the themes of secret epiphany and selective disclosure, all these have their theological ramifications, and they suggest a distinctive hermeneutical situation for Q.

Besides this trajectory dealing with the sayings of Jesus there are other streams of Christian tradition, such as that stemming from the narratives of the deeds of Christ (forming the bulk of the material codified in Mark), as well as the Pauline, the Johannine and the Petrine traditions. These traditions do not develop in total isolation from one another, but certain connections take place, as can be seen within the synoptic traditions. James is another of these streams of Christian tradition which is also not totally independent.

The picture thus emerges of the early Christian community not as a monolithic entity, but as capable of developing traditions in different centres. In the post-Pauline church the merging of traditions seems to be more common in what may be termed a syncretistic way. The development of the sayings

---

1. Kloppenborg, 'Tradition and Redaction in the Synoptic Sayings Source', 59.

tradition into the realm of Gnosticism could have been facilitated by the tendency of the sayings to come into contact with
other Christian traditions, in this instance with Gnosticism.
Brown indicates a somewhat similar development in the
realm of the Johannine community whereby the traditions of
the Gospel of John are being misused in the Gnostic circles. In
order to maintain the orthodox interpretation of John's Gospel,
it was necessary for the Johannine community to issue a cov-
ering letter (the first Epistle of John) to clarify clearly how the
Gospel is to be interpreted in reference to the person and
nature of Jesus.[1]

The article of Robinson has presented a challenging direction for the investigation of Q. As has been argued, Q falls into
the trajectory of sayings of Jesus which later were codified in
the synoptic Gospels, and then in a second development
formed part of those sayings making their way into the Gnostic writings such as the Gospel of Thomas. An examination of
the Q material shows that at least three major themes predominate,[2] namely eschatology, prophecy and wisdom. It is
specifically the theme of wisdom which forms the focus of
attention here. My intention is to examine Q from the perspective of wisdom to show that Robinson's contention that Q
belongs to a λόγοι σοφῶν trajectory is a valid insight, provided
the basis of these sayings as sayings of Jesus is maintained. At
the same time a comparison will be made with James to show
the importance that wisdom occupies in that writing.

3. *The Wisdom Character of James and Q: Practical Advice and Form of Expression*

McKenzie[3] noted that 'wisdom is viewed too narrowly when it
is viewed as wisdom literature'. My concern is not with wisdom literature as such, but with themes and forms that are
characterized as belonging to wisdom. In studies on the New

---

1. R.E. Brown, *The Community of the Beloved Disciple* (London:
Chapman, 1979), 106-109.
2. Edwards, *A Theology of Q*.
3. J.L. McKenzie, 'Reflections on Wisdom', *JBL* 86 (1967), 2.

Testament[1] the place of wisdom in early Christian thought
has not been sufficiently emphasized. In fact, just as wisdom
studies relating to the Old Testament were a much-neglected
area of research, the same is true with regard to the New
Testament. In contrast the early Patristic period showed a
lively interest in wisdom thought. Origen[2] argues that wisdom
was the most ancient title for Jesus: ὡς εἰπεῖν ἄν τινα τεθαρρη-
κότως (ὡς) πρεσβύτερον πάντων τῶν ἐπινοουμένων ταῖς
ὀνομασίαις τοῦ πρωτοτόκου πάσης κτίσεώς ἐστιν ἡ σοφία. The
Patristic period also showed much interest in the wisdom
writings of the Old Testament. Numerous commentaries
appeared on the wisdom books such as Proverbs and Ecclesiastes.[3] Consequently, this interest in wisdom and the association of Jesus with wisdom can be traced back to the very origins of Christian thought.

The period of Jesus and the emergence of the New Testament writings continued the two wisdom perspectives, namely
ethical admonitions and reflection upon the nature of wisdom,
and both can be observed in both Q and James. First, attention
will be given to the ethical admonitions in which Q and James
express their practical wisdom advice.

3.1 *Wisdom sayings and admonitions*

3.1.1 *In the Q source*
Although very prominent in Q, certain considerations of Q[4]
have tended to ignore this form of expression. Other scholars
such as Beardslee[5] and Edwards[6] have argued that the main
purpose of Q was to offer practical advice to its readers. In his

---

1. R.L. Wilken (ed.), *Aspects of Wisdom in Judaism and Early Christianity* (University of Notre Dame Center for the Study of Judaism and
Christianity in Antiquity, 1; Notre Dame: University of Notre Dame
Press, 1975), xvi.
2. Origen, *Commentaire sur Saint Jean. Tome I* (Livres I–V). *Texte
grec, avant-propos, traduction et notes par Cécile Blanc*. Paris: Editions du Cerf, 1966), 122.
3. Wilken, *Aspects of Wisdom*, xvii-xviii.
4. U. Wilckens, 'σοφία', *TDNT* 7 (1971), 515-17.
5. Beardslee, 'The Wisdom Tradition and the Synoptic Gospels'; and
Literary Criticism of the New Testament.
6. R.A. Edwards, 'An Approach to a Theology of Q', *JR* 51 (1971), 259-
60.

examination of wisdom forms in Q Edwards drew attention to a useful distinction between wisdom sayings and wisdom admonitions.

(a) Wisdom sayings are statements which arise from experience. They draw a conclusion from this experience and very often present advice on how to lead one's life. Examples of wisdom sayings in Q are: 'A disciple is not above his teacher, but every one when he is fully taught will be like his teacher' (Q 6.40); 'The good man out of the good treasure of his heart produces good, and the evil man out of his evil treasure produces evil; for out of the abundance of the heart his mouth speaks' (Q 6.45); '...Behold, I send you out as lambs in the midst of wolves' (Q 10.3).

(b) Wisdom admonitions on the other hand lay emphasis on the didactic element. They call for obedience and implementation of the advice and usually add a reason to support the admonition. Examples of such admonitions in Q abound: 'And as you wish that men would do to you, do so to them' (Q 6.31); 'Judge not, and you will not be judged; condemn not, and you will not be condemned; forgive, and you will be forgiven' (Q 6.37); 'The harvest is plentiful, but the labourers are few; pray therefore the Lord of the harvest to send out labourers into his harvest' (Q 10.2).

In their own way both the sayings and the admonitions offer practical advice for daily living. They are distinguished from each other by the direct exhortation which the admonition makes to a certain type of action. Very often that exhortation is placed within an eschatological framework in which a future result depends upon present action. In fact it appears as though traditional wisdom has been reformulated through an eschatological perspective.

With the understanding that the Son of man will return as judge, a specific dimension is added to the eschatological hope which permeates these wisdom forms. For example, 'Give, and it will be given to you; good measure, pressed down, shaken together, running over, will be put into your lap. For the measure you give will be the measure you get back' (Q 6.38). Whereas traditional wisdom saw that one's actions achieved results in the present world order, the wisdom sayings and admonitions in Q add an eschatological dimension.

3.1.2 *Epistle of James*

Both wisdom sayings and admonitions are also observable in the practical advice offered by the Epistle of James for daily life.

(a) Wisdom sayings are fairly numerous in the Epistle of James. Dibelius[1] has argued consistently for the view that these sayings are isolated and do not fit into their context. This judgment, however, is too dogmatic. While it is true that these sayings might have been originally independent, nevertheless James has woven them together in a very careful way to form an intimate part of the context. An example of such a saying is: 'For judgment is without mercy to one who has shown no mercy; yet mercy triumphs over judgment' (Jas 2.13). Dibelius[2] argues that this is an isolated saying which has no connection with the themes of the section preceding it. A close examination of this passage reveals that this is not the case because this verse forms an essential part of the context and the thought presented is in close association with the main argument of the pericope, namely that one is not to show partiality in one's actions. Most often these wisdom statements in James appear at the conclusion of a pericope. As such they are to be viewed, not simply as something appended at the end, but rather as an essential aspect of the pericope, reinforcing its argument. Similar sayings are: 'For as the body apart from the spirit is dead, so faith apart from works is dead' (2.26); 'For where jealousy and selfish ambition exist, there will be disorder and every vile practice' (3.16); 'And the harvest of righteousness is sown in peace by those who make peace' (3.18).

An examination of the last saying (3.18) shows that it brings together the development of thought in this pericope: the gift of wisdom produces the gift of righteousness which is illustrated by peace. This saying has also helped to bridge the gap to the next pericope (Jas 4.1). Chapter 3 concluded with a reference to peace, while ch. 4 opened with the question regarding the exact opposite of peace: 'What causes wars, and what causes fightings among you?' (4.1).

---

1. *James: A Commentary on the Epistle of James.*
2. *Ibid.*, 147.

(b) Wisdom admonitions concentrate attention on the teaching element. They issue a call to obedience and are eminently suited to the wisdom style which offers practical advice to its readers. Of all the wisdom forms of expression used in James this is the most frequent. James finds that the form of the wisdom admonition is the most appropriate and effective means to express his paraenetical advice. Among a few of the more important admonitions are the following:

(i)   James begins his letter with an admonition expressed in a positive way: 'Count it all joy, my brethren, when you meet various trials' (1.2). This admonition replaces the characteristic statement of thanksgiving in a Pauline letter. The passage continues with numerous other admonitions: 'And let steadfastness have its full effect...' (1.4); 'If any of you lacks wisdom, let him ask God...' (1.5); 'But let him ask in faith, with no doubting...' (1.6).

(ii) In paragraph F (1.19-27) a series of admonitions are stated which revolve around the threefold saying: 'Let every man be quick to hear, slow to speak, slow to anger' (1.19). Dibelius[1] has argued that this three-part saying is constituted from traditional wisdom sayings. Each one of the phrases is taken up in the various sections of this pericope and from them admonitions are developed.

(iii) 'My brethren, show no partiality as you hold the faith of our Lord Jesus Christ, the Lord of glory' (2.1). With this admonition James begins the body of his epistle.[2] This admonition dominates all that follows in the pericope.

(iv) 'Let not many of you become teachers, my brethren, for you know that we who teach shall be judged with greater strictness' (3.1). This admonition forms the opening of a new section dealing with guarding the tongue by means of exaggeration. James emphasizes the great responsibility falling on the shoulders of those who teach. Coupled with the admonition is the reason for its observance: εἰδότες ὅτι μεῖζον κρίμα λημψόμεθα.

---

1. *Ibid.*, 109-10.
2. Dibelius (*James*, 124) has pointed out that James has the habit of beginning a new section either with an admonition or with a rhetorical question (2.1; 2.14; 3.1).

(v) A further series of admonitions occurs in 4.7-10 whereby James offers remedies for the strife in the community. In this short section ten imperatives issue forth related admonitions which are all contained between these two parallel statements: 'Submit your-selves therefore to God. Humble yourselves before the Lord.' The concern for the type of life that one should lead shows the debt to the wisdom tradition.

(vi) The Epistle of James ends with various admonitions on a number of themes, such as not taking oaths, the exhor-tation to prayer, and the confession of sins. Finally, it concludes with the admonition: 'Let him know that whoever brings back a sinner from the error of his way will save his soul from death and will cover a multitude of sins' (5.20). The epistle ends on a high note by showing its belief in the work of salvation. This is a very suitable conclusion for it sets out the entire purpose for the admonitions: by implementing the way of life mapped out in this epistle the reader can hope to attain salvation.

A twofold direction emerges in these admonitions. First, a focus on the present shows the reader the type of life to be led here and now. Secondly, an emphasis on the future stresses the eschatological attainment of salvation. James's vision is not just directed towards the present, but also opens up the future with an eschatological vision. Through faith, illustrated by specific deeds, one comes to salvation. This eschatological per-spective has permeated the wisdom tradition of James.

Both James and Q show a concern to offer practical advice to their readers. This they express in many and diverse ways. What is noteworthy here is not so much the content of the sayings and admonitions, but rather that wisdom categories have been used to express their thought. James and Q also show a common perspective where the sayings and admoni-tions demonstrate a twofold point of reference. They are con-cerned with the *present* in that the reader is instructed on the type of life to lead; but this present perspective also looks towards the *future*. In both James and Q traditional wisdom has undergone a transformation through the influence of the eschatological dimension. While the death and resurrection of

Christ do not influence wisdom in both James and Q, the future eschatological age certainly does.

3.2 *Beatitudes*

The beatitude is a characteristic of wisdom literature. Although in more recent times the literary form of a beatitude has been shown to be at home both in the Old Testament and in the Greek world,[1] analogies for the beatitudes in the New Testament really appear in the world of the Old Testament and the Judaism of the intertestamental period. Characteristic of the New Testament beatitude is its restricted reference to persons.[2] The structure of the beatitude is usually presented in this form: μακάριος appears first in the statement; this is followed by the person who is considered blessed; and it ends with the reason or cause of the blessedness.[3] The original address of the beatitude was in the third person (as most often occurs in Matthew) while the second person formula (which appears in Luke) is secondary. Luke used the second person formula because he was attempting to bring the beatitude into correlation with the woe (which occurs in the second person address).[4]

The difference between the Old and New Testament beatitudes is attributed to the different nature of Old and New Testament wisdom. In the Old Testament the emphasis lies on practical wisdom with effects occurring in the present order, while in the New Testament the dimension is changed to the eschatological order where the results occur in an eschatological framework.[5]

---

1. F. Hauck, 'μακάριος, μακαρίζω, μακαρισμός', *TDNT*, IV (1967), 362-64.
2. *Ibid.*, 367.
3. *Ibid.*
4. *Ibid.*, 367 n. 43.
5. *Ibid.*, 367.

3.2.1 *In the Q source* eight beatitudes make their appearance.[1]
These can be divided into two groups according to their focus
of attention.[2]

(a) The beatitude as an eschatological correlative. Four of
the eight beatitudes in Q refer to the new life or the new situation in the eschatological age. This is in directly opposite correlation to what is experienced now. The following beatitudes in
the Sermon on the Mount which come from Q illustrate this:
'Blessed are you poor, for yours is the kingdom of God' (Q
6.20b); 'Blessed are you that hunger now, for you shall be sat-
isfied; blessed are you that weep now, for you shall laugh' (Q
6.21). Here the new situation, the new life, is referred to the
future: in the kingdom of God, the poor, the hungry, those who
weep, will no longer be poor, hungry or sad. 'Thus we have an
interesting combination of factors—a wisdom statement about
a condition of the future. The contrast between the now and
the then implies that the present world's criteria of worth will
be overthrown. The speaker seems to have two roles (as traditionally defined)—that of a prophet (messenger or revealer)
and that of a teacher or wise man.'[3]

In Q 6.22-23 the eschatological correlative again makes its
appearance. Those who are persecuted in the present will
receive their reward in the future kingdom of God. In true
wisdom style the past is used to explain the present in that the
prophets from the past appear as examples for the present.
Just as they were persecuted, so too the Q community experiences persecution. The Q community situates itself in the line
of the Old Testament prophets: the best way to express its own
consciousness is 'in terms of the role of a prophet'.[4]

(b) The beatitude with a paraenetic interest. The remaining
four beatitudes draw attention to the type of life required of
believers by their faith. In this sense they offer advice for the
present and have far more of a didactic interest.

---

1. Edwards ('An Approach to a Theology of Q', 263-64) speaks of only
seven beatitudes: he omits from his calculation Q 6.21b: 'Blessed are
you that weep now, for you shall laugh'.
2. *Ibid.*, 263.
3. Edwards, *A Theology of Q*, 62-63.
4. *Ibid.*, 63.

(i)	'And blessed is he who takes no offence at me'	(Q 7.23)
(ii)	'Blessed are the eyes which see what you see'	(Q 10.23)
(iii)	'Blessed is that servant whom his master when he comes will find so doing'	(Q 12.43)
(iv)	'Blessed is he who comes in the name of the Lord'	(Q 13.35c)

The paraenesis or admonition is clearly evident in (iii). The servant is blessed because he is in charge of his master's possessions, and not because he is to see the coming of the Lord, or to inherit the kingdom. The act of judging or declaring one blessed in the future depends upon urgent fidelity to the tasks that have been assigned in the present. Hence, the call is made in the present to be faithful in what one does.

The final beatitude (iv) relates to the personification of wisdom where Jesus speaks in the same way in which wisdom does in the Hebrew scriptures. The emphasis of the beatitude lies on a specific reference to the Messiah and his coming; in fact, it is a quotation from Ps. 118.26. By connecting the beatitude with a wisdom oracle, wisdom is given a messianic role. As Bultmann remarks: 'Wisdom foretells that she will remain hidden until the coming of the Messiah; for only he can be meant by the one ἐρχόμενος ἐν ὀνόματι κυρίου'.[1] In a certain sense this beatitude is unique because it does not refer, as in the other beatitudes, to a group, whether it be the community of Q or the disciples of Jesus in general. Instead the beatitude refers specifically to the Messiah where Jesus is proclaimed as the truly blessed one because he is above all the spokesman of the Lord. By implication one may argue that the Q community which saw itself in the role of the prophets, the spokesmen of the Lord, will be truly blessed as Jesus was if they exercise their function faithfully as God's emissaries.

3.2.2 *In the Epistle of James* the word μακάριος occurs on two occasions:

---

1. Bultmann, *A History of the Synoptic Tradition,* 115.

(a) Jas 1.12 is expressed according to the regular New Testament mode of expression: Μακάριος ἀνὴρ ὃς ὑπομένει πειρασμόν, ὅτι δόκιμος γενόμενος λήμψεται τὸν στέφανον τῆς ζωῆς ὃν ἐπηγγείλατο τοῖς ἀγαπῶσιν αὐτόν. It begins with the word μακάριος which is followed by the person (ἀνήρ) without the article, and finally the reason why the person is called blessed is indicated in the phrase ὃς ὑπομένει πειρασμόν. Evident too in this beatitude is the eschatological correlative: the promise of inheriting 'the crown of life' is made to the person who endures trial now. This bears a clear eschatological reference. There is a noticeable closeness in the expression of the beatitudes in Q and in the book of Revelation, where they always occur within an eschatological framework.[1] This is a further indication of wisdom being permeated by the eschatological dimension.

(b) In Jas 1.25 the word μακάριος occurs again. This time it is not used in a beatitude, but in a desriptive clause: ὁ δὲ παρακύψας εἰς νόμον τέλειον τὸν τῆς ἐλευθερίας καὶ παραμείνας, οὐκ ἀκροατὴς ἐπιλησμονῆς γενόμενος ἀλλὰ ποιητὴς ἔργου, οὗτος μακάριος ἐν τῇ ποιήσει αὐτοῦ ἔσται. Here the blessing refers to the future where present actions will lead to future blessings. The perspective is that of the eschatological correlative.

(c) Hauck[2] comments on these two verses in Jas 1.12 and 25 and his insights are worth nothing: 'Similarly, those who stand fast are called blessed in Jas 1.12, for their earthly endurance brings them eternal salvation. The thought of a sure reward is also present when the righteous doer is called blessed in Jas 1.25. In all these verses the light of future glory shines over the sorry present position of the righteous. Thus the New Testament beatitudes are not just intimations of the future or consolations in relation to it. They see the present in the light of the future.' The two references to μακάριος in James show clearly this eschatological correlation between the present and the future. The promise of blessedness is reserved for the future, to be attained as a consequence of what one does now. This future

1. Hauck, 'μακάριος', 367-68.
2. *Ibid.*, 369.

lies in that realm of God's kingdom where those who are blessed will inherit 'the crown of life'.

The eschatological correlative becomes quite marked in both Q and James. The readers are advised and exhorted to lead a specific way of life because an eschatological inheritance is promised to those that do. The wisdom character of James and Q has been determined by their appropriation a traditional Old Testament wisdom form of expression and adapted it in the same way. The aim of this wisdom form is to give the readers practical advice for their future lives.

3.3 Woes
As a literary form woes are in evidence in both the prophetic and wisdom traditions.

3.3.1 *In the Q source* an examination of the appearance of the woe shows how it has been adapted to fit the wisdom perspective. Edwards has variously identified the number of woes as six and seven.[1] In fact the number to be accepted is nine, as Jacobson[2] has rightly indicated. The nine woes are as follows: Q 10.13; Q 11.39 (Mt. 23.23); Q 11.42; Q 11.43; Q 11.44; Q 11.46; Q 11.47; Q 11.52; and Q 17.1. This list excludes the four woes found in Luke's Sermon on the Plain (Lk. 6.24-26); these latter occur only in Luke and it is uncertain whether in fact they actually formed part of Q.[3]

(a) Woes regarding the present situation. To this category belong the seven woes contained in the section Lk. 11.37-52 (Mt. 23.1-36). An examination of the context and a comparison of Lk. 11.39 with Mt. 23.25 shows Q to be closer to the formulation of Matthew. This means that Q was originally expressed in the form of a woe and not simply in the form of a

1. See Edwards, *A Theology of Q*, 67; and 'An Approach to a Theology of Q', 264.
2. Jacobson, 'The Literary Unity of Q', 374.
3. For example, Polag (*Fragmenta Q*, 84-85) includes them under 'unsichere Texte' in his appendix. As with the beatitudes two approaches and emphases are observable among the nine woes.

statement as occurs in Luke.[1] The woes are addressed to either
the Pharisees or the lawyers because of certain present actions
which they are performing. They are accused of neglecting
justice and the love of God (Q 11.42); or being too concerned
with outward observances (Q 11.39). Q 11.47 is quite revealing
for it is linked to the idea of wisdom as the sender of the
prophets. The lawyers are accused of being accomplices in the
persecution and killing of the prophets and a vindication of
their death will be required of this generation. Here the wisdom and deuteronomic traditions come together—which is
quite characteristic of Q.[2] Finally, in Q 11.52 the lawyers are
accused of not just having refused to learn from the experience of the past, but of making it impossible for others to enter
the kingdom of God.[3] Included here is the emphasis on judgment and suffering which has been the lot of the prophets in
the past.

(b) Woes with a paraenetic interest. (i) 'Woe to you
Chorazin! woe to you, Bethsaida! for if the mighty works done
in you had been done in Tyre and Sidon, they would have
repented long ago, sitting in sackcloth and ashes...' (Q 10.13).
The aim of this woe is to issue a warning to others not to put
themselves in a similar position. Here Chorazin and Bethsaida
are contrasted with Tyre and Sidon. The decided concern is to
ensure that the behaviour of Chorazin and Bethsaida is not
imitated. (ii) 'Woe to the world for temptations to sin! For it is
necessary that temptations come, but woe to the man by
whom the temptation comes!' (Mt. 18.7; cf. also Lk. 17.1 and
Mk 9.42). In Matthew and Luke Q has been joined to the
Markan account, so it is difficult to establish the reading of Q
exactly.[4] The admonition is very clear: temptations are bound
to take place, but the one responsible for the temptation is
cursed. The paraenetic interest is also evident: it is a call to the
readers to ensure that they are not a cause of temptation to

1. Jacobson ('Wisdom Christology in Q', 183-85) has examined the
sequence of the woes and in general sees the order preserved in
Matthew as being closer to Q than in Luke.
2. Jacobson, 'The Literary Unity of Q', 374.
3. Edwards, *A Theology of Q*, 70.
4. As can be seen by Polag's attempted reconstruction (*Fragmenta Q*,
74-75).

their neighbour. Above all the threat of judgment forms the centre of attention in these woes.

3.3.2 *The Epistle of James* also brings woes into harmony with the wisdom tradition. Two pericopae can be classified as belonging to the literary form of the woes: 4.13-17 and 5.1-6.

(a) The call not to neglect God: Pericope M (4.13-17). This section focuses attention on the importance wisdom gives to action: one's deeds demonstrate faith and trust in God. Although faith is not directly mentioned, it does form the background to James's thought. If one wishes to live a life of faith, one's actions must illustrate dependence upon God. The opening words of the pericope, "Αγε νῦν (Jas 4.13), are in line with the way in which a prophetic oracle would be expressed, and would in fact correspond to the expression of 'Woe to you...' so characteristic of the prophetic address (cf. Isa. 5.8ff.). This section gives attention to the passing of judgment in which a warning or a threat is issued. The final verse (4.17) of this section highlights this: 'Whoever knows what is right to do and fails to do it, for him it is a sin'. This section does not intend to condemn a specific action, but it passes judgment in general upon all those who make their plans without any reference to God. To ask, 'What circumstances gave rise to this specific example?', is in many ways a false question.[1] James wants to provide his readers with teaching which shows them how faith in action is meant to be carried out. By putting their trust entirely in themselves, they reject God. James envisages a danger which could face Christian businessmen, so he provides an illustration which warns them against the danger of excluding God from their actions. This illustration is nothing other than a concrete example of what James has considered twice before from different perspectives, namely that for a Christian faith and action are not to be separated.

(b) Condemnation of the arrogance of the rich (5.1-6). The second of the woes contained in James immediately follows the previous condemnation of those who fail to put their trust in God. It opens in the same way as the previous woe, with the phrase "Αγε νῦν. The focus of attention here is not on the pre-

---

1. Dibelius, *James*, 234-35.

sent, but on the future, on the eschatological age, which will
issue in a judgment of condemnation upon the rich. They are
condemned because of the suffering and injustice they cause
those who have placed their confidence in God. The two
aspects of the literary form of a woe are clearly evident in this
pericope, namely the passing of judgment and the emphasis on
the role of suffering for those who do God's will. An eschatological perspective also dominates the thought of this pericope. In
the previous passage emphasis had been placed on the need to
place trust solely in God. This perspective is in fact maintained
here by focusing on the rich who place their trust, not in God,
but in their own riches. Chracteristic of all New Testament
eschatology is that the kingdom of God demands that one rely
on God and not upon earthly things.[1]

The eschatological references in this section are far more
open and direct, and in fact undergo a progression of intensifi-
cation. Opening with a reference to 'the miseries that are
coming upon you' (5.1), there is a specific reference to 'the last
days' (5.3) which are finally depicted graphically as 'a day of
slaughter' (5.5). This language is clearly reminiscent of the
prophets. Contrasted with the attitude and actions of the rich
are those of the righteous man who offers no resistance. This
contrast highlights the guilt of the rich even further. One is left
with the implication that the righteous will be justified in the
eschatological age. The eschatological perspective is continued
in the following pericope O (5.7-11) whereby the righteous are
exhorted to patience. Whereas the eschatological focus in pericope N had been upon the judgment and punishment of the
wicked rich, in pericope O the focus of attention is positive: it
envisages a promise for the righteous. The prophets are held
up as examples of patient endurance under suffering.

In the above discussion one notes how the three traditions of
the prophetic, the eschatological and wisdom work together.
In fact the wisdom perspective provides the catalyst for
bringing them together in both James and Q. When speaking
of wisdom in this context of James and Q, one is viewing it as
an approach to reality in which advice is offered on how best to
lead one's life. Consequently, both James and Q utilize not only

---

1. Edwards, *A Theology of Q*, 36-37.

specific wisdom traditions, but also prophetic and eschatological ones in order to endorse and clarify the basic aim of offering advice for one's daily life. Seen from this viewpoint the wisdom perspective facilitates the use of the eschatological and prophetic traditions. This does not mean that the other traditions cease to function. Rather, in James and Q they occur in their own right, but are used for the wisdom purpose of providing advice. Both Q and James aim at providing an outline for the righteous on how to act as a true disciple in what is now envisaged as the end of time. The eschatological correlative provides the call for the disciple to act in a specific way. By means of prophetic terminology and imagery this call is made all the more urgent. 'You have lived on the earth in luxury and in pleasure; you have fattened your hearts in a day of slaughter' (5.5) provides the background to wisdom's directives on the type of life one is to lead in the present.

3.4 *Wisdom forms of comparison*
One of the most characteristic features of all wisdom writing is the use of different forms of comparison. Very often in the comparison, two things are juxtaposed and it remains for the reader to deduce the conclusion and to see the relationship which the speaker intends. The reader is no passive recipient, but is actively involved and has a distinct contribution to make to the comparison. Different types of comparison may be noted in this regard.

3.4.1 *In the Q source* three main types of comparison can be noted.[1]
  (a) Forms of contrast. A comparison is implied by placing contrasting things next to each other, thereby constructing an antithesis. 'Judge not, and you will not be judged; condemn not and you will not be condemned; forgive, and you will be forgiven' (Q 6.37).
  (b) The explicit comparison. Expressions such as more than, greater than, less than, predominate. In appealing to experience a general statement is made and then the saying is intensified. 'This generation is an evil generation; it seeks a

---

1. *Ibid.*, 73-79.

sign, but no sign shall be given to it except the sign of Jonah. For as Jonah became a sign to the men of Nineveh, so will the Son of man be to this generation... The men of Nineveh will arise at the judgment with this generation and condemn it; for they repented at the preaching of Jonah, and behold, something greater than Jonah is here' (Q 11.29-32).

(c) Parables. Parables as such also form a distinctive feature of Mark's writing. However, certain features distinguish the parable in Q from that in Mark. In Q the element of comparison is more predominant. One also notes several phrases of comparison which feature frequently in Q, but which are missing from Mark, for example πλεῖον (Q 11.31), πόσῳ μᾶλλον (Q 11.13); ἀνεκτότερον (Q 10.12).[1] Most characteristic of the Q parable is the fact that the wisdom, eschatological and prophetic perspectives all work together. Some of the characteristic Q parables are: the son's request for a fish (Q 11.11-13); the blind leading the blind (Q 6.39); the speck in contrast to the log (Q 6.41-42); the house against the flood (Q 6.47-49); the lamp and the light (Q 11.34-36); the mustard seed (Q 13.18-19); leaven (Q 13.20-21); the unclean spirit (Q 11.24-26); the householder (Q 12.39).

3.4.2 *The Epistle of James* demonstrates the same wisdom features of comparison.

(a) Forms of contrast. The simple contrast makes it easy for the reader to see the type of action one is called upon to perform. 'But let him ask in faith with no doubting, for he who doubts is like a wave of the sea' (1.6). 'But be doers of the word, and not hearers only' (1.22). 'Unfaithful creatures! Do you not know that friendship with the world is enmity with God?' (4.4). An extended form of contrast is given in pericope J (3.13-18) where a catalogue of vices is presented alongside a catalogue of virtues. The latter receives more emphasis and is presented as that for which the life of the disciple must aim.

(b) Explicit comparisons. The simple use of similes and metaphors forms the characteristic style of James's writing which is very reminiscent of Jesus' method of teaching by means of comparisons. Examples of this abound in James, and

---

1. Jacobson, 'The Literary Unity of Q', 377 n. 54.

again issue a call to the reader to apply the comparison to the life of action. 'For he who doubts is *like a wave of the sea* that is driven and tossed by the wind' (1.6); '*Like the flower of the grass* he (= the rich man) will pass away' (1.10); 'So will the rich man *fade away* in the midst of his pursuits' (1.11).

(c) Parables. The Epistle of James is one of the few New Testament writings outside the Gospels to employ the parabolic method of comparison and instruction. This is a further illustration of James's similarity to the synoptic tradition of Jesus' teaching. The parables in James differ from the synoptics in that they are much briefer and not as numerous. As with any parable, the reader is actively involved in discovering the intended teaching. (i) 'For if any one is a hearer of the word and not a doer, he is like a man who observes his natural face in a mirror; for he observes himself and goes away and at once forgets what he was like' (1.23-24). Consideration is here focused on the need to be a doer of the word by using the illustration of what a hearer of the word is actually like. (ii) 'If a man with gold rings and in fine clothing comes into your assembly, and a poor man in shabby clothing...' (2.2). This is a parabolic form of instruction in that a story or example has been painted and from this imaginary situation a lesson is derived. The point of this parable appears from the context. By highlighting the difference that is shown in the treatment of the rich and poor, the call is made to show no partiality in one's dealings with others. (iii) 'If a brother or sister is ill-clad and in lack of daily food, and one of you says to them, "Go in peace, be warmed and filled", without giving them the things needed for the body, what does it profit? So faith by itself, if it has no works, is dead' (2.15-17).[1] By means of an imaginary example James has illustrated the teaching in this section, namely that faith to be true faith has to flower forth into action.

---

1. J. Ropes (*A Critical and Exegetical Commentary on the Epistle of St. James* [Edinburgh: T. & T. Clark, 1916], 206) has referred to this as 'a little parable'.

3.5 *Practical wisdom advice with a deuteronomistic perspective*

3.5.1 *In the Q source* the Q community saw itself as living in the eschatological times just prior to the imminent return of the Son of man as judge. The community had collected the sayings of this judge and was using them as a guide for moral action. In this framework the sayings were operating within a wisdom perspective and were used as a practical guide for moral living. The community was conscious of the need for an outline of how to act as a disciple in this end time.

As in the Hebrew writings wisdom in Q has above all a practical nature: it prescribes the art of living in the world on the basis of experience. Like the words of the wise the words of Jesus now form the basis for wisdom to offer its practical advice which has been shaped in a particular context. First, a prophetic dimension operated in conjunction with this wisdom tradition. To be wise meant that one also appeared in the role of a prophet—one who was a spokesman or emissary for God's wisdom. Salvation history comprised a long line of prophets, whose lives involved suffering, persecution, death and rejection. To this line belonged John the Baptist and Jesus as the Son of man who was the pre-eminent one. The Q community saw itself within this line as those called to be prophets who were to suffer and to experience rejection.[1]

In bringing to expression this prophetic influence in the handing on of Jesus' sayings, Q is also influenced by the deuteronomistic tradition which surveys Israel's history from a specific perspective. This deuteronomistic outlook sees Israel's history in terms of disobedience being followed by a call to repentance. This Israel accepts, but it is only to be followed later by the repetition of the cycle again with disobedience to and rejection of God. If Israel repented, God would restore it by gathering those who had been scattered among the nations.[2]

---

1. As Jacobson ('The Literary Unity of Q', 383) notes: 'The study thus far strongly suggests that Q stands within a prophetic tradition. Indeed, it is clear from the redactional addition in Luke 6.23c/Matthew 5.12c that the community sees itself as successors to the persecuted prophets of the past.'
2. *Ibid.*, 384-85.

Steck has largely been responsible for showing how this deuteronomistic conception of history continued throughout Israelite thought. He saw the Hasidic movement of 250–200 BC as responsible for continuing the deuteronomistic outlook by uniting divergent groups against the threat of Hellenization. After 150 BC the Hasidic movement's thrust was taken over by other groups, among whom one may include the Qumran community.[1]

Set against this background Q also reveals strong influences from the deuteronomistic tradition. Jacobson,[2] who bases himself on Steck, presents a very good summary of these influences in which seven characteristics of the deuteronomistic tradition are clearly evident in Q. The wisdom dimension of Jesus' sayings has been thoroughly stamped by this deuteronomistic prophetic tradition. In doing so the Q community saw itself as a loyal remnant within the community of Israel which is called to remain faithful at the end of time while awaiting the return of the Son of man. In contrast to them the majority of the nation of Israel appeared to be unconcerned about the seriousness of the present moment. They were also referred to as 'this generation' (Q 11.31) who identified themselves with other evil generations who persecuted the prophets. Belonging to the line of prophets, the Q community viewed itself as being persecuted in its turn by 'this generation'. Consequently, Q bears witness to a realization among the Q community of its distinction from the nation of Israel. In fact it considered itself as the loyal group, while Israel was judged to be the impenitent nation. Going hand in hand with this polemic against Israel was the praise given to the Gentiles because their faith showed up the lack of Israel's faith (Q 7.1-10; 10.13-15; 11.31-32).

3.5.2 *In the Epistle of James* a deuteronomistic perspective is also to be found and it operates, as in the Q source, together with the wisdom tradition. In this framework one may understand the address of the Epistle of James 'to the twelve tribes of the Dispersion' (1.1). The community of James's epistle belongs to that group which God, according to his promises

---

1. Steck, *Israel*, 212.
2. Jacobson, 'The Literary Unity of Q', 384-85.

and fidelity, is gathering from the scattered nation of Israel to become 'the first fruits' (1.18). The epistle issues a call to those who are part of this community to lead a life worthy of their having experienced God's call to salvation, as those whom God has restored. To those who do not form part of this community, who do not act in the way in which they should, James extends a call to repentance. A reminder is given to his readers of the role that the prophets played in the past in calling the people back to repentance. Often in their mission they suffered and were rejected. 'As an example of suffering and patience, brethren, take the prophets who spoke in the name of the Lord' (5.10). Here the community of James's readers is compared to that of the prophets of ancient Israel. The members of this community also endure suffering and persecution because of their allegiance to God and their desire to lead others to repent and to embrace the new community that God himself is creating.

James sees his task as urging his readers to remain faithful to this calling while they await the coming of the Judge who 'is standing at the doors' (5.9). This deuteronomistic approach to history situates James's community within that important stage when God is reconstituting the chosen people according to his promises. At the same time this deuteronomistic-prophetic dimension operates with the wisdom perspective which outlines the type of life that the member of this reconstituted community is to lead in order to remain loyal and faithful until the Lord's coming.

3.6 *Conclusion*
The *Sitz im Leben* of the community of Q and that of the Epistle of James appear to be very similar. Both show that they are emerging from a context in which the members are living at the end time and are awaiting the return of Jesus which is imminent. Both James and Q issue a call to their readers to remain faithful to their calling as they wait for the coming of the Lord, the Judge.

Seen in this light, the Q sayings of Jesus have a vital role to fulfil: they give a specific direction to people on how to lead their lives in a world that is about to attain its fulfilment. Wisdom, eschatology, prophecy, and the deuteronomistic view of history all combine to present this teaching. It is clear that this would be a development which would have taken place early in the spread of the Christian gospel, certainly prior to AD 70.[1] The most likely location for this development would be northern Palestine or Syria, because of its firm roots in Judaism, as well as the absence of the influence of Pauline thought and of the Passion kerygma.

Our aim has not been to try to uncover the original sayings of Jesus; rather, the investigation has aimed at taking Q as it is and analysing the main themes which emerge from the document as well as the way in which they were expressed. The Q community did not make a distinction between the historical Jesus and the words which they spoke as prophets in his name.[2] Instead, they saw themselves as handing on the message of Jesus in their own setting. In doing so they have given great weight to the wisdom dimension of the sayings of Jesus in order to offer practical advice to their community living in the eschatological age. It is in this sense that one can apply the phrase 'sayings of the wise' to the sayings of Jesus. Havener[3] expressed this well when he said:

> There has been a definite shift away from trying to recover the 'very words' (*ipsissima verba*) of the historical Jesus to a less precise 'very voice' (*ipsissima vox*) of the historical Jesus, that is, the type of material rather than the precise wording that may have come from Jesus during his earthly existence. Undoubtedly Q has some of the latter and, perhaps, also some of the former, but this material is embedded in a theological document, Q, which has its own way of looking at the person and role of Jesus, as he continues to speak to the Q community.

The Epistle of James also has as its main purpose the giving of practical wisdom advice to its readers on how to lead their lives. In this sense James appears above all as a wisdom teacher concerned with providing advice that his readers should follow. James, too, combines the eschatological, prophetic, and deuteronomistic perspectives with wisdom.

1. Edwards, *A Theology of Q*, 150.
2. D. Zeller, *Kommentar zur Logienquelle* (Stuttgart: Katholisches Bibelwerk, 1984), 11-14.
3. Havener, *Q: The Sayings of Jesus*, 106.

The above investigation has argued for a very close similarity between Q and James. They are both wisdom documents in that they are concerned with presenting practical advice on the way of life a Christian is to follow. This advice is presented in wisdom categories and use is made of the traditional wisdom forms of expression. If Q and James demonstrably have a similar wisdom outlook, then they should be viewed as emerging from a similar worldview or from a community or communities with very similar perspectives.

Chapter 3

THE NATURE OF WISDOM IN JAMES

The New Testament traditions of James and Q do more than simply offer paraenetical wisdom advice to their hearers or readers. They follow the approach adopted by the biblical and the intertestamental wisdom writings and examine the very nature of wisdom. This present chapter and the following one will illustrate how the New Testament traditions of James and Q continued the biblical personification of wisdom. In this way the role of wisdom in these two traditions emerges more clearly and the closeness of these writings will again be evident from the similarities in their understanding of the nature of wisdom.

Three main pericopae in James (1.2-8; 2.1-13; 3.13-18) give attention to the nature of wisdom. From them emerges a particular understanding of wisdom similar to that in the Hebrew traditions. At the same time James gives that understanding a stamp of his own with a specific direction within the context of Christianity.

1. *Faith, Steadfastness and Wisdom: Pericopae B and C (1.2-8)*

This section comprises two pericopae (see Appendixes 1 and 2). Pericope B (1.2-4) concerns the testing of faith which produces steadfastness, while pericope C (1.5-8) deals with the question of asking for wisdom in faith. Although these are two separate pericopae, they are connected through their common interest in the theme of wisdom, which they treat in different ways.

1.1 *Pericope B: The testing of faith produces steadfastness*
(1.2-4)

The letter begins with an introductory formula of joy. Structurally, this opening formula has been united to its context by
means of a catchphrase using the word χαράν (v. 2) which
refers back to χαίρειν (v. 1). The line of thought develops in
vv. 2 and 3 in a chiastic way:

χαράν....................................περιπέσητε
τὸ δοκίμιον......................ὑπομονήν

Joy is the proper response to trials which in their turn produce
the steadfastness of faith. The structure of these verses shows
a carefully developed progression of thought, which is led
further by the bonding of vv. 3 and 4 through the words
κατεργάζεται (v. 3) and ἔργον... ἐχέτω... (v. 4). The steadfastness produced by joy in the time of testing flowers forth into
perfection.

1.1.1 *Joy amidst trials (vv. 2 and 3)*. From the context of the
letter it appears that the trials envisaged here are those persecutions and sufferings that befall the faithful on account of the
faith that they profess. This is reminiscent of Job whose sufferings were presented as a test of his faith. Amidst these sufferings Job never turned his back on God despite his inability to
grasp why he was suffering. The emphasis on joy and rejoicing is important because it places what follows in a particular
context. The readers of this letter are to be perfectly happy[1]
when they encounter πειρασμοί. The concept of a faith that is
tested is best understood against the background of Jewish
tradition where from the earliest days special attention was
given to people who either endured testing successfully or
failed dismally. Abraham (Gen. 22) was the best example of a
man who through his testing proved to be faithful. The outstanding example of unfaithfulness in time of trial was that of
the Israelites in their wanderings through the desert (Num.

---

1. The use of the adjective πᾶς to qualify joy conveys the notion that it
is a perfect joy which is to be communicated (cf. R. Hoppe, *Der theologische Hintergrund des Jakobusbriefes* [Würzburg: Echter, 1977], 20).

14.20-24). The wisdom tradition gave detailed attention to suffering and testing (cf. Sir. 2.1-6; 4.17-18; Wis. 2.17-19)[1] and a connection was forged between suffering and joy.

This Jewish wisdom tradition provides the best background for James's view that one should rejoice in the trials that come one's way. Yet a shift of emphasis is to be noticed when one compares closely James's thought with this wisdom heritage. Whereas Jewish tradition looked upon the trials (or πειρασμοί) as an end in themselves, or at the very least as having an educative role, James viewed trials as future-orientated. Through suffering one attains the perfection of God's eschatological kingdom.[2] Affliction and trials are, then, not an end in themselves, but they look forward to the attainment of the gift of perfection in the eschatological kingdom. The path to this kingdom lies in the patient endurance of suffering, not for its own sake, but for the sake of the future kingdom.

1.1.2 The testing of faith leads to endurance (vv. 2 and 3)
The thought in James is very specific: the sufferings and trials are a means of testing (δοκίμιον)[3] the faith and this ultimately

1. In referring to the deuterocanonical/apocryphal books of Sirach, the Wisdom of Solomon as well as 1 and 2 Maccabees, the text and translation that will be referred to and quoted is that of the *Revised Standard Version, Catholic Edition* (London: Catholic Truth Society, 1966). In referring to the pseudepigraphical works such as the book of *Jubilees*, the *Testaments of the Twelve Patriarchs*, etc., the text and translation that is referred to and quoted is that of the two volumes of J.H. Charlesworth (ed.), *The Old Testament Pseudepigrapha*, vol. 1: *Apocalyptic Literature and Testaments* (Garden City: Doubleday, 1983); and *The Old Testament Pseudepigrapha*, vol. 2: *Expansions of the 'Old Testament' and Legends, Wisdom and Philosophical Literature, Prayers, Psalms, and Odes, Fragments of Lost Judeo-Hellenic Works* (London: Darton, Longman & Todd, 1985).
2. Hoppe, *Der theologische Hintergrund*, 22. However, M. Dibelius (*James: A Commentary on the Epistle of James*, 72) fails to perceive this future direction. He puts James in opposition to the views of early Christianity which placed the value of suffering in the eschatological hope.
3. Some manuscripts read δόκιμον in place of δοκίμιον. The evidence of the manuscripts is largely in favour of δοκίμιον and 'the reading δόκιμον shows a tendency to regularize the unusual δοκίμιον, which occurs only here and in 1 Peter 1.7' (P.H. Davids, *The Epistle of James: A Commentary on the Greek Text* [Exeter: Paternoster, 1982], 68). Dibe-

leads to endurance (ὑπομονή). In the period between the two testaments the question of suffering was examined in depth. In wrestling with this problem examples were chosen from the past to show not only the heroic nature, but also the educative function of suffering. In the book of *Jubilees* Abraham's faith was tested by ten trials: 'This (is) the tenth trial with which Abraham was tried. And he was found faithful, controlled of spirit' (*Jub.* 19.8). In the *Testament of Joseph*, Joseph is referred to in much the same vein: 'In ten testings he showed that I was approved, and in all of them I persevered, because perseverance is a powerful medicine and endurance provides many good things' (*T. Jos.* 2.7). The *Testament of Job* also presents Job as an example of pious endurance (*T. Job* 1.5; 4.5-6; 27.3-7). In the course of his letter James refers to both Abraham (2.21) and Job (5.11) as specific illustrations of those who demonstrated endurance in their lives. This steadfast endurance showed that suffering had an educative value. James demonstrates once more that he is at home in this world of Jewish wisdom thought. True to his heritage he affirms that without trials and sufferings one cannot show steadfast endurance. The one who has endured trials, who has shown

lius (*James*, 72-73) notes that δοκίμιον can have a twofold meaning: (i) genuineness and (ii) the means of testing. He argues that it is in the first sense, namely as genuineness, that it is used in 1 Pet. 1.7. This accords with the way it is used in the LXX, for example in 1 Chron. 29.4 and Zech. 11.13, James does not have this use in mind. He sees δοκίμιον in the second sense, namely as a means of testing. In this sense it appears in the LXX text of Prov. 27.21: 'the furnace is a means of testing (δοκίμιον) for silver and gold'.

1 Peter uses δοκίμιον πίστεως in the sense of the genuineness of faith which is understood above all from the eschatological event of Jesus' revelation (Hoppe, *Der theologische Hintergrund*, 23). Faith shows that it is genuine in the future as a result of its perseverance through suffering. James, on the other hand, does not focus as Peter does on the result, namely the genuineness of faith: instead, he refers specifically to the means of testing the faith. The sufferings and trials that have been experienced are a way to test their faith.

This distinction in usage between Peter and James tends to be supported by more recent interpreters such as Davids (*The Epistle of James*, 68), W. Grundmann ('δόκιμος', *TDNT*, II [1964], 259), and Hoppe (*Der theologische Hintergrund*, 23).

his heroism, is the one to be highly valued (as is gold which emerges from the furnace).

1.1.3 *Endurance leads to perfection (v. 4)*. Although steadfast endurance (ὑπομονή) occupies an important place in James's thought, it remains a link which leads to something even more important: perfection. This development in thought reaches its culmination here with the final member of the chain of catchwords: from *testing* one is led to *patient endurance* and then finally to *perfection*. The purpose of the whole development is found in the statement: ἵνα ἦτε τέλειοι καὶ ὁλόκληροι. This final clause is dependent upon the exhortation, 'let steadfast endurance produce a perfect work' (ἡ δὲ ὑπομονὴ ἔργον τέλειον ἐχέτω). A clear development occurs in James's line of catchwords: the phrase ἔργον ἔχειν corresponds to the verb κατεργάζεται (v. 3). This exhortation leads one to expect that James will indicate some particular perfect work to be done; but no such reference is made. In its place is the idea of perfection itself. In effect he says: 'You are that perfect work'.[1] By means of this admonition James calls the Christian to perfection. His view is not expressed by means of a categorical statement: 'Steadfast endurance makes you perfect'. Rather, he issues a call to allow steadfast endurance to work its full effect—and this will produce perfection.

What actually does James understand by perfection? Again, the wisdom literature of the biblical and extra-biblical writings provides help in answering the question. In the Judaic tradition Noah was the perfect man, and Gen. 6.9 was the origin for this thought: 'Noah was a righteous man, blameless (תָּמִים) in his generation'. The wisdom tradition of Sir. 44.17 and *Jub.* 23.10 took up and repeated this thought. A very interesting direction developed in the wisdom tradition which indicated the importance of wisdom for the perfect man. If wisdom was lacking, then he could no longer be called perfect, 'for even if one is perfect among the sons of men, yet without the wisdom

1. Dibelius (*James*, 74). To support this interpretation Dibelius (*James*, 74) argues: 'Only this interpretation is justified both by the correspondence between "perfect" (τέλειοι v. 4b) and "perfect work" (ἔργον τέλειον v. 4a) and by the schema of the concatenation; furthermore, it creates no linguistic difficulties'.

that comes from thee he will be regarded as nothing' (Wis. 9.6). In the context of this saying the importance of the law and its observance are also emphasized (Wis. 9.5). Here we have brought together the wisdom ideas of perfection and law. This is significant for James where these thoughts are also united.

The paraenetical nature of James is evident in these verses. Dibelius[1] has emphasized this aspect well; but he has tended to ignore the eschatological dimension inherent in this call to perfection. The concatenation of ideas that takes place in these verses comes to a climax with this idea of a perfection, which can only be realized in the framework of eschatology.[2] Herein lies the real motive for the joy with which this pericope commenced: it will be joy experienced in the culmination of a perfection attained in the eschatological kingdom.

1.2 *Pericope C: Asking for wisdom in faith (1.5-8)*

1.2.1 *Wisdom as a gift from God (v. 5).* Contrary to the view of Dibelius[3] the connection between pericopae B and C is not superficial. An essential aspect of perfection is the possession of wisdom as the wisdom tradition has emphasized: 'For even if one is perfect among the sons of men, yet without the wisdom which comes from thee he will be regarded as nothing' (Wis. 9.6). Consequently, the reference to wisdom in 1.5 is to be expected from the context of pericope B.

The focal point of this pericope is the request to God for wisdom which emerges as the horizon for obtaining perfection. Wisdom is above all a gift from God obtained through prayer and not through one's own self-realization. The Jewish wis-

---

1. *Ibid.*

2. F. Mussner (*Der Jakobusbrief: Auslegung*, 67) draws attention to this eschatological emphasis very well when he says: 'Der eschatologische Klang der Termini ὑπομονή, τέλειος, ὁλόκληρος ist unüberhörbar. Der Perfectionismus des Jakobus ist ein eschatologischer!... Der eschatologische Perfektionismus resultiert bei ihm aus seiner Forderung nach einem entschiedenen Christentum.'

3. Dibelius (*James*, 77). Besides the catchword λείπεται, which externally unites vv. 4 and 5, the theme of wisdom binds the two together. Pericope B has emphasized the virtue of perfection for which the Christian strives in life.

dom traditions consistently emphasize this view of wisdom as God's gift. 'All wisdom comes from the Lord and is with him forever' (Sir. 1.1; cf. also 1.26; 17.11; 24.2; 39.6). 'Therefore I prayed, and understanding was given me; I called upon God, and the spirit of wisdom came to me' (Wis. 7.7; cf. also 7.15; 8.21; 9.4). James certainly depends upon this Jewish wisdom tradition which sees God as the fount of all wisdom who gives 'generously without reproaching' (ἁπλῶς καὶ μὴ ὀνειδίζοντος). The word ἁπλῶς has provoked much discussion. Dibelius[1] shows how it can have two meanings: (i) 'in/with kindness' or (ii) 'unreservedly'. He opts for 'unreservedly', as does Davids.[2] This interpretation is supported by a later Christian tradition, such as Hermas, *Mandates* 2.4.6, which seems dependent on James.[3] The second phrase καὶ μὴ ὀνειδίζοντος depends without doubt on the Jewish wisdom tradition which emphasized that all giving should be undertaken without any form of grumbling. 'My son, do not mix reproach with your good deeds...' (Sir. 18.15; see also 20.14; 41.21). The same thought endures in the Christian tradition where it appears in the two ways of the *Didache* 4.7: οὐ διστάσεις δοῦναι οὐδὲ διδοὺς γογγύσεις. In James God is presented as the one who gives without any form of grudge and without any reservation. As the Jewish tradition has confidently proclaimed, God is always committed to his people and they can always be confident in approaching him.

1.2.2 *Requests made in faith (vv. 6-8)*. Having expressed the faith that God is the giver of wisdom and of all gifts, James turns to consider the human response. He advises one to pray in faith for what one needs and thus reproduces an old Jewish wisdom tradition rich in its emphasis on prayer offered in the certainty of faith: 'Do not be fainthearted in your prayer' (Sir. 7.10). This thought appears again in Jas 5.16: 'The prayer of a righteous man has great power in its effects'. The Gospels also hand on this tradition in a somewhat different way (Mk

---

1. *Ibid.*, 77-79.
2. Davids, *The Epistle of James*, 72.
3. S. Laws, *A Commentary on the Epistle of James* (London: Black, 1980), 55.

11.23-24; Mt. 21.21-22; Lk. 17.5; Mt. 17.20). Attention will be devoted to this link between James and the Gospel tradition in Chapters 5 and 6.

1.3 *Wisdom as the horizon for attaining perfection in the eschatological age*

The Jewish wisdom tradition helps to provide the background from which the thought of James develops. Pericope C continues the view of pericope B that perfection is the hope of those who are steadfast. The focal point of this pericope is the request for wisdom. If one lacks this wisdom needed for perfection, one has to ask for it from God who alone can grant it. Opposed to this stance is the person who doubts. Above all, one is to appreciate with joy the fact that one can approach God and request from him this gift of wisdom. In using this tradition, James had undoubtedly given it a stamp and direction of his own. By means of the method of concatenation in 1.1-4 he has brought his thought to the intended climax, namely a call to perfection. In effect he is saying, 'Let steadfast endurance make you perfect'.[1] In the underlying wisdom tradition the notion of perfection demands the idea of wisdom (Wis. 9.6). For this reason pericope B is incomplete in that perfection demands a reference to the possession of wisdom. This is provided in pericope C. Consequently, pericope C is expected, given the context of pericope B.

The analysis of the epistle has shown that the theme of steadfastness amidst trials occurs twice in the introductory sections (1.2-4, 12-18). It is not taken up again in the body of the epistle, but appears again in the concluding section of the epistle (5.7-11). Taking these three passages together, one sees a theme progressively developing and a full picture ultimately emerging. Wisdom in James, as in Jewish wisdom literature, is the horizon for attaining perfection (1.5). Because wisdom is God's gift enabling one to stand the test, it is to be sought in prayer from God with firm confidence. This is a clear illustration of the gospel tradition of 'ask and it will be given you' (Lk. 11.9). Elsewhere in the Epistle of James where reference is made to trials, suffering and patient endurance (pericopae E

---

1. Dibelius, *James*, 74.

and O) the eschatological perspective is present to give them meaning. Through patient endurance under trial one comes to obtain eschatological life.

Whether trials are external on account of one's faith, or internal on account of inordinate desires, they can only be faced with the wisdom which comes from God. In this sense wisdom is the all-embracing horizon influencing the present life and directing the believer towards the eschatological age. This is the reason for rejoicing.

2. *Belief in Jesus, the Lord of Glory and the Wisdom of God: Pericope G (2.1-13)*

The actual body of the letter commences with this pericope. The theme of the relationship of rich and poor forms the focus of attention in which a profession of belief is made in Jesus as the Lord of glory. This theme was already introduced in pericope D (1.9-11) together with the other major themes that will be taken up in the epistle. This topic of rich and poor is referred to again at the end of the body of the epistle (pericope N 5.1-6) thereby ensuring that the entire body of the epistle forms an *inclusio* within this consideration of rich and poor. This pericope unfolds in this way:

(a) Announcement of command not to make distinctions among people (2.1)
(b) Example which illustrates the command (2.2-4)
(c) Four arguments corroborating the command and the example (2.5-13):
   (i)   election of the poor by God (2.5-6a)
   (ii)   persecution by the rich (2.6b-7)
   (iii) statement of the law (2.8-11)
   (iv)   judgment (2.12-13)

Attention will be focused only upon those elements that illustrate the wisdom dimension. Since 2.2-13 presents examples to illustrate the command expressed in 2.1 not to make distinctions, attention will be directed first to those examples insofar as they illustrate the command.

2.1 An example illustrating the command to avoid partiality: discrimination in the church between rich and poor (2.2-4)
James's use of paraenetic material shows clear evidence of belonging to the wisdom tradition of Israel's past. This example, which graphically contrasts rich and poor, illustrates the command not to show partiality in one's action. Dibelius[1] emphasizes that this is a hypothetical example, rather than a concrete situation within the community to which James is writing. James chooses an example which contains a gross disregard for human persons and presents it in completely unrealistic terms. This use of hyperbolic examples is similar to Jesus' use of parables in which he expressed his message by means of exaggeration and unrealistic elements. This belongs to the method of wisdom teaching which uses the language of comparisons, examples, contrasts, exaggerations. The book of Sirach is a good example of this illustrative language when it also considers partiality between rich and poor (Sir. 13.21-23).

James argues in true wisdom fashion that showing partiality is not reconcilable with faith in Jesus Christ as the Lord of glory. In this context Jesus as the Lord of glory is the source of the wisdom which enables a person to act as a true Christian, for whom showing partiality in dealings with the rich and poor would be totally contradictory.

2.2 Four arguments which corroborate the command and the example (2.5-13)
The above example is supported in what follows by two sets of double arguments. The action of God in his choice of the poor becomes the focal point.

(a) God has chosen the poor to be rich (2.5-7). Jas 2.1 and 2.5 are parallel to each other. In 2.5 the phrase ἀδελφοί μου ἀγαπητοί refers back to ἀδελφοί μου in 2.1. By drawing attention back to 2.1, the reader is reminded of the requirement of faith in Jesus as the Lord of glory not to show partiality. But 2.5 gives a further reason why the Christian should show no par-

---

1. 'The author nowhere implies that he has been prompted to write because of reports about one or more Christian churches. Therefore, we cannot with any certainty infer some crisis in the Christian churches from an admonition in James' (Dibelius, *James*, 129).

tiality for the rich: God has chosen the poor. God's action in choosing is a fundamental biblical theme. His choice is illustrated primordially in the selection of Israel as a nation (Deut. 26.5-9; 26.7). God also chose others to form a new people (Eph. 1.4). Among these God has a special care for the poor (Ps. 72.13). The equation between the poor and the pious develops during the later wisdom writings: 'It is not right to despise an intelligent poor man, nor is it proper to honour a sinful man' (Sir. 10.23). All these ideas stand behind the tradition to which James is witness.[1]

In the second argument (2.6b-7) the rich are presented as the enemies of Christianity. A threefold development occurs in the argument. First, the rich are responsible for oppressing the Christian; then, they are accused of dragging the believer into court; and finally, they are accused of blaspheming the name of God. Oppression by the rich is a theme very common in Judaism, above all in the prophetic and wisdom traditions. For example: 'Hear this, you who trample upon the needy, and bring the poor of the land to an end' (Amos 8.4). In the wisdom tradition it is the ungodly man who says: 'Let us oppress the righteous poor man; let us not spare the widow nor regard the grey hairs of the aged' (Wis. 2.10).

---

1. Elsewhere in the New Testament Paul develops a similar approach. In 1 Cor. 1.26ff. he urges his readers to consider their call: 'For consider your call, brethren; not many of you were wise according to worldly standards, not many were powerful, not many were of noble birth; but God chose what is foolish in the world to shame the wise, God chose what is weak in the world to shame the strong... He is the source of your life in Christ Jesus, whom God made our wisdom, our righteousness and sanctification and redemption.' Paul presents Jesus as the wisdom of God who is the source of the life of the Christian, whom God has chosen. God's choice did not take place according to human standards. In fact what the world considers wise, God has rejected. His choice instead has been for the weak in the world, for what is despised. This corresponds to the thought that James has expressed about God's choice of the poor. At the same time it lends support to the view that Jas 2.1-4 is to be understood against the background of wisdom. One is not arguing for a literary connection between Paul and James, but what is significant is that both are illustrative of traditions within the early church which are operating with similar concepts.

The ultimate accusation levelled against the rich is that they 'blaspheme that honourable name by which you are called' (2.7). This alludes to a well-known Old Testament way of expressing God's control over something through the invocation of his name. In the context of James the reference is to Jesus[1] whose name is invoked over Christians at baptism, by which act they become his property. In this section a twofold tendency has emerged. James stands within the framework of the wisdom tradition and speaks in a way quite characteristic of this tradition. At the same time he presents his instruction within a clear Christological perspective. The wisdom advice derives from the belief in Jesus as the eschatological Lord of glory.

(b) Further development of the argument: law and judgment (2.8-13). A second set of two arguments substantiates the basic argument of the entire section. 2.8-11 uses the example of the law, while 2.12-13 concentrates upon the notion of judgment.

(i) In the first section (2.8-11) the law of love is termed the royal law (νόμος βασιλικός). The exact meaning of this appears from an analysis of some wisdom traditions. For example: 'The beginning of wisdom is the most sincere desire for instruction, and concern for instruction is love of her, and love of her is the keeping of her laws, and giving heed to her laws is assurance of immortality and immortality brings one near to God; so the desire for wisdom leads to a kingdom' (Wis. 6.17-20). Here is a clearly stated view that wisdom which is attained through the observance of law leads to the inheritance of a kingdom. Consequently, such an expression in James as νόμος βασιλικός becomes understandable: it is that law which leads to wisdom and the inheritance of a kingdom.

In a similar way Sir. 6.23-31 speaks of the observance of laws which grant wisdom. The reward appears in regal terms (a 'crown of gladness') which comes close to James's νόμος βασιλικός and offers a background to his thought. He is steeped in wisdom traditions and only from that background can he be understood. The advice to fulfil the royal law in 2.8 is balanced by the encouragement given, namely καλῶς ποιεῖτε ('you do

1. Davids, *The Epistle of James*, 113.

well'). This is in line with the purpose of all wisdom instruction, which aims at providing guides or norms to a successful life.

(ii) The second section (2.12-13) is an essential element of pericope G.[1] The passage ends with the statement that judgment is overcome by mercy. This refers back to the opening verse of ch. 2 where the admonition was given not to show distinctions among people.

2.12 refers to the νόμος ἐλευθερίας which from its context is identical to the νόμος βασιλικός. Previously, reference was made to the νόμος ἐλευθερίας in 1.25 where it was identified with the νόμος τέλειος. Consequently, the perfect law, the law of freedom and the royal law are all expressions which refer to the same reality. Jewish tradition also thinks of the law in terms of perfection: 'The law of the Lord is perfect, reviving the soul; the testimony of the Lord is sure, making wise the simple...' (Ps 19.7). Here wisdom, law and perfection are all united in one breath. Because the law comes from God, it is perfect and its observance leads to wisdom. Attention has already been focused on Wis. 6.17-20. In this context wisdom is personified and stands beside God. She gives herself as a gift to those who love and seek her. One shows a desire for wisdom by keeping her laws. 'And giving heed to her laws is assurance of immortality, and immortality brings one nearer to God; so the desire for wisdom leads to a kingdom' (Wis. 6.18-20). Elsewhere, the same ideas are also emphasized. In Wis. 9.5-10 the task of wisdom is to help one to decide on what laws to perform and how to perform them. Without wisdom 'I am... a man... with little understanding of judgment and laws...' (Wis. 9.5). Perfection comes through the carrying out of laws inspired by wisdom.

In a similar way James urges his readers to put into practice his wisdom advice. 2.13 concludes with the assurance that if one follows out these admonitions one will overcome judgment. This idea of judgment takes us back to the eschatological image of the Lord of glory in the opening verse of the chapter. In James wisdom and law go hand in hand as they did in the

1. This is contrary to Dibelius (*James*, 147), who claims that v. 13 is an isolated saying.

intertestamental wisdom literature. Wisdom shows the type of life to be lived.

2.3 *Faith in Jesus, the Lord of glory (2.1)*

The above analysis of pericope G has shown how v. 1 subsumes the entire pericope in its ambience. Faith in Jesus as the Lord of glory forms the basis for all the paraenetical material developed in the rest of this pericope. Attention was given first of all to the wisdom paraenetical material in order to illustrate clearly the dependence of this material on the understanding of Jesus as the Lord of glory.

Showing partiality is completely irreconcilable with a faith in the Lord Jesus Christ, the Lord of glory: ἔχετε τὴν πίστιν τοῦ κυρίου ἡμῶν ’Ιησοῦ Χριστοῦ τῆς δόξης. The correct translation of this string of genitives has been much disputed. Some scholars have argued that the words form an insertion which aimed at christianizing a pre-existent Jewish document.[1] However, there is no textual evidence in favour of any form of textual corruption. Consequently, the interpretation must be based upon the text as it stands. Davids[2] lists four ways in which this text can be interpreted:

(i)   τῆς δόξης modifies τὴν πίστιν meaning either 'the glorious faith' or 'faith in the glory of...'
(ii) τῆς δόξης modifies κυρίου meaning 'faith in our Lord of glory Jesus Christ...'
(iii) τῆς δόξης is in apposition to Jesus Christ, that is, 'our Lord Jesus Christ, the glory...'

---

1. For example, A. Meyer, *Das Rätsel des Jacobusbriefes* (Giessen: Töpelmann, 1930), 118-21.
2. Davids, *The Epistle of James*, 106. This translation focuses attention on the words τῆς δόξης. In all four possibilities offered by Davids the reference to Jesus Christ is understood as an objective genitive, namely 'faith in our Lord Jesus Christ'. However, it would also be possible to understand it as a subjective genitive in that it could refer to the 'faith *of* our Lord Jesus Christ'. However, this does not alter the basic concern here with investigating the relationship of Jesus to glory and wisdom.

(iv) τῆς δόξης is a genitive of quality modifying 'our Lord
Jesus Christ' and the whole phrase should be translated
'our glorious Lord Jesus Christ'.[1]

This last interpretation appears to be the best since it represents the word order in the Greek text and takes the expression τῆς δόξης as a genitive which qualifies and expands a title
for Jesus: 'our Lord Jesus Christ' (Eph. 6.24; Gal. 6.18). The
Old Testament reference to the glory of God (כָּבוֹד) was a way
of expressing the manifestation of God to Israel especially with
a view to granting Israel salvation. Against this background
the application of this term to Jesus Christ carries with it a
reference to the exalted Lord who will be manifested at the end
of time to bring judgment and salvation to humanity. By
applying the glory of God to the person of Jesus in this particular eschatological context, James identifies Jesus with the
qualities of God. Just as God is manifested in Israel by granting
salvation, so in the eschatological age Jesus will be manifested
as God by granting salvation to those who have faithfully
adhered to his instruction, to the wisdom that he had granted
them.

The wisdom implied throughout the examples and argu-
mentation of this pericope derives its source from Jesus, the
Lord of glory. James has emphasized elsewhere that all wisdom comes from God (1.5). In this pericope Jesus, as the
eschatological Lord of glory, is also to be identified with wisdom, because he is its source. Consequently, Jesus is to be
viewed in the light of the wisdom of God. Although it is not
stated explicitly, this is the understanding which emerges
from the structure of this entire pericope whereby faith in
Jesus the Lord of glory is the all-embracing basis for the wisdom direction that the lives of the believers must follow. All the
wisdom advice stems from this one source.

Hoppe[2] gives support to this particular interpretation of
Jesus as the wisdom of God by referring to a similar tradition
found in the writings of Paul. The genitive τῆς δόξης occurs on

1. Dibelius, *James*, 128; J. Ropes, *A Critical and Exegetical Commentary on the Epistle of St. James* (Edinburgh: T. & T. Clark, 1916), 187;
Mussner, *Der Jakobusbrief*, 116.
2. Hoppe, *Der theologische Hintergrund*, 72-78.

only a few occasions in the New Testament. Eph. 1.17 emphasizes that the Father of glory (πατὴρ τῆς δόξης) communicates
the gift of the spirit of wisdom. God, as the Father of glory, is
also intentionally brought into relation with the person of Jesus
Christ. This in turn leads to an association between Jesus
Christ and wisdom as well. This idea is clearly spelled out later
in the same letter (Eph. 3.10-12) where the author says:
'...that through the church the manifold wisdom of God might
now be made known to the principalities and powers in the
heavenly places. This was according to the eternal purpose
which he has realized in Christ Jesus our Lord...' This same
Jesus Christ makes known the wisdom of God. In this context
the specific reference to Jesus Christ in Eph. 1.17 and 3.10-12
must be understood in terms of the means by which God, the
Father of glory, communicates the spirit of wisdom to
humanity.

In 1 Cor. 2.6-8 Jesus Christ is called the 'Lord of glory'. This
occurs in the context of God granting his gift of wisdom 'for
our glorification'. Because they did not possess this wisdom of
God, those wise in the ways of the world crucified Jesus. Consequently, the gift of the wisdom of God is closely associated
with recognizing Jesus as the Lord of glory. This phrase κύριος
τῆς δόξης is connected with the person of Jesus in a wisdom
context because in 1 Cor. 1.30 Jesus has been identified with
wisdom. This represents a tradition in the early Church which
associates τῆς δόξης with the person of Jesus in a wisdom context. The argument is not about dependence of either James on
Paul or vice versa; but, in a tradition distinct from James,
there is evidence for the use of κύριος τῆς δόξης to refer to
Jesus in a wisdom context. This gives support to the interpretation of Jas 2.1 against the background of wisdom thought:
Jesus as the eschatological Lord of glory is the wisdom of God.

This is the only christological pericope in the entire epistle.[1]
It begins with a reference to Jesus Christ in 2.1 and in doing so
attributes to Jesus one of the most significant of titles, namely
the Lord of glory (κύριος τῆς δόξης). Jesus will appear as the
eschatological exalted Lord at the end of time when he comes
to bring judgment and salvation to humanity. This is a title

1. *Ibid.*, 98.

which is applied to Jesus not as the earthly Messiah, but as the heavenly Messiah exalted at the right hand of the Father.[1] This identification of Jesus with wisdom shows a striking difference from the way it appears in Paul and James. Hoppe[2] has failed to notice this significant difference despite the fact that he draws attention to the Pauline traditions in this connection. In Paul the reference to Jesus as the Lord of glory (1 Cor. 2.8) is to the earthly, crucified Jesus. Consequently, when Paul speaks of Jesus in this vein he sees him as the wisdom of God-incarnate: it is in his earthly life that he is to be seen as the wisdom of God. In James the matter is completely different. As the Lord of glory Jesus exercises this role only as an eschatological figure, and not as the earthly suffering Jesus, as in Paul's mind. Consequently, when James identifies Jesus as God's wisdom it is because of the eschatological role that he has to play. This is highly significant for any attempt to trace a development in the concept of Jesus' relationship to wisdom in the different traditions of the New Testament.

3. *The Wisdom from Above: Pericope J (3.13-18)*

This is the most obvious pericope in the entire epistle dealing with wisdom. An examination of the compositional relationships among the pericopae[3] reveals that pericopae J and K together form the very heart and centre of the body of the epistle. The focus of attention centres upon the wisdom from above and around that all other themes in the body form an embrace. In fact it is the nature of wisdom which is the central theme and that gives meaning to the actual consideration of these other wisdom ideas.

This section is a well developed unity which unfolds in a threefold way. 3.13 presents the criterion for true wisdom. This leads, then, to a consideration of a negative definition of a lifestyle led without wisdom in 3.14-16. Finally, we return to a positive definition of wisdom in 3.17-18. Judged from the view-

---

1. This is the interpretation given by Davids (*The Epistle of James*, 107): 'The one exalted Lord Jesus Christ whose glory will be fully revealed in eschatological judgment'.
2. Hoppe, *Der theologische Hintergrund*, 98.
3. See Chapter 1, §3.1.3.

point of content the structure of an *inclusio* is evident in this passage:

criterion for true wisdom	(3.13)
negative lifestyle without wisdom	(3.14-16)
positive definition of wisdom	(3.17-18)

A consciously constructed unity has been achieved. The author has given a very special stamp to this section which occupies an important position within the epistle itself.[1] One is indeed dealing with a new thought, a new argument, in this section. This explains the few linguistic connections with what precedes. However, there are in fact two specific connections: the word πικρόν (3.11 and 3.14) and the word ἀκατάστατον (3.8) which corresponds to ἀκαταστασία (3.16). The new argument is not completely independent of the context. James inserts wisdom consciously into this context because of the relationship between the σοφός and the διδάσκαλος. In fact the two terms later became identical.[2]

Jas 3.1 begins with the reference to the teacher (διδάσκαλος) which dominates what follows. By referring at the beginning of the next pericope (3.13) to the σοφός, a parallel is made to the teacher. 3.1-12 and 3.13-18 are similar in that they both have in mind teachers who are capable of dividing the community.[3] Jas 3.1-12 was concerned above all with the divisions which arose within the community and the author feared that teachers could inspire and fuel these divisions. Jas 3.13-18 also turns attention to the qualities of selfish ambition and disorder (3.16) and invokes wisdom in order to overcome these false divisive elements.

Viewing the relationship of 3.13-18 to what follows in 4.1-10, Dibelius[4] placed these sections into a larger unity which dealt with sayings against contentiousness. The content of the two

---

1. Dibelius (*James*, 207) on the other hand states categorically: 'There is no indication of a connection with the preceding section, and the Interpretation [*sic*] will reveal that there is no connection in thought either'. This very negative assessment is not substantiated by a critical analysis of the preceding context of these verses.
2. As Mussner (*Der Jakobusbrief*, 168-69) has argued.
3. Davids, *The Epistle of James*, 149.
4. Dibelius, *James*, 207.

pericopae demonstrates some form of connection. In 4.1-4 the author issues a strong criticism of what can be categorized as a life led without wisdom (3.15). The advice that James gives in 4.7-10 is an application of the concept of wisdom from above as discussed in 3.17.[1] Consequently, the two themes of 3.13-18 reappear in 4.1-10. At the same time 4.1-10 is not as closely connected to 3.13-18 as Dibelius[2] has tended to argue. James 4.1-10 introduces themes which do not appear in the preceding pericope, and which are fundamental to the whole epistle.

Jas 3.18 forms the bridge between the two pericopae. Dibelius[3] has argued that this verse was originally an independent saying. This is probably true. However, it has been woven intentionally into its context. Jas 3.18, viewed in relation to 4.1, forms quite a contrast. εἰρήνη at the end of 3.18 stands in direct contrast to the πόλεμοι of 4.1. In fact 4.1 makes specific what 3.13-18 implies.[4]

3.1 *A wise man leads a good life (3.13)*
An analysis of this verse reveals the emphasis placed on wisdom. It begins with σοφός and concludes with the word σοφίας. The concept of wisdom includes the whole section. The function of this verse is to embrace the whole section.[5] As such wisdom gives direction to the whole pericope, and in fact to what follows in 4.1-10 as well.[6]

---

1. Hoppe, *Der theologische Hintergrund*, 44.
2. Dibelius, *James*, 207.
3. *Ibid.*, 208.
4. Davids, *The Epistle of James*, 149.
5. Davids (*The Epistle of James*, 150) describes it as the topic sentence of this paragraph dealing with virtues and vices.
6. In expressing the theme, σοφός is connected to another similar adjective, ἐπιστήμων. The phrase also appears in the philosophy of the age in which σοφός is characterized by the intellectual aspect of knowledge (ἐπιστήμη) (Hoppe, *Der theologische Hintergrund*, 45). One should be careful, however, not to give overdue emphasis to this influence, which is a general failing of both Hoppe and Dibelius who tend at times to overstate the case for a direct Greek influence. James is influenced by the world out of which he comes. The influence of Judaism and its writings help above all to explain the thoughts of James. Where the influences from Greek popular philosophy appear, they are indirect influences in that they have influenced the world and thought patterns of the society. Popular philosophy has influenced

Structurally, v. 13 is well ordered, with τὰ ἔργα appearing at
its very centre. The same words occurred in the discussion on
faith and works (pericope H); but now they are at the heart of
the discussion on wisdom. The relationship between works and
wisdom is similar to that between works and faith. 'Show me
your faith apart from your works, and I by my works will
show you my faith' (2.18). Jas 3.13 argues that the way of life
should demonstrate that works are influenced by wisdom.
These works will show wisdom, just as they illustrated faith.
Wisdom, then, must be demonstrated in action. It is not just an
intellectual concept, but something that involves the very life
of the believer. There are two ways in which wisdom illustrates herself in action, in works. First, wisdom reveals herself
through the type of life one leads. Secondly, wisdom is demonstrated by means of the virtue of meekness. Attention will be
given to both these aspects.

(a) ἐκ τῆς καλῆς ἀναστροφῆς. The wise person shows wisdom
by leading the good life. This is very close to the thought
expressed by *1 Clem.* 38.2: 'Let the wise manifest his wisdom
not in words but in good deeds'.[1] Davids[2] translates ἐκ τῆς
καλῆς ἀναστροφῆς as 'by a proper lifestyle', which captures the
intended thought very well. Fundamental to the Christian
message is the teaching that one's lifestyle bears witness to
one's belief. 1 Pet. 2.12 and 3.2 as well as Heb. 13.7 also use this
thought, which shows that it is a characteristic teaching found
in the early Christian paraenesis.[3] This harmonizes well with
the central view of the Old Testament on wisdom.

(b) ἐν πραΰτητι σοφίας. Dibelius[4] considers this genitival
expression, 'in meekness of wisdom', as possibly a Semitic construction equivalent to the phrase 'in meek wisdom'. The
meaning is clear: the Christian shows wisdom in conflict sit-
uations by demonstrating the virtue of meekness. It is a particularly New Testament attitude to praise and promote the

James via the common heritage of ordinary thought rather than exercising a directly causal influence.
1. This translation is taken from that of *1 Clement* by K. Lake
(trans.), *The Apostolic Fathers*, vol. 1 (London: Heinemann, 1965).
2. Davids, *The Epistle of James*, 150.
3. *Ibid.*
4. Dibelius, *James*, 209.

virtue of meekness: Gal. 6.1; Eph. 4.2; 2 Tim. 2.25; Tit. 3.2; 1 Pet.
3.15. The term πραΰτης appears elsewhere in the epistle in Jas
1.21 where it is contrasted with ὀργή (1.20). Similarly, in the
use of πραΰτης in Jas 3.13, meekness is opposed to the conflicts
of bitter jealousy and selfish ambition (3.14). A call to work is
also issued: 'Let him show his works' (3.13). Consequently, the
uses of πραΰτης in both 1.21 and 3.13 are roughly parallel. This
verse (3.13) emphasizes, then, that through the virtue of
meekness (πραΰτης) one demonstrates that one possesses wisdom.[1] The implication is that the Christian is the truly wise
person who demonstrates wisdom through meekness and a
specific lifestyle.

3.2 *A negative lifestyle without wisdom (3.14-16)*
(a) Bitter jealousy and selfish ambition (3.14). In this and the
next section James contrasts a lifestyle led without wisdom
(3.14-16) to that of a lifestyle led with wisdom (3.17-18). The
proper lifestyle of one who is wise should exclude all bitter jealousy and selfish ambition (ζῆλον πικρὸν καὶ ἐριθείαν). Both
these words appear in Paul's catalogue of vices in 2 Cor. 12.20;
Gal. 5.20. The sense of the second term ἐριθεία is difficult to
determine because it appears only in James and Paul in the
New Testament; but the meaning of 'party spirit' seems to be
the best suited.[2] Within the church jealousy has led to party
splits and a group has formed under a leader intending to
withdraw from the church. These members have decided that
they have to withdraw if they wish to remain loyal to wisdom
and the truth. The opening chapters of 1 Corinthians also deal
with the problem of groups within the church and to this is
connected the search for wisdom (1.10-13; 1.18–2.16; 3.18-21).
For James the person who claims to have wisdom, yet acts in
this way, lies against the truth. James calls upon those who are
filled with contentiousness to be honest and to cease claiming

1. Davids (*The Epistle of James,* 150) notes the significance of this
concept of meekness in relation to wisdom when he says: 'This cardi-
nal virtue of NT vice and virtue lists (e.g. Gal. 5.23) is the sign of wisdom; therefore this verse functions as a topic sentence to a paragraph
which is itself a list of virtues and vices'.
2. As Dibelius (*James,* 209-10) and Davids (*The Epistle of James,* 151)
both propose.

inspiration from God's wisdom. They cannot possess God's wisdom if at the same time they are full of jealousy and cause dissensions.[1]

(b) This lifestyle is not influenced by the wisdom from above (3.15). On a number of occasions James clearly teaches that true divine wisdom comes down from heaven (Jas 1.5; 1.17; 3.17). Anything else cannot make a claim to the title of wisdom. In the Jewish wisdom tradition it was axiomatic that true wisdom is divine in origin, and comes down from heaven (Prov. 2.6; 8.22-31; Sir. 1.1-4; 24.1-12; Wis. 7.24-27; 9.4, 6, 9-18). At the same time a stream runs throughout Israel's traditions which identifies wisdom with God's spirit which is communicated to humanity. A number of examples illustrate this:

(i)   'And Pharaoh said to his servants, "Can we find such a man as this, in whom is the Spirit of God?" So Pharaoh said to Joseph, "Since God has shown you all this, there is none so discreet and wise as you are"' (Gen. 41.38-39).

(ii)   '...And I have filled him with the Spirit of God, with ability and intelligence, with knowledge and all craftsmanship, to devise artistic designs, to work in gold, silver and bronze' (Exod. 31.3-4). The description of the fruits of the Spirit's communication to humanity illustrates Israel's concept of practical wisdom.

(iii)   'And Joshua the son of Nun was full of the spirit of wisdom, for Moses had laid his hands upon him...' (Deut. 34.9).

(iv)   'And the Spirit of the Lord shall rest upon him, the spirit of wisdom and understanding...' (Isa. 11.2).

(v)   In later wisdom literature a development took place. In the Book of Wisdom 'what in earlier times was always considered to be the function of the Divine Spirit in the affairs of Israel... is now invariably assigned to the Wisdom of God'.[2]

---

1. As Dibelius (*James*, 210) expresses it: 'The boast which defies the truth is their claim of wisdom, for true wisdom cannot be contentious'.
2. J.A. Kirk, 'The Meaning of Wisdom in James: Examination of a Hypothesis', *NTS* 16 (1969/70), 34.

(vi) 'As an eschatological gift for the future age, the Divine Spirit and Wisdom also play the same role'.[1] In the prophets the gift of the Spirit occurs as an eschatological gift leading to moral consequences (Isa. 11.2ff.). In the *Book of Enoch* this same concept is applied to Wisdom. 'In those days... to the elect there shall be light, joy and peace, and they shall inherit the earth... And then wisdom shall be given to the elect. And they shall all live and not return again to sin... but those who have wisdom shall be humble' (*1 En.* 5.6-9).

(vii) A similarity also emerges between James's description of wisdom and the Qumran description of the spirit of truth in contrast to the spirit of deceit in 1QS 4.3-11.

From these numerous examples scattered throughout the biblical as well as the intertestamental literature one notes the interconnection of notions such as: to be wise, to have wisdom, to be filled with God's spirit. In the New Testament writings these ideas also tend to coalesce. A number of examples also illustrate this point.

(i) 'And the child grew and became strong, filled with wisdom; and the favour of God was upon him' (Lk. 2.40).

(ii) 'Therefore, brethren, pick out from among you seven men of good repute, full of the Spirit and of wisdom, whom we may appoint to this duty' (Acts 6.3).

(iii) 'To one is given through the Spirit the utterance of wisdom, and to another the utterance of knowledge according to the same Spirit' (1 Cor. 12.8).

(iv) There are also similarities between James's description of wisdom and what Paul lists as the 'fruits of the Spirit' in Gal. 5.22ff., as well as the description in Hermas, *Mandates* 11.8, of the man who has the spirit from above.

For James the communication of wisdom is the same as the communication of God's spirit. Both wisdom and the spirit are divine in origin; and both wisdom and the spirit produce effects

1. J.C. Rylaarsdam, *Revelation in Jewish Wisdom Literature* (Midway reprint; Chicago: University of Chicago Press, [1946] 1974), 114.

in the life of the believer. When James uses the concept of wisdom he is expressing what the New Testament traditions express elsewhere by means of the concept of the Holy Spirit.

James reserves the use of the term wisdom for the gift which comes down from God. He refuses to identify exactly what these people have who are causing divisions; but whatever it is, it does not bear the title of wisdom. The Greek text expresses this view far more clearly than the English translation does. A literal translation would be: 'This (lifestyle) is not the wisdom itself which comes down from above'. Nowhere in the text of James is the word wisdom used in the way in which Paul uses it when he refers to human wisdom and hence makes a comparison between two different wisdoms, one from above and one belonging to the world. Most commentators on James have failed to appreciate this point.[1] James does not operate with a dualistic concept of wisdom. His aim is to emphasize that there is only one wisdom and it comes from above and is incompatible with a lifestyle that is characterized by jealousy, bitterness and party spirits. Laws[2] has perceived this point and supports this interpretation by saying: 'His point is not that there is a different wisdom in opposition to the true one, but that a claim to true wisdom cannot be upheld in the context of an inconsistent style of life'.

In 3.15 James goes on to specify the attitude adopted by the opponents. This is stated in a form of crescendo progressing from the least to the most evil aspects of their style of life. Very brief attention will be given to the three aspects that are mentioned to show that this lifestyle is not influenced by the wisdom which comes from above.

(i) ἐπίγειος. This description should also be viewed against the background of the remote context of Jas 4.4 in which James regards friendship with the world as enmity with God. A sharp contrast between the earthly to the heavenly is intimated with the former being in direct opposition to the latter. This is not a neutral term, nor is it simply indicative of something that is inferior to a higher reality. It is presented as a lifestyle which is opposed to that influenced by the true wisdom which comes

1. Such as Hoppe (*Der theologische Hintergrund,* 59-61).
2. Laws, *A Commentary on the Epistle of James,* 163.

from God. The term ἐπίγειος is used in the writing of Hermas in a similar sense to that in James. The reference is specifically to an earthly spirit which is opposed to God: 'You see, then, he said, that faith is from above, from the Lord, and has great power; but double-mindedness is an earthly spirit (ἐπίγειον πνεῦμα), from the devil, and has no power' (Hermas, *Mand.* 9.11; cf. 11.6.11-19).

(ii) ψυχική. This is the second characteristic of that lifestyle which does not come from God: it is unspiritual or devoid of the Spirit.[1] The meaning of ψυχικός here is similar to its sense elsewhere in the New Testament. For example, 1 Cor. 2.14 refers to 'the natural man who lives without the eschatological gift of the πνεῦμα and who thus belongs to the world (v. 12) and not to God (v. 10)'.[2] I am not arguing that James depends on Paul,[3] but that the term ψυχικός bears a specific meaning in the early Christian tradition. Jas 3.15 emphasizes that people so characterized are leading lives without the gift of the πνεῦμα; consequently, they belong to the world and not to God. As has been argued above, James is not opposing two types of wisdom; but rather he opposes the true wisdom from above to the ethical lifestyle which some members of the community are leading. He argues that their lifestyle is in fact a decided contradiction to the wisdom which comes from above.

(iii) δαιμονιώδης. The lifestyle which does not conform to the wisdom from above is termed δαιμονιώδης. 'It would seem more reasonable to take James as intending that such deeds were inspired by demons. "You claim", says James, "to have the Holy Spirit. Impossible! You are inspired all right—you are inspired by the devil!"'[4]

---

1. The word ψυχικός became an important concept in the Gnostic systems. However, one is not to see the use in James as having any connection with the Gnostic views or use. Rather, James uses terminology which later found its way into the Gnostic system without in any way endorsing the Gnostic content which these terms later gained (Ropes, *The Epistle of St. James*, 247-48; Davids, *The Epistle of James*, 152; Dibelius, *James,* 211-12).
2. E. Schweizer, 'ψυχικός', *TDNT*, IX (1974), 663.
3. Davids, *The Epistle of James*, 152.
4. *Ibid.*, 153.

Jas 3.14-16 has painted a picture of the negative aspects of those who live without the wisdom which comes from above. The emphasis is not on the construction of another form of wisdom, human wisdom, competing with the divine wisdom, as is the case in Paul's 1 Corinthians. Instead of a competing wisdom, James describes the style of life which is led without any influence from the wisdom from above. The lifestyle is characterized as earthly, unspiritual and demonic. It shows jealousy and selfish ambition and results above all in disorder within the community.

3.3 *The true wisdom from above (3.17)*

(a) ἄνωθεν σοφία. The main focus of this whole section is on true wisdom, ἄνωθεν σοφία. This phrase occurred first in 3.15, but in the order σοφία ἄνωθεν. The changed order of the words here is not the normal sequence of words in Greek and has the effect of emphasizing ἄνωθεν which draws attention to the origin of true wisdom.

The understanding of this text emerges from the background of 1.17-19. Jas 1.17 states: 'Every good endowment and every perfect gift is from above, coming down from the Father of lights...' This verse opposes 1.13-15 and implies that nothing evil comes from God. Instead, all good gifts come from God. This gift from above, this wisdom, results in the Christian receiving the word of truth (λόγος ἀληθείας) which has as its purpose 'that we should be a kind of first fruits of his creatures' (1.18). Although this phrase is interpreted in different ways, the more logical interpretation understands it as a reference to Christians who are the first to be reborn in God's process of redemption.[1] Wisdom, as the greatest gift of God from above, results in the person being reborn. The allusion to 'the word of truth' (λόγος ἀληθείας, 1.18) is explained in 1.21 as the ἔμφυτος λόγος. Although the meaning of ἔμφυτος has been variously interpreted as inborn, innate, natural, the more commonly accepted translation today is that of implanted.[2] This interpre-

---

1. *Ibid.*, 89. See also Dibelius, *James*, 104-105; Mussner, *Der Jakobusbrief*, 94-95; J.B. Adamson, *The Epistle of James* (Grand Rapids: Eerdmans, 1976), 76-77.

2. Dibelius, *James*, 113; Davids, *The Epistle of James*, 95; Adamson, *The Epistle of James*, 98-100; Mussner, *Der Jakobusbrief*, 101.

tation satisfies the context in that what is implanted takes place through the proclamation of the Gospel.[1]

With these thoughts as the background and context to 3.17 it becomes clear that the wisdom from above is not simply a gift directed to a specific moral type of life. It implies more than ethical direction; it also brings with it regeneration and rebirth. The gift of wisdom has a twofold consequence: an ethical way of life, as well as rebirth to new salvation.[2] The characteristics attributed to wisdom are strongly reminiscent of the promises made by the prophets for the eschatological age (Jer. 31.31-36).

James has presented a catalogue of virtues which stem from the acceptance of the wisdom from above. Kirk[3] asks: 'Is not Wisdom in Jas iii.17 equivalent to Spirit in Gal. v. 22, or at least the fruit of the Spirit'. For example, Gal. 5.22, 'But the fruit of the spirit is love, joy, peace, patience, kindness...', is analogous to Jas 3.17: 'But the wisdom from above is first pure, then peaceable, gentle, open to reason, full of mercy...' A further similarity is observed between Jas 3.17 and Hermas, *Mand.* 11.8: 'In the first place, he who has the spirit which is from above, is meek and gentle, and lowly-minded and refrains from all wickedness and evil desire of this world...' What is noteworthy in comparing this passage to Jas 3.17 is the interchangeability of σοφία and πνεῦμα whereby both terms are expressed as coming from above (ἄνωθεν). In the tradition of the early Church there was a tendency to hand on lists of virtues and vices in much the same format, namely a listing of adjectives without comment. One is not arguing here for a literary dependence of this list in Hermas upon James. What, however, these texts do show is that they belong to the same stream of tradition which tended to present lists of virtues and vices in much the same form.

---

1. As Davids (*The Epistle of James*, 95) says: 'Thus the God who regenerates (begets) the Christian by the word of truth [,] will save him by the same word implanted in him if he receives it'.
2. Hoppe, *Der theologische Hintergrund*, 51-52.
3. Kirk, 'The Meaning of Wisdom in James', 27.

(b) πρῶτον ἀγνή. In this context the notion of pure (ἀγνός) refers to the person who is inspired to follow God's ways fully.[1] Jas 4.7-8 calls upon sinners to 'purify' their heart, to submit to God. As a result of the gift of wisdom from above Christians are reborn. They stand in a new relationship with God, a relationship which enables them to walk in the ways of the Lord. Seen in this perspective this term ἀγνός is indeed highly suitable as the crown of the virtues mentioned. Wisdom is first of all pure in that, through rebirth, the life of the recipient of this wisdom lives according to God's ways, according to God's directives.

(c) εἰρηνική, ἐπιεικής, εὐπειθής. This is the first of a threefold group giving the characteristics of wisdom. First, wisdom is peaceable (εἰρηνική). Jas 3.18 returns to this concept by joining righteousness and peace together. Both terms are related to the relationship of people with God and one another. Fundamental to the view of the New Testament is the belief that the true relationship between God and humanity, and between person and person, had been destroyed. Wisdom is peaceable in that it brings with it a relationship with God and one another, a relationship of righteousness. The salvific qualities of wisdom are consequently being emphasized.

In addition wisdom is characterized as gentle (ἐπιεικής). In Paul's writings this word is frequently applied to Jesus. In 2 Cor. 10.1 Paul says to the Corinthians: 'I myself entreat you by the meekness and gentleness of Christ' (διὰ τῆς πραΰτητος καὶ ἐπιεικείας τοῦ Χριστοῦ). Christ as example forms the model for

---

1. Dibelius (*James,* 213) feels that 'the priority given to "pure" (ἀγνός) does not fit well with the train of thought, for "pure" in this case sounds very general'. However, a brief survey of the use of this word does indicate its suitability for its context in James. In the LXX it refers to a range of meanings such as cultic purity; the purity of God's words; the inward disposition of the individual; and moral chastity (F. Hauck, 'ἀγνός', *TDNT*, I [1964], 122). In James this term refers either to the purity of God's words ('The promises of the Lord are promises that are pure', Ps. 12.6) or to the purity of those whose ways are righteous ('The way of the guilty is crooked, but the conduct of the pure is right', Prov. 21.8). Davids (*The Epistle of James,* 154) expresses this well when he says: 'This purity, then, means that the person partakes of a characteristic of God: he follows God's moral directives with unmixed motives'.

the way in which the Christian is to act. Here πραΰτης and
ἐπιείκεια are used together as synonyms: gentleness is a syno-
nym for meekness. In Jas 3.17 the quality of wisdom
implanted in the lives of Christians is that of gentleness or
meekness.

Finally, wisdom is described as friendly (εὐπειθής).[1] The use
of this word in conjunction with ἐπιεικής emphasizes two different aspects of the reasonable quality of wisdom. 'They may
be seen as a complementary pair, two sides of a coin: wisdom is
reasonable or gentle both in a dominant and a subordinate
position.'[2]

These three adjectives show that wisdom that is communicated from above brings with it certain essential qualities.
Peace, which is akin to righteousness, emphasizes its salvific
quality. Gentleness invokes the supreme quality of Jesus himself in the life of the Christian. Finally, openness to reason calls
the Christian to obedience and to listen carefully to the other.

(d) μεστὴ ἐλέους καὶ καρπῶν ἀγαθῶν. This is the second
description of wisdom's character and contains a more developed presentation of qualities.

Wisdom is full of mercy (μεστὴ ἐλέους). The whole biblical
tradition pays attention to the concept of ἔλεος which in the
LXX translates the Hebrew *hesed* (חֶסֶד). 'In the OT חֶסֶד denotes
an attitude of man or God which arises out of a mutual relationship. It is the attitude which the one expects of the other in
this relationship, and to which he is pledged in relationship to
him.'[3] In the New Testament context the mercy of God is evident above all in the person of Jesus and this becomes the basis
for all human mercy. 'But God, who is rich in mercy, out of the
great love with which he loved us, ...made us alive together
with Christ' (Eph. 2.4-5; see also Tit. 3.5 and 1 Pet. 1.3: 'By his
great mercy we have been born anew to a living hope through
the resurrection of Jesus Christ from the dead'). The refer-

1. Davids (*The Epistle of James,* 154) defines this term in this way: it
'does not indicate a person without convictions who agrees with everyone and sways with the wind (cf. 1.5-8), but the person who gladly
submits to true teaching and listens carefully to the other instead of
attacking him'.
2. Laws, *A Commentary on the Epistle of James,* 163.
3. R. Bultmann, 'ἔλεος', *TDNT*, II (1964), 479.

ence in Jas 3.17 to wisdom being full of mercy is to be interpreted against this background. Above all the Jewish concept
of God's mercy (חֶסֶד) must be taken into account (in contrast to
his anger and judgment). When one is called upon to exercise
the quality of mercy (Mt. 5.7), one implements something
which comes from God himself. The wisdom of God communicates this quality, which is to be exercised in one's actions.

Wisdom is also full of good works (καρπῶν ἀγαθῶν). In the
tradition of the Gospels the καρποὶ ἀγαθοί have an eschatological relevance because they form the basis for the eschatological judgment. 'You will know them by their fruits' (Mt. 7.16).
The good fruits (with the emphasis on the adjective good) are
consequently the good works of those who are justified. The
two virtues expressed here (μεστὴ ἐλέους καὶ καρπῶν ἀγαθῶν)
are closely united, as Davids[1] shows: 'The next two virtues fit
together in that ἐλέους is the practical mercy or concern for
the suffering that manifests itself in alms (ἐλεημοσύνη) i.e.
bears "good fruit" (cf. 1.26-27, 2.18-26)'.

(e) ἀδιάκριτος, ἀνυπόκριτος. This is the last statement about
the qualities of wisdom. The two terms have been joined
together because of the assonance of ά.

Wisdom is firstly ἀδιάκριτος. In post-New-Testament writings, especially in the letters of Ignatius, a number of uses of
this term appear which help to give a specification to this term
in James. What is particularly noticeable about the use is its
appearance in a positive sense which is intended by the context
of James. Dibelius[2] surveys the evidence in this manner:

> In *Mg.* 15.1 it obviously means 'simple' or of 'one accord' or
> 'harmonious': 'Farewell in godly concord and may you possess a
> harmonious spirit, for this is Jesus Christ' (ἔρρωσθε ἐν ὁμονοίᾳ
> θεοῦ, κεκτημένοι ἀδιάκριτον πνεῦμα, ὅς ἐστιν Ἰησοῦς Χριστός)
> [Loeb modified]. The same is true for *Tr.* 1.1: 'I have learned that
> you possess a mind free from blame and of one accord in
> endurance' (ἄμωμον διάνοιαν καὶ ἀδιάκριτον ἐν ὑπομονῇ ἔγνων
> ὑμᾶς ἔχοντας).

Against this background James appears to use this term
ἀδιάκριτος to emphasize his view that true wisdom is impartial

---

1. Davids, *The Epistle of James*, 154.
2. Dibelius, *James*, 214.

and makes no distinctions among people. It is, as Ignatius uses it and Dibelius[1] expresses it, 'simple or harmonious'.

The meaning of the term ἀνυπόκριτος is more easily determinable than ἀδιάκριτος. Appearing on a number of occasions in the New Testament (Rom. 12.9; 2 Cor. 6.6; 1 Tim. 1.5; 2 Tim. 1.5) it receives the meaning: without hypocrisy or sincere.[2] Wisdom, as true wisdom, is impartial, simple and harmonious (ἀδιάκριτος). At the same time it is without hypocrisy, absolutely sincere (ἀνυπόκριτος). Impartiality and sincerity are two aspects of the same thing.

(f) Conclusion. The main focus of 3.17 has been on the ἄνωθεν σοφία. Wisdom comes down from above and is the greatest gift that God communicates to humanity (Jas 1.17). This wisdom from above produces salvific results within the recipient. The receiver is reborn through the word of the truth (1.18), the implanted word (1.21). The wisdom from above brings with it a twofold consequence: a rebirth to a life of salvation, and an ethical way of life.

In the presentation of the catalogue of virtues that the Christian receives as a consequence of his acceptance of the gift of wisdom, the emphasis is placed on the quality of being pure (ἀγνός). Through bringing a new relationship with God wisdom enables the Christian to walk in the ways of God. The threefold grouping of the qualities of wisdom specifies further the nature of this wisdom from above. Taken together these adjectives show the manner of life that the recipient is to lead. Just as wisdom effects qualities and works within Christians, so Christians bring these to effect within their own life. In this sense the whole life of Christians is touched by the wisdom of God.

Noteworthy in James's description of wisdom and the qualities she bestows is the fact that James lies without doubt within the main stream of Jewish and Christian wisdom thought. The Jewish wisdom tradition continues through into the Christian era when a specific Christian wisdom tradition is produced.

1. *Ibid.*
2. Davids, *The Epistle of James*, 154; Dibelius, *James*, 214.

3.4 A harvest of righteousness for those who work peace (3.18)
The phrase τοῖς ποιοῦσιν εἰρήνην can be translated as either (i)
by those who make peace (the dative of agent), or (ii) for those
who make peace, that is, for the peacemakers. Following
Laws[1] and Hoppe,[2] I think that the second translation is to be
adopted, since the first is little more than a repetition of what
had already been said. This promise to the peacemakers is
reminiscent of Jesus' beatitude in Mt. 5.9: 'Blessed are the
peacemakers'.

The promise of the fruit of righteousness forms part of the
promise of wisdom from above. Since peace is a distinct quality
of this wisdom (3.17), those who possess peace, the peacemakers, are the ones who also possess wisdom; and wisdom
brings with it the fruit which is righteousness. As Laws[3]
observes: 'The promise of the fruit of righteousness will then be
a coherent and satisfactory conclusion to this section, because
it is implicitly a promise of the true wisdom from above'.
Hoppe[4] draws attention to the eschatological direction of the
promise of righteousness towards which the ethical admonitions are all directed. Jas 3.18, as the conclusion to this section,
ends with this eschatological promise. This accords with what
was indicated previously concerning the eschatological direction of James's ethical teaching which aimed at acquiring perfection. Only in the eschatological age is perfection to be
attained. At the same time the one who has lived by the qualities of wisdom will possess the fullness of the gift of righteousness in the life to come. This future eschatological promise of
the fullness of righteousness is in no sense realized by humans.
The καρπὸς δικαιοσύνης comes solely as a gift through Jesus
Christ. This is well expressed in Phil. 1.10-11 where Paul uses
the identical expression: 'so that you may approve what is
excellent, and may be pure and blameless for the day of Christ,
filled with the fruits of righteousness (καρπὸς δικαιοσύνης),
which come through Jesus Christ, to the glory and praise of
God'. Christians will be filled with the fruits of righteousness

1. Laws, *A Commentary on the Epistle of James*, 165.
2. Hoppe, *Der theologische Hintergrund*, 67.
3. Laws, *A Commentary on the Epistle of James*, 166.
4. Hoppe, *Der theologische Hintergrund*, 67.

when they appear on the Day of Christ. God is the one who grants the eschatological gift of righteousness and peace to those who have in their lives been doers of peace.[1]

4. *Significance of This Investigation*

James has adopted the traditional Jewish view of wisdom in which true wisdom has its origin from above. What the Christian has to do is to receive it and actualize it. Jas 3.13-18 continued the reflection on the nature of wisdom and two lifestyles were contrasted. The lifestyle of the one without wisdom is earthly, unspiritual, even demonic. James does not depict a human wisdom as though it is competing with divine wisdom. Instead, James describes an ethical lifestyle which knows no divine wisdom. Its characteristics are well presented and show that jealousy coupled with selfish ambition lead to disorder within the community. In contrast to this is the lifestyle of the one who has received the gift from above, the gift of wisdom. Through the actualization of this wisdom the Christian influences action. Wisdom brings faith to action and will bring the eschatological gift of righteousness.

This section has emphasized wisdom's qualities: it comes from God, is exercised in action and lifestyle, and carries with it the promise of the eschatological gift of righteousness. In the recipient the wisdom from above works rebirth which is illustrated through action. The quality of peace characterizes those who are the recipients of this wisdom from above. This provides the transition to the next section which gives attention to the opposite of peace: those who promote wars and dissensions.

Of extreme importance in this section is the prominence given to the two dimensions of wisdom. First, the nature of wisdom as coming from above has emphasized its divine origin and its quality as gift, influencing the life of its recipients.

---

1. 'Solcher eschatologische Charakter der Verheissung der Gerechtigkeit geht auch aus dem σπείρεται hervor: das Tun des Friedens wird... von Gott fruchtbar gemacht (καρπὸς ... σπείρεται) zum eschatologischen Besitz der "Gerechtigkeit in Frieden". Der abschliessende Satz Jak 3,18 hat also eschatologischen Verheissungscharakter' (Hoppe, *Der theologische Hintergrund*, 70).

Secondly, the section has stressed the qualities and lifestyle of those who have received this wisdom from above.

In his article on the meaning of wisdom in James, Kirk[1] has drawn attention to two main aspects that appear in the New Testament consideration of wisdom: 'In the first place Christ himself is connected with wisdom and in the second place Wisdom is never viewed as a neutral attribute'. Both these aspects appear in the Epistle of James. First, the relationship of Jesus to wisdom emerged in the examination of pericope G, where Jesus as the eschatological Lord of glory is identified with the wisdom of God. Secondly, in this present consideration of pericope J the practical dimension of wisdom as God's gift has been set forth. The qualities inherent in one who has received this gift of God are clearly spelled out. It is in this latter case that the relationship between divine wisdom and God's Spirit has been highlighted.

In the reflection on wisdom which developed in the wisdom literature, qualities were attributed to wisdom which were previously reserved for God's Spirit.[2] In Prov. 8.22-36 the role of wisdom at creation is analogous to that of God's Spirit. Whereas in Gen. 1.2 it was God's Spirit who was hovering over the waters prior to the creation, now in Prov. 8.27 it is personified wisdom who was present there with God. Even in Qumran the close association between wisdom and God's Spirit is maintained. Wisdom is a gift which the members of Qumran receive through the communication of God's Spirit.[3]

In the light of this tradition from the past one can understand the line of thought which developed in James. As a gift communicated from above wisdom gives the believer a share in many virtues. Davids[4] draws attention to four lists of virtues which are very similar to one another, namely James 3; 1QS 4; Mt. 5 and Gal. 5. In Mt. 5 one is simply called to put these virtues into practice; the beatitudes are the design for the life of the believer. In Gal. 5.22 these virtues are specified as the gifts of the Spirit; they are 'the fruit of the Spirit'. In James similar

1. Kirk, 'The Meaning of Wisdom in James', 28.
2. See above, §3.3.
3. Kirk, 'The Meaning of Wisdom in James', 36-37.
4. Davids, *The Epistle of James,* 54.

virtues are characterized as the results of the gift of wisdom which comes down from above. What Paul expresses as the effects of the gift of the Spirit, James expresses as the effects of the gift of wisdom.[1]

In the Jesus tradition handed on by Luke it is said that God will give the gift of the Spirit to the one who asks (Lk. 11.13). This parallels the teaching of James who instructs his readers to ask for the gift of wisdom (Jas 1.5). James has consistently attributed to wisdom a role and function which in other traditions (Q and Paul) are attributed to the Spirit. One could in fact speak of a wisdom pneumatology in James.[2] He does not use the term Spirit of God, but the way in which wisdom functions shows that it exercises the same role that the Spirit of God exercises elsewhere. This wisdom pneumatology is clarified in the following features: (1) wisdom comes down from above from God; (2) it is communicated through requests; (3) it brings with it the necessary virtues of the Christian way of life; and (4) above all it works rebirth and regeneration in the heart of the believer who becomes 'a kind of first fruits of his creatures' (1.18).

The focal point to which pericope J has given attention is the divine origin of wisdom. True wisdom is a gift from God enabling the Christian to lead a specific type of life. The practical dimension of wisdom is a consequence of the reception of the very gift of the Spirit. All practical advice stems from the conviction that this advice can only be carried out as a result of the communication of God's gift of wisdom. This gift alone gives the believer the belief to lead a specific lifestyle. Good deeds bear witness to this wisdom which comes from God.

1. 'The point at issue in demonstrating the similarity of context and thought in these two passages is not whether one has borrowed from the other or whether there may be some common source or community of ideas, but whether there is sufficient equality of meaning and terminology to make probable an identical use of Wisdom in James with Spirit in Paul' (Kirk, 'The Meaning of Wisdom in James', 28).
2. As Davids (*The Epistle of James,* 56) observes.

Chapter 4

THE PERSONIFICATION OF WISDOM IN Q

The two tendencies within wisdom literature are also evident
in Q. While reflection on the nature of wisdom may not be as
dominant in Q as the practical wisdom advice, this tradition
does offer some important reflections particularly with regard
to the relationship between Jesus and wisdom personified.

There are five passages in Q which require a very special
consideration because of the use of wisdom terminology. They
introduce reflection on Jesus in terms of wisdom. A brief consideration of each of these passages will be undertaken to discover the exact relationship between Jesus and personified
wisdom. In the Old Testament Proverbs 8 initiated reflection
on wisdom. Like a town crier she stands at the entrance to the
city calling on her hearers to give heed to her wisdom (Prov.
8.1-6). The scene painted here is quite revealing. Wisdom is
presented as being like a great thinker, teacher, or wise person, who assembles a number of pupils to instruct them in the
ways of wisdom. They in turn become her messengers. Sirach
(1 and 24) continues this speculation on wisdom whose role is
to communicate herself to the believer. The Wisdom of
Solomon shows how wisdom in its personification is clearly
inserted into the whole of Israel's salvation history. Chapter 10
illustrates this very clearly. It is in terms of this tradition that
the five wisdom passages in Q are to be understood.

1. *Wisdom's Role of Doom (Lk. 11.49-51; Mt. 23.34-36)*

In this passage wisdom is involved in salvation history just as
she was in Wisdom 10.1-4. The prophets act as spokesmen of
wisdom, and speak on her behalf. They meet opposition, persecution and death. This rejection of the emissaries of wisdom is

repeated again in another wisdom passage on which more will be said later: 'O Jerusalem, Jerusalem, killing the prophets and stoning those who are sent to you' (Q 13.34). Q presents the final chapter in the long saga of salvation history extending from Abel to Zechariah in which all wisdom's spokesmen are persecuted and killed. To this context belongs Jesus: as a spokesman for wisdom he too is rejected and persecuted.[1]

In examining the text as it appears in Matthew and Luke one notes the closeness of the two accounts. My intention is not to enter into the discussion of the exact wording of Q, nor to try to substantiate a particular reading.[2] What is of special relevance is the quotation; who is actually speaking these words? According to Lk. 11.49 the wisdom of God is speaking this saying, while in Mt. 23.34 the saying is attributed to Jesus himself. It is hard to imagine why Luke would change an original 'I' saying and transform it into a wisdom saying. It is more conceivable that Matthew would change a wisdom saying into an 'I' saying, especially in view of the tendency he has to equate Jesus and wisdom.[3] It appears therefore that Luke has preserved the more original form of Q. A further argument in support of the originality of the saying as coming from the wisdom of God (and not Jesus) emerges from the use of the aorist verb εἶπεν. If Jesus was referring to himself as the wisdom of God, as he did in the case of the Son of man, the verb would have been in the present (λέγει), and not in the past, in the aorist.

Form critical analysis shows that this passage is very close to the Old Testament form of an oracle of doom. In the prophets such an oracle very frequently followed a speech of reproach rather like a conclusion drawn from the speech by means of a

---

1. J.M. Robinson, 'Jesus as Sophos and Sophia: Wisdom Tradition and the Gospels', *Aspects of Wisdom in Judaism and Early Christianity* (ed. R.L. Wilken; University of Notre Dame Center for the Study of Judaism and Christianity in Antiquity, 1; Notre Dame: University of Notre Dame Press, 1975), 5.

2. A. Polag (*Fragmenta Q: Textheft zur Logienquelle* [Neukirchen-Vluyn: Neukirchener Verlag, 1979], 56) gives a reconstruction of Q which agrees in essence with Luke.

3. M.J. Suggs, *Wisdom, Christology, and Law in Matthew's Gospel* (Cambridge, MA: Harvard University Press, 1970), 14.

'therefore'.[1] In both Matthew and Luke the oracle of reproach is presented by a series of woes against the Pharisees and lawyers (Lk. 11.37-48 and Mt. 23.1-33). This is followed by the wisdom passage which is joined by 'therefore' (διὰ τοῦτο) to the woe and has the characteristics of an oracle of doom. The phrase 'the wisdom of God' is best understood as a formula which introduces an oracle of reproach taken from some pre-existing wisdom work.[2] This view, then, sees the passage as a quotation from a wisdom work where wisdom is personified. As has already been indicated, in the Wisdom of Solomon a special role was attributed to wisdom within salvation history. 'Though she is but one, she can do all things; and while remaining in herself, she renews all things; in every generation she passes into holy souls and makes them friends of God, and prophets' (Wis. 7.27). In Q 11.49-51 the emissaries of the wisdom of God are prophets, who are given the characteristic reception of all wisdom's spokesmen, namely persecution. The totality and all-inclusiveness of this rejection of wisdom's emissaries is demonstrated by the persecution of God's holy ones from Abel (the very first to be killed) to Zechariah (judged to be the last). In this passage the extension of the persecution of wisdom's envoys to include this generation is significant: 'Yes, I tell you, it shall be required of this generation' (Lk. 11.51). This generation is associated with Jesus, who as wisdom's envoy encountered hostility and death as did all of wisdom's emissaries. The association of this generation with the generation of Jesus shows the early nature of this Q passage. It corresponds to the outlook of Mk 9.1 (Mt. 16.28; Lk. 9.27) in which Jesus says: 'There are some standing here who will not taste death before they see that the Kingdom of God has come with power'. What is of special significance in the deaths of the prophets is not that they have a vicarious value, but that they will be vindicated; there is absolutely no concept of vicarious suffering.[3]

---

1. A. Bentzen, *Introduction to the Old Testament*, vol. 1 (Copenhagen: G.E.C. Gad, 1948), 199.
2. Suggs, *Wisdom*, 16.
3. According to Suggs (*Wisdom*, 27) this corresponds to the presentation of the suffering of the righteous in wisdom and apocalyptic literature.

Johnson[1] takes issue with the view outlined above, which was first presented by Suggs.[2] In fact his objection to the view of Suggs is based on two points. First, Johnson[3] refuses to accept that 'the crucial point for Suggs' thesis, and one which needs much closer scrutiny, is that in every generation Wisdom sends forth her personal representatives to speak her message'. In rejecting Suggs's view, he attempts to discredit the evidence which Suggs put forward for his position. The arguments of Johnson do not appear very convincing. In interpreting Prov. 9.3, 'She has sent out her maids to call from the highest places in the towns', he refuses to accept the meaning in its most obvious sense that wisdom sends out envoys. He argues by quoting Dahood[4] that the cultural context of the time would not allow women slaves to give an invitation to men. This seems to be a very tendentious argument; it is wrong to exclude the most obvious interpretation of a text, above all on the basis of what is proclaimed to be improper for a Semite! Further, Johnson[5] states: 'The idea of Wisdom sending envoys or prophetic messengers is foreign to the conception of Wisdom in Ben Sira'. In support of this contention he quotes F. Christ,[6] but a closer examination of Christ shows that Johnson does not understand what Christ has said. In no way does Christ support his argument. Christ[7] states that 'Sirach ist der "Kanal" der Weisheit' in Sir. 24.30-34. From this perspective Sirach appears as the envoy of wisdom, her messenger, sent to proclaim the message of wisdom. 'I will again pour out teaching like prophecy, and leave it to all future generations. Observe I have not laboured for myself alone, but for all who seek instruction' (Sir. 24.33-34). Contrary to the view of John-

---

1. M.D. Johnson, 'Reflections on a Wisdom Approach to Matthew's Christology', *CBQ* 36 (1974), 44-64.
2. Suggs, *Wisdom*.
3. Johnson, 'Reflections on a Wisdom Approach', 46.
4. M. Dahood, *Proverbs and Northwest Semitic Philology* (Rome: Pontifical Biblical Institute, 1963), 16-18.
5. Johnson, 'Reflections on a Wisdom Approach', 49.
6. F. Christ, *Jesus Sophia: Die Sophia-Christologie bei den Synoptikern* (Zurich: Zwingli Verlag, 1970), 33.
7. *Ibid.*

son, wisdom does make a communication to the individual who is meant to pass this wisdom on to others.

In commenting on Wis. 7.27 which reads, 'In every generation she passes into holy souls and makes them friends of God, and prophets', Johnson[1] interprets the view in this way: 'The centre of attention is clearly placed on the status of those seeking wisdom, not on their revelatory function; as such it is too much to call them "envoys of Sophia"'. This interpretation is not as clear as Johnson wishes. In fact he has distorted the biblical concept of a prophet, as one who is God's spokesman. A prophet never exists for what he is in himself, but for what he can communicate to others. Again in Wis. 11.1 wisdom is brought into connection with the prophets: 'Wisdom prospered their works by the hand of a holy prophet'. Since a prophet is meant to fulfil the role of God's spokesman, in these contexts the prophets fulfil the role of wisdom's spokesmen, her envoys, communicating to people her understanding and instruction. To try to reject this interpretation, as Johnson has done, betrays a lack of insight into the role of a biblical prophet, and distorts the use of the biblical evidence.

Johnson's second rejection of Suggs's argument is 'his [Suggs's] insistence on the centrality of Wisdom both in Q and Matthew'.[2] Johnson continues: 'We must conclude that in Q we have the conscious desire of an early Christian community to continue the crisis proclamation of Jesus and that the Sophia motif is limited to two passages (Lk. 7.35; 11.49)... Thus, in spite of the brilliance of Suggs' argument, perhaps it is best that the wisdom motif remain in the scholarly footnotes where he found it'.[3] Unfortunately for Johnson this is not the case. Wisdom cannot be limited in Q to two passages. The investigation in the thesis of Jacobson[4] has shown how essential wisdom is to the whole composition of Q. At the same

---

1. Johnson, 'Reflections on a Wisdom Approach', 50.
2. *Ibid.*, 53.
3. *Ibid.*, 64.
4. A.D. Jacobson, 'Wisdom Christology in Q' (PhD thesis, Claremont Graduate School, 1978).

time the whole approach to practical wisdom themes deserves very great attention.[1]

The objections of Johnson are rejected as being without foundation.[2] The view proposed by Suggs[3] is accepted, namely that part and parcel of the concept of wisdom in Judaism is the idea of wisdom being personified and sending forth emissaries throughout the course of salvation history. Against this background Q speaks of sending prophets and apostles who will be persecuted (Lk. 11.49-51; Mt. 23.34-36). According to this passage the deaths of the prophets (from Abel to Zechariah—and now included among these are those of this generation, incorporating Jesus) are to be vindicated. There is no interest in the idea that their deaths had a vicarious value. This corresponds to the whole Q outlook which has no passion–resurrection–redemptive account; instead, this tradition places Jesus in the line of the martyred prophets whom wisdom is to vindicate.[4]

The examination of this passage has revealed a number of important insights with regard to the relationship between Jesus and wisdom. In Q Jesus adopted a saying or passage from traditional Jewish wisdom literature where personified wisdom speaks. Wisdom tells of her envoys, the prophets, who have been persecuted and put to death throughout salvation history. Jesus' generation experiences the same reaction to their message with Jesus himself being in this line of prophets who have been put to death. Matthew developed this passage further and identified wisdom and Jesus. He simply put the saying in the mouth of Jesus, making it an 'I' saying. Wilckens[5] fails to see the development that is going on in the Gospel of Matthew and simply argues that the identification of

---

1. As R.A. Edwards has argued in 'An Approach to a Theology of Q' *JR* 51 (1971), 247-69 and *A Theology of Q: Eschatology, Prophecy and Wisdom* (Philadelphia: Fortress, 1976).

2. The wisdom myth as proposed by R. Bultmann (*The History of the Synoptic Tradition* (trans. by J. Marsh from the 2nd German edition (1931); rev. edn, Oxford: Basil Blackwell, 1972], 114-15) is not really considered here, because this would take us too far afield in this investigation.

3. Suggs, *Wisdom*, 20-29.

4. *Ibid.*, 27-28.

5. U. Wilckens, 'σοφία', *TDNT*, VII (1971), 515.

Jesus with wisdom was present in Q. It is true, as Suggs[1] observes, that 'Q is moving in the direction of a Wisdom Christology'. There is a wisdom christology present in Q only to the extent that Jesus is seen as wisdom's envoy. Anything further than this belongs to later developments which have taken place in Matthew, Paul and John, who identify Jesus, in different ways, with wisdom herself. But, for the period of Q, to which Luke has remained faithful and bears witness (because he has no interest in developing wisdom speculation) Jesus remains as one of wisdom's envoys.

2. *Wisdom's Children and Wisdom in the Market Place (Lk. 7.31-35; Mt. 11.16-19)*

The final verse of the parable is of special interest:

> Yet wisdom is justified by all her children (Lk. 7.35)
> Yet wisdom is justified by her deeds (Mt. 11.19)

It is important to examine this saying as it occurs in the two contexts because each version has a decidedly different purpose and teaching in mind.

2.1 *The Q form*

Polag[2] presents the reading 'Yet wisdom is justified by her children' (Q 7.35) as the Q form which Matthew and Luke each used in his own way. There is a growing tendency to view this section (Lk. 7.18-35 and Mt. 11.2-19) as the conclusion to the first section of Q.[3] The unity of this first section of Q emerges from an examination of the Lucan order, which is generally accepted as reproducing the original order:

---

1. Suggs, *Wisdom*, 28.
2. Polag, *Fragmenta Q*, 42-43.
3. J.M. Robinson, 'Basic Shifts in German Theology', *Interp.* 16 (1962), 83; Suggs, *Wisdom*, 37-38; Jacobson, 'Wisdom Christology in Q', 24-98.

Luke		Matthew	
John the Baptist	3.1-6	John the Baptist	3.1-6
John's preaching	3.7-9, 16f.	John's preaching	3.7-12
Temptations	4.1-13	Temptations	4.1-11
Jesus' preaching	6.20ff.	Jesus' preaching	5.3ff.
Centurion's servant	7.1-10	Centurion's servant	8.5-13
John and Jesus	7.18-35	On following Jesus	8.19-22
On following Jesus	9.57-60	'Mission charge'	9.35ff.
'Mission charge'	10.1ff.	John and Jesus	11.2-19[1]

One can trace the line of thought by using the order of Luke. Q introduced the Baptist (Lk. 3.1-6) and gave his teaching (3.7-9.16f.). Then Jesus was introduced (4.1-13) and his teaching presented (6.20ff.). This was interrupted by an account of one of Jesus' miracles (one of the few narratives in Q). This first section of Q ends with this unit on John and Jesus (Q 7.18-35) in which the relationship between them is indicated.

Jacobson[2] sees this unit (Q 7.31-35) as belonging to what he terms the compositional stage of Q. By presenting Jesus and John as messengers of wisdom, it forms the foundation for the whole of this first section of Q. However, Jacobson shows some confusion in making a distinction between wisdom's children on the one hand, and Jesus and John on the other hand. 'The "children" of wisdom are those who, in contrast to "this generation" respond to the call to repentance issued by John and Jesus, and who thus "justify" wisdom because they acquiesce in wisdom's judgment on this generation, uttered by her messengers John and Jesus.'[3] Robinson[4] gives a similar interpretation: 'Here Sophia's children vindicate her by affirming both John and Jesus'.

However, I adopt the opposite viewpoint. Jesus and John are to be associated with the children of wisdom. As wisdom's 'children' or emissaries John and Jesus experience rejection: John is condemned for having a demon, while Jesus, as the Son of man, is identified as a 'glutton and drunkard, a friend of tax collectors and sinners' (Lk. 7.34). Although Jesus and John are mentioned together as wisdom's envoys, the context in which

1. Jacobson, 'Wisdom Christology in Q', 24.
2. *Ibid.*, 24-98.
3. *Ibid.*, 96-97.
4. Robinson, 'Jesus as Sophos and Sophia', 5.

they appear does tend to make a distinction between them—
they are not placed on an equal level. Of John in Q 7.28b it is
said: 'Yet he who is least in the Kingdom of God is greater than
he'. The word translated 'least' (μικρότερος) is a comparative,
and not a superlative as it is translated in English. Hence it
should read 'the lesser (of the two) is greater than he in the
Kingdom'.[1] In the order of salvation history there was a time
when Jesus was a disciple, that is, 'lesser'; but now he is ranked
higher than John. This interpretation is further supported by
the presence of the title 'Son of man' which is applied to Jesus.
It is an eschatological title and denotes the role of eschatological judge.

In this particular passage wisdom is personified. She acts in
the same way as in the Jewish wisdom tradition as well as
elsewhere in Q, namely by sending forth emissaries who are
rejected by their hearers. Among these stand John and Jesus,
who are both presented in an eschatological light.[2] Through
the activities of John and Jesus the righteousness of wisdom is
demonstrated. As the Son of man Jesus exercises a more
important function than John.

2.2 *The Matthean formulation*
Matthew developed this passage further and in the final verse
Matthew replaced Q's 'wisdom is justified by her children'
with the phrase 'wisdom is justified by her deeds'. This was
done consciously in order to identify Jesus once more with
wisdom. This section of Mt. 11.2-19 begins and ends with a
reference to deeds (ἔργα) which produces an *inclusio*: the
whole passage is included between the reference to works. Mt.
11.2 speaks of 'the works of Christ' whereas Mt. 11.19 speaks

---

1. O. Cullmann ('The Significance of the Qumran Texts for Research
into the Beginnings of Christianity', *JBL* 74 [1955], 219), and F. Blass &
A. Debrunner (*A Greek Grammar of the New Testament and Other
Early Christian Literature* [a translation and revision of the ninth–
tenth German edition incorporating supplementary notes of A.
Debrunner by R.W. Funk; Chicago: University of Chicago Press, 1961],
32-33) give indirect support to this interpretation.
2. Wilckens ('σοφία', 516) also interprets the phrase 'children of wisdom' in the way indicated, namely as referring to John and Jesus, as
wisdom's emissaries.

of 'the works of wisdom'. In this way the phrases parallel each other. The following verse (Mt. 11.20) continues to speak about the 'mighty works' (δυνάμεις) of Christ. Following this line of thought, it is clear that the deeds of wisdom are to be identified with the deeds of Christ himself. As in 23.34-36 Matthew has here again taken Q's concept of wisdom further by identifying Jesus and wisdom. Jesus is in fact wisdom incarnate.

2.3 *The Lucan formulation*

A very good examination and interpretation of this passage has been given by Du Plessis[1] in which the context is used as an aid to interpret the identity of 'wisdom' and 'the children'. He contends that Luke has fully incorporated this Q saying within his ch. 7 and this tends above all to give a special understanding to Lk. 7.35. Du Plessis[2] notes that a chiastic parallelism has been constructed between vv. 29 and 35 in which he observes the following structure:

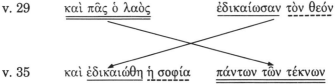

v. 29   καὶ πᾶς ὁ λαὸς   ἐδικαίωσαν τὸν θεόν

v. 35   καὶ ἐδικαιώθη ἡ σοφία   πάντων τῶν τέκνων

The reference to 'the children' in the Q original ('But wisdom is justified by her children') now goes far beyond Jesus and John to include all those who accept and carry out the will of God in their lives. Further, θεός and σοφία are used in a parallel way, showing that σοφία now refers to God himself, and not simply to the personification of wisdom, as was the case in the Q original.[3] God, therefore, is justified by all those who carry out his will in their lives.

A noteworthy development has taken place in this saying, as has been observed in the preceding discussion. In the Q origi-

1. I.J. Du Plessis, 'Contextual Aid for an Identity Crisis: An Attempt to Interpret Luke 7.35', *A South African Perspective on the New Testament: Essays by South African New Testament Scholars Presented to Bruce Manning Metzger during his Visit to South Africa in 1985* (Leiden: Brill, 1986), 112-27.
2. *Ibid.*, 124.
3. *Ibid.*, 124-25.

nal, wisdom is personified and in this way she sends forth her emissaries, John and Jesus, who through their activities demonstrate the righteousness of wisdom. In *Matthew* development takes place with an identification being made between Jesus and wisdom: he becomes wisdom incarnate who demonstrates his righteousness by his works. In *Luke* wisdom is effectively identified with God himself and is no longer a mere personification. God is proved right by all who carry out his will. Each of the sources has developed the saying in its own way, giving it its own specific thrust and understanding. The understanding of the Q original is most important for this study because it reveals that at this stage in the thought processes of the early Church wisdom is a personification, and Jesus is represented as one of her emissaries. There is no identification of Jesus and wisdom. This occurs only at a later stage, and is evidenced by the Gospel of Matthew.

3. *Jerusalem Killing the Prophets* (Lk. 13.34-35; Mt. 23.37-39)

The form of this saying is almost identical in Matthew and Luke; but its position differs. In Matthew it follows wisdom's oracle of doom (Mt. 23.29-36) which concerns those who kill 'the prophets, and wise men and scribes' (23.34). In Luke the words are connected to Jesus' reply to the news that Herod is intent on killing him (13.31-33). Although one may not be able to solve the riddle of its original position in Q, the more important question to answer concerns the passage's relationship to wisdom. Without doubt it originally belonged to traditional Jewish wisdom in which the speaker, wisdom, was personified. Christ[1] discovers a connection here between the deuteronomic-prophet statement and the wisdom tradition. In Q it has been adapted from this tradition and presented as a word of wisdom in line with Q's interest in wisdom.

A different development takes place in Luke and Matthew. Luke places the words in the mouth of Jesus and ignores the wisdom focus completely. Luke wishes to summarize Jesus' Galilean ministry and by means of the lament he gives a per-

---

1. Christ, *Jesus Sophia*, 139.

spective on the journey to Jerusalem. Matthew, however, by placing it in the context of wisdom's oracle of doom (Mt. 23.34-36), preserves the wisdom emphasis. In doing so, Matthew has implicitly identified Jesus with wisdom: it is a saying of Jesus, wisdom-incarnate.

The lament commences with wisdom charging Jerusalem as the place where her emissaries, the prophets, and those who had been sent to Jerusalem, are being killed. Once again (as in Mt. 23.34-36 and Lk. 11.49-51) reference is made to the killing of the emissaries of wisdom. The tenderness and compassion of wisdom is contrasted with the violence with which her emissaries were met: she would 'have gathered your children together as a hen gathers her brood under her wings' (Lk. 13.34). Wisdom's greatest desire is for humanity to accept her and her will to guide and protect. Throughout the wisdom tradition this was quite a common theme (Prov. 8.4-5; Sir. 24.1-11; Bar. 4.1-12). These passages indicate how deeply the oracle of doom in Q is steeped in the wisdom tradition and show that it can only be understood against this background.

'Behold, your house is forsaken' (Lk. 13.35) implies that because she has not been accepted, wisdom has left her dwelling in Jerusalem and in the temple to return to her heavenly abode. This idea finds expression in the wisdom tradition of *1 Enoch* 42.1-3: 'Wisdom could not find a place in which she could dwell; but a place was found (for her) in heaven. Then Wisdom went out to dwell with the children of the people, but she found no dwelling place, (so) Wisdom returned to her place and she settled permanently among the angels'.

This saying in the Q original was an oracle of wisdom. While Luke did not preserve this as a wisdom oracle, Matthew has certainly done so by placing it in the immediate context of an oracle of doom. Matthew put this wisdom saying in the mouth of Jesus and once again has forged an identification between Jesus and wisdom: Jesus is wisdom incarnate.[1] A similar line of development took place in the previous pericope which we discussed (Q 7.31-35).

---

1. 'As this figure, Jesus can say—as no merely historical individual might—"I would have gathered your children under my wings". Jesus is Wisdom incarnate' (Suggs, *Wisdom,* 71).

4. Thanksgiving and Revelation (Lk. 10.21-22; Mt. 11.25-27)

The forms of this saying in Matthew and Luke are virtually identical: a few variations occur in the manner in which they are expressed.[1] Jacobson[2] has analysed this passage as forming part of what he terms the second section of Q which extends from Lk. 9.57 to 10.22. Just as the first section (Lk. 3.1-6 to 7.18-25) begins and ends with wisdom themes, so too does the second section. Jacobson[3] argues that 'Lk. 9.58 par. stood immediately adjacent to the saying in Lk. 7.35 par.—"Wisdom is justified by her children"'. This means that the sayings in Lk. 9.58 are to be interpreted in a wisdom framework as wisdom sayings. According to Jacobson[4] the sequence of material in this second section of Q is as follows:

Following Jesus	Lk. 9.57-60	Mt. 8.19-22
The 'Mission Charge'	Lk. 10.1-12	Mt. 9.37f.; 10.7-16
Woes over Galilean cities	Lk. 10.13-15	Mt. 11.21-23
Saying about messengers	Lk. 10.16	Mt. 10.40
Jesus' thanksgiving	Lk. 10.21-22	Mt. 11.25-27

The character of this pericope on wisdom (Q 10.21-22) has occasioned considerable discussion. Lk. 10.21 (Mt. 11.25-26) is a thanksgiving unit, while Lk. 10.22 (Mt. 11.27) is revelatory. It is important, however, to treat this passage as a unity; the aspect of thanksgiving implies knowledge communicated in connection with eschatological mysteries, while the word of revelation speaks about an intimate knowledge of the Father. Once again the correct approach in understanding this Q passage is to view it against the background of Jewish wisdom

---

1. Polag (*Fragmenta Q,* 46-48) offers a reconstruction of Q which is closer to Matthew's formulation.

2. Jacobson, 'Wisdom Christology in Q', 127-46.

3. *Ibid.,* 132.

4. *Ibid.,* 144. Whereas Jacobson sees this section of Q ending with Q 10.21-22, Polag (*Fragmenta Q,* 24) incorporates a further saying as a conclusion to what he terms the section on the mission of the disciples (Lk. 9.57–10.23-24).

thought which has received a specific eschatological-apocalyptic stamp.[1]

The closest parallel to this present passage has been found in the Wisdom of Solomon, which refers to one who 'professes to have knowledge of God, and calls himself a child of the Lord... and boasts that God is his Father. Let us see if his words are true, and let us test what will happen at the end of his life; for if the righteous man is God's son, he will help him' (Wis. 2.13-18). In Wis. 4–5 this son appears in a scene of eschatological judgment in which he is vindicated before those who have opposed him.[2] With this background in mind, one must again read this passage in Q (as Luke has portrayed it) with Jesus as a spokesman for wisdom. This Q passage commences with a hymn of thankfulness for eschatological mysteries which have been revealed to God's chosen ones. Above all this revelation has been made known by the Father to the Son. Whereas elsewhere Jesus is a spokesman or emissary of wisdom, here he is presented in the role of the one to whom the Father has revealed himself, and the Son in turn communicates this revelation to others. Suggs sums up this understanding of the passage in Q well when he says: 'The Q hymn thus opens with thankfulness for the eschatological secrets given to the elect; it speaks of the revelation entrusted to the Son who is not known by men, and—even if paradoxically—of that Son's revelation of the Father to his followers'.[3]

In the Gospel of Matthew this passage underwent a further transformation in line with the way in which the other wisdom passages were transformed. Jesus is not simply the revealer of the Father, but is again identified with wisdom as wisdom incarnate. Immediately after the saying on Jesus as

---

1. Suggs, *Wisdom*, 83. This eschatological-apocalyptic stamp has been emphasized by the fact that within its context in Q it appears immediately following the woes which have been pronounced against the Galilean cities.

2. Suggs (*Wisdom*, 92) concludes his argument: 'Thus, the Wisdom of Solomon furnishes the background against which the revealed knowledge in Mt. 11.25-27 can be seen in its relation to election, to eschatological knowledge, to the intimate relation of Father and Son, and the failure of men to know the Son as well as the Father'.

3. *Ibid.*, 95.

the revealer of the Father, Matthew adds a saying exclusive to himself about coming to Jesus and bearing his yoke (Mt. 11.28-30) which has similarities in wisdom literature, such as Sir. 51.26-27. In the mouth of Jesus this saying again presents him as wisdom incarnate. Matthew has developed Q further to identify the Son with wisdom.[1]

Many scholars[2] have failed to perceive the distinction and the development that have taken place here between Q and Matthew. They see an identification between Jesus and wisdom already at the stage of Q. This forces them to conclude that this passage in Q is a very late addition to Q because of the development in thought.[3] What they have failed to appreciate is that in Q the Son still remains the revealer of wisdom. The Son is in a special relationship to the Father: he is his spokesman, the one who communicates the knowledge of the Father to others. Just as the Son here is in relation to the Father, so elsewhere Jesus stands in relation to wisdom as her spokesman. In Matthew this thought is expressly developed so that

1. Supporters of this approach are Christ, *Jesus Sophia*, 117-19; Robinson, 'Jesus as Sophos and Sophia', 9-11. On the other hand G.N. Stanton ('Salvation Proclaimed: X. Mt. 11.28-30: Comfortable words?' *ET* 94 [1982], 3-9) presents the opposite view where he refuses to see Jesus as identified with wisdom incarnate in these verses or for that matter in the Gospel of Matthew: 'In short, it is not at all clear that Matthew identifies Jesus as Sophia. The use of the same Wisdom themes in 11.28-30 is not being disputed, but they do not seem to be the key to the passage as it now stands in Matthew's gospel' (p. 6). At the heart of Stanton's opposition lies his refusal to see any influence of the sapiential literature, especially Sir. 51 or 24, on this passage. However C. Deutsch (*Hidden Wisdom and the Easy Yoke: Wisdom, Torah and Discipleship in Matthew 11.25-30* [Sheffield: JSOT, 1987]) has examined the background to Mt. 11.25-30 very carefully and to my mind has successfully argued against Stanton: 'We believe the presentation of 11.28-30 is analogous to the way in which Wisdom is represented in Sirach 24. There Wisdom comes to reside in Torah, thus becoming "incarnated" in and identified with Torah. So in Matthew, Wisdom is identified with Jesus as its incarnation' (p. 134).

2. For example, Robinson ('Jesus as Sophos and Sophia', 8-10); S. Schulz (*Q: Die Spruchquelle der Evangelisten* [Zurich: Theologischer Verlag, 1972], 224-25); and Jacobson ('Wisdom Christology in Q', 141-43).

3. Jacobson, 'Wisdom Christology in Q', 142; and Robinson, 'Jesus as Sophos and Sophia', 10.

Jesus is no longer the revealer, but the one who is identified with wisdom.

It is my contention that Matthew has consistently developed the Q thought on the relation of Jesus to wisdom by identifying Jesus with wisdom, as wisdom incarnate. This tendency or development occurred elsewhere as is evident in the writings of Paul (1 Corinthians) and John. The teaching of Jesus and its expression in Q have been reflected upon and the same understanding of this teaching has made its appearance in three different centres of the early community (Corinth, Syria and later Ephesus). At the same time as this development took place it was brought into connection with a passion christology: the wisdom that Paul proclaimed was a Christ who was crucified; Matthew inserted the wisdom speculation side by side with the passion structure of the gospel genre; and John developed speculation on the pre-existent Word who became incarnate, died and returned to the Father.

5. *Greater than the Wisdom of Solomon (Lk. 11.31; Mt. 12.42)*

The wording of this saying in Matthew and Luke is almost identical: the only difference is that Luke has μετὰ τῶν ἀνδρῶν τῆς γενεᾶς ταύτης while Matthew has simply μετὰ τῆς γενεᾶς ταύτης.[1] This saying on the wisdom of Solomon forms part of a larger Q pericope dealing with the sign of Jonah (Lk. 11.29-32 and Mt. 12.38-42). Jacobson[2] observes a threefold development in this pericope. It begins with the statement: 'This generation is an evil generation; it seeks a sign, but no sign will be given it except the sign of Jonah' (Lk. 11.29b = Mt. 12.39b)—this is the core statement. It is then expanded to explain what the sign of Jonah is (Lk. 11.30; Mt. 12.40). To this then is added the wisdom saying (Lk. 11.31f. = Mt. 12.41f.).

This passage is again at home in the realm of thought of the wisdom tradition. Just as in Lk. 11.49-51 (Mt. 23.34-36),[3] the background to this picture of wisdom is that wisdom contin-

---

1. Polag (*Fragmenta Q*, 52-53) sees Luke as having added these words (τῶν ἀνδρῶν) to Q.
2. Jacobson, 'Wisdom Christology in Q', 166-68.
3. According to Jacobson ('Wisdom Christology in Q', 187-95) Lk. 11.49-51 (Mt. 23.34-36) brings the third section of Q to a conclusion.

ually sends messengers or spokesmen. The reaction of Israel to these emissaries of wisdom is always that of rejection and persecution. In contrast to this negative response of rejection is the positive acceptance by the Gentiles who welcome wisdom's envoys. The queen of the South travels great distances to hear the wisdom of Solomon. The men of Nineveh responded positively to Jonah's preaching. A parallel is drawn here between the wisdom (σοφία) which is in evidence in Solomon, and the preaching (κήρυγμα) of Jonah. One may therefore infer that the wisdom of God lies behind both the wisdom of Solomon and the preaching of the prophets.

Placed alongside this consistent picture of Israel's rejection is that of the acceptance by the Gentiles. In this way the wisdom tradition is being permeated with a deuteronomistic concept of history. In contrast to Israel's response there stands the favourable response of Gentiles to the appeal of σοφία and the κήρυγμα addressed by wisdom through her spokesmen and emissaries. The conclusion of this third section of Q (Lk. 11.49-51 = Mt. 23.34-36) emphasizes the impenitence of Israel. In this context Jesus is referred to as the Son of man and appears as the greatest of wisdom's representatives: 'and behold, something greater than Solomon is here' (Q 11.31). This accords with the picture presented elsewhere in Q of Jesus' relationship to wisdom. Matthew leaves this picture as it stands in Q without developing it according to his custom of identifying Jesus with wisdom.

6. *The Development of the Personification of Wisdom in the Jesus Traditions*

A common approach and thread runs through the five wisdom passages in this category. In an attempt to express an understanding of the role of Jesus, Q combines the sayings of Jesus with traditional Jewish wisdom. As has been argued previously, the Q community did not distinguish between the historical Jesus and the words they spoke as prophets in his name. The intention of Q was to present faithfully the community's understanding of the person of Jesus as he continued to lead them to a deeper understanding of himself and his teaching. Jesus belongs to the long line of emissaries sent by wisdom in the course of salvation history. Among these the prophets in particular experienced persecution and death (Q 11.49-51) as they exercised their role as wisdom's spokesmen. In seeing Jesus in this role as one of wisdom's envoys who encountered suffering, no thought was given to the notion of vicarious suffering—this was something which the traditional Gospel Gattung introduced with its emphasis on the Passion and Resurrection. As spokesman for wisdom, Jesus is placed in a very special position. In Q 7.33-35 Jesus appears alongside John the Baptist; but as the eschatological Son of man Jesus is ranked higher than John.

In Q the highlight of the relationship between Jesus and wisdom finds expression in the thanksgiving and revelation oracle of Q 10.21-22. Whereas elsewhere Jesus is a spokesman or emissary of wisdom, here he exercises the role of the one to whom the Father has revealed himself, and who in turn communicates this revelation to others. In the rejection of wisdom's envoys, a contrast is drawn between the rejection by Israel and the interest and acceptance on the part of the Gentiles. In Q 11.29-32 the focus of attention lies on the positive response given by the Gentiles to wisdom's representatives. The implication to be drawn is that they will give the same response to Jesus, the greatest of wisdom's representatives.

An analysis of the appearance of these wisdom passages in Luke and in Matthew has shown the tendency in Luke to remain faithful to their meaning in Q. Characteristic of this tendency is the personification of wisdom, and the fact that Jesus exercises the consistent role of spokesman or emissary for wisdom. Even in Lk. 10.21-22 Jesus remains the one to whom the revelation is communicated and he in his turn communicates this revelation to others. Luke appears at times to wish to avoid referring to wisdom as personified alongside God. This is evident in Lk. 7.31-35 where God and wisdom are identified.

Matthew on the other hand has developed these wisdom passages in a consistent way. His reflection on Jesus and the role that he exercised led to an identification of Jesus with wisdom as wisdom incarnate. The wisdom passages bear this particular stamp and transformation. One can speak of a wisdom christology evolving in Matthew's reflection. In Mt.

23.34-36 the wisdom saying is placed in the mouth of Jesus thereby identifying Jesus with wisdom. In the context of Mt. 11.19 Jesus appears as wisdom incarnate when his deeds and the deeds of wisdom are identified. But what must be the peak of this identification appears in the thanksgiving and revelation hymn of Mt. 11.25-27. In Lk. 10.21-22 (and hence Q) Jesus is presented in the role of the one to whom the Father has revealed himself and who in turn communicates this revelation to others. To this saying on Jesus as the revealer of the Father Matthew adds a further saying from traditional wisdom about coming to him and bearing his yoke (Mt. 11.28-30): no longer is it wisdom personified speaking, but it is Jesus himself as wisdom incarnate who calls and invites.

7. *James and Q: Reflection on the Nature of Wisdom*

In comparing briefly the results of this investigation on the personification of wisdom in James and Q some noteworthy points emerge.

James tends to focus his attention on the communication of God's gift of wisdom to humanity. This is analogous to the gift of God's Spirit as represented in later traditions. The effects of both are the same: they lead to rebirth and regeneration which enable the Christian to conduct a specific lifestyle. In one passage (2.1) a relationship between Jesus and wisdom can be implied. There Jesus as the eschatological Lord of glory exercises the role of wisdom. As eschatological Lord, Jesus is presented as the heavenly exalted Lord, who will be seen by all in this way at the end of time. This title 'Lord of glory' is applied to Jesus, not with reference to his earthly function as Messiah, but to his exalted role now that he is seated at the right hand of the Father. Jesus as the Lord of glory is the origin of all the paraenetical wisdom advice developed in this pericope (2.1-13).

Although not explicitly stated, the understanding which emerges from the structure of this entire pericope is that Jesus is the wisdom of God. As the Lord of glory Jesus is the all-embracing source of the wisdom direction that the lives of the believers must follow. If one compares this thought in James with that presented in the Jesus traditions, the following perspective emerges with regard to the relation between Jesus and wisdom.

(a) In Q Jesus appears as the emissary of wisdom who has come to instruct humanity on the wisdom direction life should take. Just as the prophets were persecuted in the past, so too Jesus and his followers will meet persecution and opposition. In line with the whole Old Testament and intertestamental period wisdom is viewed as personified. Although the notion of suffering and persecution is presented, no emphasis is really placed upon the cross and death of Jesus.

(b) James tends to have developed these thoughts a little further. Whereas for Q Jesus was wisdom's envoy, now in James it is Jesus exalted to the right hand of the Father who is identified as carrying out the role of wisdom. This is in line with the eschatological direction of James's thought. At the same time the nature of James as a paraenetical writing means that great emphasis is placed on the gift of wisdom which comes down from above, a gift which works a regeneration and rebirth in the hearts of those who receive her. In this way the gift of wisdom is analogous to the gift of the Spirit appearing in other New Testament traditions. One can see here the germ of what would later flower forth into trinitarian theology. In the identification of Jesus Christ with wisdom one sees emerging the profession of belief in the divinity of Jesus Christ. The communication of wisdom to humanity is equivalent to the communication of the gift of the Spirit by God, the Father, and the Son to humanity. In James, then, the focus has shifted from Jesus as being the emissary of Heavenly Wisdom in Q to the relationship between the exalted Jesus Christ and wisdom.

(c) In the Gospel of Matthew the relationship of Jesus to wisdom has further progressed to the point where the evangelist can refer to Jesus in the role of wisdom incarnate. The earthly Jesus is now identified with wisdom. Jesus himself speaks as wisdom and acts in this role. In the Gospel of Luke the author has tended to remain closer to the perspective of Q, and that accords with the general tendency of Luke. Nevertheless, a development did take place in that wisdom is not seen as a personification but as God himself.[1]

In these four documents there is a progressive developing understanding of wisdom in relationship to Jesus. A deeper perception of the person and role of Jesus emerges through their reflections. At the same time the investigation helps to position the Epistle of James within this line of development. From a content perspective James is midway between Q and Matthew. He shows how the development from the personification of wisdom in Q took place. The identification of Jesus with wisdom in his exalted role (James) made it possible for further reflection to take place which saw the earthly Jesus as wisdom incarnate (Matthew). This intermediate position of James was necessary before the further step in Matthew could take place. The tradition of Luke, on the other hand, tended to take a different direction. It absorbed the Q tradition and further aspects of Q, but developed them in a setting removed from that in which James and Matthew moved.

This does not mean that I am arguing for a direct line of use of documents extending from Q through James to Matthew. Rather, we are dealing with a common thought world in which certain traditions are developed against a common cultural and ideological background. What this examination of the nature of wisdom and its relationship to Jesus has shown is that the thought of Q must be presumed by James, and that the latter has shown a development of the Q thought. At the same time, while Matthew certainly knows Q and its tradition, his gospel also shows a development in its thought. Each one of these documents is representative of a stage in which the Jesus tradition developed within the early Christian community. From this it appears that Q, James and Matthew lie along the same line of development in the tradition, with James representing a stage intermediate between that of Q and Matthew. Matthew, however, does not demonstrate a direct use of James himself, but rather a further development (over two decades) of those traditions that James has used.

In a general sense James and Q can be termed wisdom documents provided that this is not seen in any exclusive way.

1. Du Plessis, 'Contextual Aid for an Identity Crisis', 124-25.

The examination of this and the previous chapter on the role of wisdom in James and Q has revealed that the twofold Hebrew perspective on wisdom has been maintained in both. The investigation has shown that Q and James have a similar wisdom outlook which tends to indicate that they emerge from a similar worldview. This conclusion will be tested in more detail in the following chapters by examining the relationship between James and Q with regard to specific texts.

PART II

TEXTUAL RELATIONS BETWEEN JAMES
AND THE JESUS TRADITION

Chapter 5

JAMES AND THE SERMON ON THE MOUNT/PLAIN: A COMPARATIVE EXAMINATION

While James makes no direct quotations of the words of Jesus, his writing does show a striking closeness to Jesus' words in the Gospels. In fact Kittel[1] remarked very succinctly: 'Es gibt keine Schrift des NT ausser den Evangelien, die so mit Anklängen an Herrnworte gespickt ist wie er'. Although most commentators on James draw attention to these correspondences, not all agree on their exact composition. In this and the following chapters the correspondences between James and Q will be investigated by paying attention to specific texts in which agreements may be observed. First, an overall chart of these correspondences will be presented. Then, attention will be devoted to those correspondences that are seen to exist between James and the Q Sermon on the Mount. Finally, in the next chapter, attention will be given to other correspondences that exist textually between James and Q (excluding the Sermon on the Mount) as well as other synoptic traditions outside Q.

The Q text of Polag (1979) will be used when referring to Q because it is the best complete text of Q in Greek to have been published to date. However, it has to be kept in mind that this is not the definitive text of Q. In examining the relationship of James to Q, notice will always be taken of how Matthew and Luke differ in order to see whether James shows a tendency to lie closer to Matthew's version of Q or to that of Luke.

---

1. G. Kittel, 'Der geschichtliche Ort des Jakobusbriefes', *ZNW* 41 (1942), 84.

1. *Chart of Correspondences between James and the Synoptic Tradition*

NO	JAMES	MATTHEW	LUKE	SOURCE	LOCATION IN Q*	TOPIC
1	1.2	5.11-12	6.22-23	Q	Sermon on Mount (B)	Joy under persecution
2	1.4	5.48		M		Call to perfection
3	(a) 1.5 (b) 1.17 (c) 4.2-3	7.7 7.11 7.7-8	11.9 11.13 11.9-10	Q Q Q	Prayer (E)	Asking
4	1.6	21.21		Mk 11.23		Faith and doubting
5	(a) 1.22 (b) 1.23	7.24 7.26	6.46-47 6.49	Q Q	Sermon on Mount (B)	Doers of the Word Doers of the Word
6	2.5	5.3, 5 (11.5)	6.20 (7.22)	Q Q	Sermon on Mount (B) John the Baptist (C)	Poor
7	2.8	22.39-40	10.27	Mk 12.28-34		Law of love
8	2.10	5.18-19	16.17	Q	Parables (I)	Obligation to keep whole law
9	2.11	5.21-30		M		Do not kill or commit adultery
10	2.13	5.7	 6.36	M Q	 Sermon on Mount (B)	Mercy
11	2.15-16	25.34-35	 3.11	M L		Clothe the naked
12	3.12	7.16-18	6.43-44	Q	Sermon on Mount (B)	Fruit of good works
13	3.18	5.9		M		Peacemakers

NO	JAMES	MATTHEW	LUKE	SOURCE	LOCATION IN Q*	TOPIC
14	4.4	(a) 12.39	11.29	Q	Contro-versies (F)	Unfaith-ful crea-tures
		(b) 6.24	16.13	Q	Parables (I)	Serving two masters
15	4.8	5.8		M		Pure in heart
16	4.9		6.25	L		Mourn and weep
		(5.4)	(6.21b)	Q	Sermon on Mount (B)	
17	4.10	23.12	14.11; 18.14	(?) Q	Possibly Q	Humility & exalta-tion
18	4.11	7.1-2	6.37-38	Q	Sermon on Mount (B)	Do not judge
19	5.1		6.24-25	L		Weep
20	5.2-3	6.19-21	12.33-34	Q	On proper concerns (H)	Treasure in heaven
21	5.6	(7.1)	6.37	Q	Sermon on Mount (B)	Do not condemn
22	5.9	24.33		Mk 13.29		Judge at doors
23	5.10	5.11-12	6.23	Q	Sermon on Mount (B)	Suffering prophets
24	5.12	5.34-37		M		Oaths
25	5.17		4.25	L		Elijah example
26	5.19-20	18.15	17.3	Q	On the responsi-bilities of disciples (J)	Relation to sinful brother

* Different scholars have presented different lists of correspondences (for example: Kittel, 'Der geschichtliche Ort', 84-94; J.B. Mayor, *The Epistle of St. James: The Greek Text with Introduction, Notes, Comments and Further Studies in the Epistle of St. James* [3rd rev. edn; Grand Rapids: Zondervan, [1913] 1954], lxxxv-lxxxviii; W.D. Davies, *The Setting of the Sermon on the Mount* [Cambridge: Cambridge University Press, 1964], 402-403; F. Mussner, *Der Jakobusbrief: Auslegung* [4th edn; Freiburg: Herder, 1981], 48-50; P.H. Davids, *The Epistle of James: A Commentary on the Greek Text* [Exeter: Paternoster, 1982], 47-48; P.H. Davids, 'James and Jesus', *Gospel Perspectives*, vol. 5 *The*

In the above survey the correspondences are limited to what appear to be close associations or allusions. Many other more general echoes or parallels in thought have also been noted,[1] but these are not referred to here. The latter have meaning or significance only against the background of the more obvious or more striking similarities. They will be considered once the more noteworthy correspondences have been investigated.

This material will be examined in order to illustrate the correspondences and similarities. The intention is not to give a detailed exegesis of the passages concerned, but to show the high degree of relationship between the documents involved and to draw some conclusions from these relationships. The investigation in this and the following chapters will proceed in the following way:

(a) By examining the striking correspondences between James and the Sermon on the Mount.

Jesus Tradition outside the Gospels, vol. 5 [ed. D. Wenham; Sheffield: JSOT, 1985], 66-67).

The correspondences presented here are those that appear to be close associations or allusions. These will be the subject of investigation in this and the following chapter. The structure of Q adopted here is that of the reconstruction of A. Polag, *Fragmenta Q: Textheft zur Logienquelle* (Neukirchen-Vluyn: Neukirchener Verlag, 1979), 23-26. In this presentation he gives eleven sections to the Q document, namely:

(A) Introduction
(B) Sermon on the Mount
(C) John the Baptist
(D) Mission of the disciples
(E) On prayer
(F) Controversies
(G) On acknowledgment
(H) On proper concerns
(I) Parables
(J) On the responsibilities of disciples
(K) On judgment

The above translation is based on the translation of Polag's text by I. Havener (*Q: The Sayings of Jesus: With a Reconstruction of Q by Athanasius Polag* [Wilmington: Michael Glazier, 1987], 117-22), who introduces the alphabetical sequence of I, J, K, whereas Polag has I, K, L.

1. Davids, *The Epistle of James*, 48; and 'James and Jesus', 66-67.

(b) By investigating the further correspondences between James and the Q source.
(c) By inquiring into the other correspondences appearing in James and the M source and L source.
(d) With the above as the background, by examining the other more general echoes or parallels in thought between James and the synoptic traditions.

2. *James and the Q Sermon on the Mount/Plain*[1]

In the twenty-six parallels given in the chart, Matthew's[2] version of the Sermon on the Mount bears twenty-one correspondences to James,[3] while the reconstructed version of Q which depends upon the order of Luke has nine correspond-

---

1. The substance of this examination appeared in a revised and shortened form as 'James and the Sermon on the Mount/Plain', in D.J. Lull (ed.), *Society of Biblical Literature 1989 Seminar Papers* (Atlanta: Scholars Press, 1989), 440-57 (presented to the Q Seminar of the SBL).
2. As in the case of James, the use of the terms Matthew and Luke does not intend to imply anything as regards actual authorship.
3. The following twenty-one correspondences between James and the Matthean Sermon on the Mount are noted:

1	Jas 1.2 = Mt. 5.11-12
2	Jas 1.4 = Mt. 5.48
3	Jas 1.5 = Mt. 7.7
4	Jas 1.17 = Mt. 7.11
5	Jas 4.2-3 = Mt. 7.7-8
6	Jas 1.22 = Mt. 7.24
7	Jas 1.23 = Mt. 7.26
8	Jas 2.5 = Mt. 5.3, 5
9	Jas 2.10 = Mt. 5.18-19
10	Jas 2.11 = Mt. 5.21-22
11	Jas 2.13 = Mt. 5.7
12	Jas 3.12 = Mt. 7.16-18
13	Jas 3.18 = Mt. 5.9
14	Jas 4.4 = Mt. 6.24
15	Jas 4.8 = Mt. 5.8
16	Jas 4.9 = Mt. 5.4
17	Jas 4.11 = Mt. 7.1-2
18	Jas 5.2-3 = Mt. 6.19-21
19	Jas 5.6 = Mt. 7.1
20	Jas 5.10 = Mt. 5.11-12
21	Jas 5.12 = Mt. 5.34-37

ences.[1] Consequently, most of the parallels between James and the Q tradition occur in the material of the Sermon on the Mount. While some noteworthy differences between the two sermons are observable, there is sufficient similarity to support the hypothesis that within Q there was 'a nucleus sermon'[2]

1. The following nine correspondences between James and the reconstructed version of Q depending on the Lucan order are noted:

1	Jas 1.2 = Lk. 6.22-23
2	Jas 1.22 = Lk. 6.46-47
3	Jas 1.23 = Lk. 6.49
4	Jas 2.5 = Lk. 6.20
5	Jas 2.13 = Lk. 6.36
6	Jas 3.12 = Lk. 6.43-44
7	Jas 4.11 = Lk. 6.37-38
8	Jas 5.6 = Lk. 6.37
9	Jas 5.10 = Lk. 6.23

2. J.A. Fitzmyer, *The Gospel according to Luke (1–9): Introduction, Translation and Notes* (The Anchor Bible; Garden City: Doubleday, 2nd edn, 1983), 627. The agreement of Matthew and Luke in the sermon is very striking and this supports the hypothesis that within Q there was a 'nucleus sermon'. Fitzmyer (*The Gospel According to Luke [1–9]*, 628) has analysed the similarities between the sermon appearing in Matthew and Luke in the following way: *subject-matter* (teaching about conduct expected of disciples [or following crowds]); *exordium* (the beatitudes); *content* (almost all of the Lucan sayings are found in the Matthean sermon; also an eschatological dimension of Jesus' words; and above all, the teaching about love of one's neighbour and even of one's enemies); *conclusion* (the parable of the two houses, challenging listeners to become doers); *occasion* (early in Jesus' one-year ministry and preceding the cure of the centurion's servant); *relation to a common place* (in Mt. 5.1, on the 'mountain'; in Luke, after descent from 'the mountain' [6.12, 17]).
    Given the appearance of a sermon in Q, the least amount of material that it would represent would be that containing the similarities indicated above.
    What is noteworthy in the content of this sermon would be the following outline provided by Polag (*Fragmenta Q*, 23); and Havener (*Q: The Sayings of Jesus*, 117-18) of the similarities:

		MATTHEW	LUKE
(a)	Beatitudes	5.3-12	6.20b-23
(b)	Love of one's enemies	5.44	6.27-28
	Patience	5.39b-41	6.29
	Giving and lending	5.42	6.30
	Decisive behaviour	5.45-47	6.32-35

which has been developed by the incorporation of other tradi-tions. The Q form of this sermon can be reconstructed with some degree of certainty because of the very numerous simi-larities existing between the presentation of the sermon in Matthew and Luke. This reconstruction extends above all to the order, sequence, and content, although the exact wording

	Merciful like the Father	5.48	6.36
	Judge not	7.1-2	6.37-38
(d)	The golden rule	7.12	6.31
(e)	Blind leaders	15.14	6.39
	Disciple and teacher	10.24-25	6.40
(f)	Log and speck	7.3-5	6.41-42
(g)	Good and bad tree	7.16-20	6.43-44
	Heart's treasure	12.34b-35	6.45
(h)	'Lord, Lord' sayer	7.21	6.46
	House construction	7.24-27	6.47-49
(i)	Conclusion	7.28	7.1a

D. Lührmann (*Die Redaktion der Logienquelle: Anhang: Zur weiteren Überlieferung der Logienquelle* [Neukirchen-Vluyn: Neukirchener Verlag, 1969], 53) presents the similarities between the two sermons in a similar way:

Macarisms	Lk. 6.20-23/Mt. 5.3-12
Woes	Lk. 6.24-26
Sayings	Lk. 6.27-36/Mt. 5.38-48
Sayings	Lk. 6.37-42/Mt. 7.1-5
Sayings	Lk. 6.43-45/Mt. 7.15-20
Parable	Lk. 6.46-49/Mt. 7.21-27

This comparison shows the similarity in the basic structure of the sermon as it occurs in Matthew and Luke. Luke's sermon is shorter and probably comes closest to that of the original Q sermon (A.D. Jacobson, 'Wisdom Christology in Q' [PhD thesis, Claremont Gradu-ate School, 1978], 50). This agrees with the general hypothesis that Luke reproduces the order of Q more faithfully. To this structure the Gospel of Matthew has added additional material which appeared in Q. As Fitzmyer (*The Gospel according to Luke [1–9]*, 628) noted: 'In many of these episodes Luke has preserved the more original order of "Q" and sometimes even a more natural (perhaps the original) setting for sayings or pronouncements, whereas Matthew has topically arranged otherwise scattered, but related, sayings. For instance, con-trast the use of the Our Father in Mt. 6.9-13 and Lk. 11.2-4.' Matthew's expansion occurs briefly in ch. 6, as well as in 5.13-37 (containing the antitheses of the law), and 7.6-14. These additions contain mostly Q material which appears in Luke in different contexts.

at times is difficult to establish with certainty. This view endorses the argument of Bauckham[1] that the Q source developed from blocks of material that were originally independent of one another. The Q sermon, according to this argument, would have an independent development as an entity or a block of material in its own right before it formed part of the Q source itself.

Both Matthew and Luke bear witness to the context of the Q sermon within the Q source. In both Gospels the sermon is preceded by the temptations of Jesus, while the story of the centurion's servant follows the sermon. Another interesting feature of similarity is the change in audience. Both sermons present Jesus instructing his disciples (Lk. 6.20a and Mt. 5.1); yet they both conclude by referring to 'the people' (Lk. 7.1) or 'the crowds' (Mt. 7.28). Because the same change took place in both Gospels, the logical conclusion is that it occurred in the original Q sermon. Betz[2] has made an important study of the development that the sermon underwent before it was incorporated into the Gospel of Matthew. For him it had a history independent of the evangelist Matthew and was formed within the community of Matthew.[3] I do not intend to enter into a detailed examination of this thesis of Betz. What is important is the attention he has drawn to the need to see three elements in Matthew's sermon: the Q material, the further development of Q within the Matthean community, and the hand of the evangelist, Matthew. Whether the Ser-

1. R. Bauckham, 'The Study of the Gospel Traditions', *Gospel Perspectives*, vol. 5: *The Jesus Tradition outside the Gospels* (ed. D. Wenham; Sheffield: JSOT, 1985), 378-79.
2. H.D. Betz, 'Die Makarismen der Bergpredigt (Matthäus 5,3-12): Beobachtungen zur literarischen Form und theologischen Bedeutung', *ZThK* 75 (1978), 3-19.
3. Betz ('Die Makarismen der Bergpredigt', 3-4) opts for the view that the Sermon on the Mount was composed prior to and independently of the redactor Matthew. Among the reasons given by Betz the following are the most noteworthy: (a) The material which does not come from Q cannot be attributed to the sole composition of Matthew, the evangelist. (b) A formal analysis of the Sermon on the Mount shows that it is best understood as a unity in itself. (c) The theology of the Sermon on the Mount shows features which mark it as independent of that of the Gospel of Matthew and as being in itself quite distinctive.

mon on the Mount was in a final format and was merely
introduced into the Gospel of Matthew as it existed, or whether
Matthew had more of a constructive part in the formation of
the Sermon on the Mount is a point that is not easily solved.
What does emerge is that there was material present in the
Matthean community (M) in addition to the Q material. A
specific feature of this material was its Jewish-Christian
flavour and interest.

In comparing the relationship between James and the
Gospel tradition, the distinction between the M material and
the evangelist Matthew must be kept in mind. Too often a
formal identity is made between Matthew and the source
peculiar to him. This results in the similarities between James
and Matthew being seen as being between the epistle and the
Gospel, whereas we ought to keep in mind the possibility that
the relationship may be between the epistle and the tradition
peculiar to Matthew.

2.1 *The relationship between James and the beatitudes*

In examining the similarities between James and the beati-
tudes/woes as found in Matthew and Luke, one has to try to
establish wherein the relationship actually lies. To what stage
in the development of the beatitudes do the connections actually extend?[1] In the handing on of the Jesus tradition, is one to
see the similarities as being with the common source Q; are

---

1. I have discussed the development of the beatitudes elsewhere (cf.
'James and the Q Sermon on the Mount/Plain', 442-46). The results of
that investigation will be used here. Briefly, this development can be
described in this way: (a) The Q Sermon was composed of an original
four beatitudes (Lk. 6.20-22; Mt. 5.3, 4, 6 and 11-12: the poor, those who
hunger, who weep and who are reviled). (b) These original four beatitudes were developed within the Matthean community into a larger
group now comprising eight beatitudes and making use of existing Q
material. (They are referred to as the Q[Mt] beatitudes: the meek, the
merciful, the pure and the peacemakers: Mt. 5.5, 7, 8, 9.) (c) Finally,
the influence of the redactor Matthew on the beatitudes can be observed
in a number of respects. He constructed a beatitude of his own at 5.10
(blessed are the persecuted) with the intention of creating a cohesive
unity among all the beatitudes. He realigned the original beatitudes
with Isa. 61.1-3 by referring to 'the poor in spirit', by transposing the
beatitude of those who mourn to the second position, and finally by
focusing the fourth and eighth beatitudes upon righteousness.

they to be established with the further development into Q^{Mt} or
Q^{Lk}; or are they to be found in the final composition of the
Gospels of Matthew and Luke? An answer to these questions
emerges from an examination of a number of striking similarities between James and the beatitudes.

2.1.1 *The poor (Jas 2.5; Mt. 5.3; Lk. 6.20)*

James 2.5. οὐχ ὁ θεὸς ἐξελέξατο τοὺς πτωχοὺς τῷ κόσμῳ
πλουσίους ἐν πίστει καὶ κληρονόμους τῆς βασιλείας ἧς
ἐπηγγείλατο τοῖς ἀγαπῶσιν αὐτόν; The reference to πτωχοὺς τῷ
κόσμῳ is not an attempt to distinguish the poor further, nor to
restrict the concept of the poor. Instead, the τῷ κόσμῳ is a *dati-
vus commodi*: they are 'poor in the view of the world'.[1] The
antithesis is illustrated by showing that the values of this world
are reversed in the world of the kingdom. Those who are poor
in the eyes of the world are now considered to be rich as heirs
of the kingdom of God. This bears a striking resemblance to
the first beatitude in Q, which read: μακάριοι οἱ πτωχοί, ὅτι
αὐτῶν ἐστιν ἡ βασιλεία τοῦ θεοῦ.[2]

---

1. Davids, *The Epistle of James*, 112.
2. The striking difference between Matthew and Luke regarding the
first beatitude is that Matthew specifies the reference to πτωχοί as the οἱ
πτωχοὶ τῷ πνεύματι. Isa. 61.1 helps to throw light on this designation of
'the poor in spirit' where reference is made to the poor, the '^{a}nāwîm;
who in a synonymous phrase are referred to as the 'broken hearted'
(לבשר ענוים שלחני לחבש לנשברי־לב). The first line refers simply to the poor or
the afflicted ('he has sent me to declare good tidings to the afflicted')
while the second line creates a synonymous parallelism with 'to bind
up those broken in heart': 'the afflicted' are further determined as
'those broken in heart'. If Isa. 61.1 had an influence on the beatitudes,
it is understandable that this could have been responsible for an elaboration from the original πτωχοὶ to the specific πτωχοί τῷ πνεύματι taking
place through the hand of the redactor Matthew. Consequently, it is
proposed that the Q form of the first beatitude read as follows:

μακάριοι οἱ πτωχοί,
ὅτι αὐτῶν ἐστιν ἡ βασιλεία τοῦ θεοῦ.

Polag (*Fragmenta Q*, 32) supports this reading, as do the reconstructions of R.D. Worden ('The Q Sermon on the Mount/Plain: Variants
and Reconstruction', *Society of Biblical Literature 1983 Seminar
Papers* [ed. K.H. Richards; Chico: Scholars Press, 1983], 469) and U.
Luz ('Sermon on the Mount/Plain: Reconstruction of Q^{Mt} and Q^{Lk}', in

James and Q have a number of features in common. They both refer to 'the poor' in unqualified terms. Whereas Matthew has further specified the poor as 'the poor in spirit', James does not show this development. He lies closer to the Jesus tradition of the simple οἱ πτωχοί, as is the case with the Gospel of Luke. James also refers to 'the kingdom' (ἡ βασιλεία) just as Q does. While the exact antithesis between the poor and the kingdom is not too obvious in Q, this antithesis has been clearly spelled out in James's formulation: the poor in the eyes of this world are to be considered blessed for they will become rich as heirs of the kingdom. Poor is contrasted to rich; the world is contrasted to the kingdom. James emerges as a reflection and development upon the Jesus tradition recorded in Q. Just as Matthew and Luke reformulated the beatitudes within their own framework, so James reworked the same Q tradition in this context.

The development of the Q beatitudes in the community of Matthew shows the construction of a beatitude parallel to that of the poor, namely μακάριοι οἱ πραεῖς, ὅτι αὐτοὶ κληρονομήσουσιν τὴν γῆν (Mt. 5.5). Noteworthy in this beatitude is the use of the verb κληρονομήσουσιν. When Jas 2.5 makes a promise of the kingdom, he uses the noun κληρόνομος. Kittel questions whether this is an accidental similarity.[1] It seems that James knew of this development of the Q beatitudes within the Matthean community. Jas 2.5 used the language of both synonymous beatitudes: the reference to 'heirs of the kingdom' is an amalgamation of terminology derived from both beatitudes. This indicates James's knowledge, not only of the Q-beatitude group, but also of its further development within the context of the Matthean community. James keeps the emphasis upon the poor, and has not developed it into 'the poor in spirit' as did the redactor Matthew. This example would point to a knowledge by James of the development of Q within the Matthean community, but prior to its final form in the Gospel. An isolated example of this kind is not sufficient to prove the point conclusively, but taken together with other evi-

---

Richards, *Society of Biblical Literature 1983 Seminar Papers*, 474) in their reconstruction of Q^{Mt} and Q^{Lk}.

1. Kittel, *Der geschichtliche Ort*, 86.

dence, which will be advanced in the further discussion, it is a clear marker pointing in this direction.

2.1.2 *Those who mourn and weep (Jas 4.9; Mt. 5.4; Lk. 6.25)*

It has been proposed that the Q form of the beatitude dealing with those who mourn read: μακάριοι οἱ πενθοῦντες, ὅτι αὐτοὶ παρακληθήσονται.[1] James also speaks about mourning in 4.9: ταλαιπωρήσατε καὶ πενθήσατε καὶ κλαύσατε. ὁ γέλως ὑμῶν εἰς πένθος μετατραπήτω καὶ ἡ χαρὰ εἰς κατήφειαν. The only real similarity between Jas 4.9 and this beatitude lies in the use of the one verb πενθέω (to mourn). A far closer relationship can be established with the Lucan woe of 6.25: οὐαί, οἱ γελῶντες νῦν, ὅτι πενθήσετε καὶ κλαύσετε. Linguistically, there are three points of contact between Jas 4.9 and Lk. 6.25: ὁ γέλως (cf. the participle γελῶντες), and the use of the verbs πενθέω and κλαίω in conjunction.[2] The very fact that there is much discussion on

---

1. The actual reading of this beatitude has been much discussed: Was it πενθοῦντες (according to Matthew) or κλαίοντες (according to Luke)? It is a difficult question to decide; but a number of important arguments point to the conclusion that the term πενθοῦντες appeared in the Q source. This is contrary to Polag (*Fragmenta Q*, 32) and R.A. Guelich ('The Matthean Beatitudes: "Entrance-Requirements" or Eschatological Blessings?', *JBL* 95 [1976], 427). The verb which Luke uses (κλαίω) is a characteristically Lucan verb (N. McEleney, 'The Beatitudes of the Sermon on the Mount/Plain', *CBQ* 43 [1981], 9) and is used in line with the traditional New Testament understanding of the term. 'This kind of weeping arises when man recognizes his total inadequacy in face of God and when he sees that he cannot evade this...' (K.H. Rengstorf, 'κλαίω', *TDNT*, III [1965], 723). Further, in the Lucan woe which corresponds to the beatitude both the verbs πενθέω and κλαίω appear: this seems to indicate that πενθέω is a relic of the Q source as this is Luke's sole use of πενθέω (McEleney, 'The Beatitudes', 9). Further support for the use of πενθοῦντες in the beatitude could be adduced from the alliteration of π because this consonant π also appears in the other two beatitudes of the common source. Consequently, all three beatitudes of the common source refer by means of the π consonant to those who are blessed (C. Michaelis, 'Die π-Alliteration der Subjektsworte der ersten 4 Seligpreisungen in Mt. v.3-6 und ihre Bedeutung für den Aufbau der Seligpreisungen bei Mt., Lk. und in Q', *NT* 10 [1968], 148-61).

2. 'Es wird nicht Zufall sein, dass γελάω in NT nur Lk. 6,21.25, nur γέλως Jak. 4,9 begegnet' (H. Schürmann, *Das Lukasevangelium* [Freiburg: Herder, 1969], 339).

whether the Lucan woes originally formed part of the Q sermon shows that they do have a close relationship with Q. Their insertion into the Q Sermon on the Mount in the Lucan community reflects a development of Q material within the Lucan context.

The closeness of Jas 4.9 to this woe, not in form but in content, indicates James's awareness of this saying and its terminology. I am not arguing that James was aware of the development of Q within the Lucan community. But the similarity in content suggests that James and Luke have utilized a traditional saying of Jesus and have adapted it to the context of their own teaching.[1] Once again James is shown to have a relationship with the Jesus tradition. In this instance James demonstrates an awareness of this material before it was firmly fixed in the form and structure of the woes as expressed in Q^{Lk}.

2.1.3 *Those who are merciful (Jas 2.13; Mt. 5.7; Lk. 6.36)*
Jas 2.13 reads: ἡ γὰρ κρίσις ἀνέλεος τῷ μὴ ποιήσαντι ἔλεος· κατακαυχᾶται ἔλεος κρίσεως. While it is quite possible that this originally circulated as an independent saying,[2] James has incorporated it well into his text and argument. In fact from the viewpoint of content this saying draws together what has been said in the previous section and then looks forward to the section which is to come: '...it makes an excellent bridge in that it captures and summarizes aspects of what precedes and yet throws thought forward into the topic of charity, which the following verse will take up'.[3]

In the Jesus tradition much teaching is given to the theme of mercy—which explains the importance this theme holds in the group of beatitudes: μακάριοι οἱ ἐλεήμονες ὅτι αὐτοὶ ἐλε-

---

1. Davids (*The Epistle of James,* 167) sees this connection in the same way: 'Perhaps remembering the words of Christ (Lk. 6.21, 25: οὐαί, οἱ γελῶντες νῦν, ὅτι πενθήσετε καὶ κλαύσετε) and in tune with the OT...'
2. M. Dibelius (*James: A Commentary on the Epistle of James* [trans. from the German, Der Brief des Jakobus; 11th rev. edn prepared by H. Greeven, 1964; English trans. M.A. Williams; ed. H. Koester for Hermeneia; Philadelphia: Fortress, 1975], 147-48); Mussner, *Der Jakobusbrief,* 126.
3. Davids, *The Epistle of James,* 118.

ηθήσονται (Mt. 5.7). This beatitude is found in that non-common group of beatitudes belonging exclusively to Matthew.

Possibly the Matthean community used the Q saying about being merciful as the Father (Lk. 6.36) to construct this beatitude. In doing so they replaced the saying itself with a reference to perfection, which is a characteristic theme of the Jesus tradition in the Matthean community.

A distinct difference is observable in the choice of words used for merciful in Matthew and Luke. Mt. 5.7 has ἐλεήμονες, while Lk. 6.36 prefers οἰκτίρμονες. The use of the term ἐλεήμονες in the beatitude of Mt. 5.7 is reflected in Jas 2.13 where the word ἔλεος occurs.[1] Whether James himself composed 2.13 or not is open to discussion. However, by inserting this saying here, James shows his knowledge of the traditional importance of the concept of mercy, which the Matthean community had developed into a beatitude in order to spell out the type of life a Christian should lead.

Kittel[2] argues that the thought content in Jas 2.13 and Mt. 5.7 is identical. The beatitude of Mt. 5.7 shows that the person who exercises mercy on earth acquires God's mercy; implied in this is the fact that the one who shows no mercy cannot expect any mercy from God. This latter implication Jas 2.13 spells out when it says: 'Judgment is without mercy to him who shows no mercy'. When Jas 2.13 goes on to add 'mercy triumphs over judgment', this is indeed what the beatitude claims when it declares 'blessed are the merciful'. On account of the similarity of the term ἔλεος and of the thought content it is legitimate to conclude that James is aware of the Jesus tradition which lies behind the beatitude 'blessed are the merciful'.[3]

---

1. G. Strecker, 'Die Makarismen der Bergpredigt', *NTS* 17 (1970/71), 266. C.L. Mitton (*The Epistle of James* [London: Marshall, Morgan & Scott, 1966], 98) argues for a reflection of this beatitude here in the saying of James: 'Yet, it would not be improper for James here, in his own way, to enforce what he understands to be the meaning of the Lord's beatitude: "Blessed are the merciful, for they shall receive mercy"'.
2. Kittel, *Der geschichtliche Ort,* 88.
3. Davids (*The Epistle of James,* 119) supports this conclusion and argues in this way: 'Here (Jas 2.13), then, is the negative statement of that saying (Mt. 5.7) phrased in good Jewish form, juxtaposed (thus

At the same time James shows an awareness of the Q tradition as expressed in Lk. 6.36 where reference is made to the mercy of God which the individual must imitate. Lk. 6.36 uses the term οἰκτίρμων for merciful while the same phrase occurs in Jas 5.11 in reference to God: ὅτι πολύσπλαγχνός ἐστιν ὁ κύριος καὶ οἰκτίρμων. Since Lk. 6.36 has been judged to be the original Q formulation of this phrase,[1] the echo contained in Jas 5.11 must be to that of the Q phrase.

When James, then, makes reference to the quality of mercy in his writing, he shows a twofold connection. First, he betrays an awareness of the Q tradition that God is merciful (ὁ πατὴρ ὑμῶν οἰκτίρμων ἐστίν) through his use of the same adjective οἰκτίρμων in Jas 5.11. Secondly, he shows an awareness of the development of this Q tradition within the Matthean community whereby this saying has been developed into a beatitude on mercy (ἔλεος) which is further echoed in Jas 2.13. This lends further support to our suggestion about James's knowledge of the Q tradition and its subsequent development within the Matthean community.

2.1.4 *Those who make peace (Jas 3.18; Mt. 5.9)*

Matthew 5.9	James 3.18
μακάριοι οἱ εἰρηνοποιοί, ὅτι αὐτοὶ υἱοὶ θεοῦ κληθήσονται.	καρπὸς δὲ δικαιοσύνης ἐν εἰρήνῃ σπείρεται τοῖς ποιοῦσιν εἰρήνην.

James uses what may indeed be a traditional saying which, as Dibelius[2] argues, was originally independent of the context. Yet, an examination of its use in James has shown how it has been woven into the context in order to form an essential part of James's discussion. The entire chapter 3 has dealt with those involved with fighting and disturbing the peace. Consequently, the sayings form a suitable conclusion to the passage and at the same time point forward to 4.1 which concerns those fighting and waging war.

the lack of any connective particle) with a positive proverb following from it'.

1. See the reconstructions of Polag (*Fragmenta Q*, 34) and Worden ('The Q Sermon on the Mount/Plain', 470).

2. Dibelius, *James*, 214-15.

'The fruit of righteousness' is understood as a genitive of definition, namely 'the fruit which is righteousness'.[1] The aim is to show how just and righteous deeds are to be performed: they are 'sown in peace by those who make peace'. The concept of peace in the New Testament writings embraces three thoughts: '(a) Peace, as a feeling of peace and rest; (b) peace as a state of reconciliation with God; and (c) peace as the salvation of the whole man in an ultimate eschatological sense'.[2] In this latter sense the reference is not to peace between God and humanity, nor among people, but to salvation which comes from God.

People themselves are not capable of achieving this type of peace. Only two texts in the New Testament speak of making peace, namely Mt. 5.9 and Jas 3.18. A close similarity in thought exists between these two passages—they each speak about making peace, which stems from a special relationship with God. In Jas 3.18 the gift of righteousness comes from the gift of wisdom from above and belongs to the catalogue of virtues outlined in 3.17 as expressive of this wisdom. As a consequence the gift of righteousness is illustrated by those who sow peace, by the peacemakers. In Mt. 5.9, which belongs to the non-common group of beatitudes, a special relationship is also established between God and the believers: they are referred to as 'his sons'. A characteristic of these 'sons of God' is that they also make peace. In both instances a special relationship is attributed to God and the believer: in James it is a relationship of righteousness, while in Matthew it is that of 'sons of God'. This relationship is characterized by both in terms of leading a life which establishes peace among humanity. This indicates a close bond between the two texts especially seeing that they are the only two in the New Testament to speak of making peace. This points to an awareness by James of the expanded Q tradition of the beatitudes emerging within the context of the Matthean community.

1. Davids, *The Epistle of James,* 155.
2. W. Foerster, 'εἰρήνη', *TDNT,* II (1964), 412.

2.1.5 *Those who are pure in heart (Jas 4.8; Mt. 5.8)*

James 4.8	Matthew 5.8
ἐγγίσατε τῷ θεῷ καὶ	μακάριοι οἱ καθαροὶ τῇ
ἐγγιεῖ ὑμῖν. καθαρίσατε	καρδίᾳ, ὅτι αὐτοὶ τὸν θεὸν
χεῖρας, ἁμαρτωλοί, καὶ	ὄψονται.
ἁγνίσατε καρδίας, δίψυχοι.	

The connection between these two texts is not as clear and evident as the previous examples. In the context of Judaism the
concept of being 'pure' (καθαρός) was usually associated with
cultic cleanness and cultic cleansing.[1] However, from a very
early stage in the New Testament world a change occurred
whereby religious and moral purity replaced the ritual and
cultic purity of the Old Testament. According to the teaching
of Jesus the Jewish concern for ritual or cultic purity was
inadequate because its pre-occupation was chiefly with exter-
nals (Mt. 23.25-26). The New Testament community, on the
other hand, saw itself in a personal relationship with Jesus
Christ. This influenced its concept of purity whereby the personal and moral dimension received emphasis. 'It consists in
full and unreserved self-offering to God which renews the
heart and rules out any acceptance of what is against God.'[2]
The beatitude in Mt. 5.8 developed against this background
within the context of the Matthean community. The language
only makes sense in the context of a community that is familiar with cultic rituals such as the various purification rites
within Judaism. The beatitude takes over the cultic language
and applies it in line with the teaching of Jesus to the personal
and moral level. The reference is no longer to the purification
of one's hands, but to the purification of one's heart where it
has taken on an entirely moral aspect.

The text in James is also understandable against this background where he, too, shows a knowledge of the Jewish cultic
usage of the term 'to purify' (καθαρίζω). He utilizes it in its
cultic sense of purifying one's hands, but then shows that he
wishes it to be taken entirely in its moral, personal relationship
by adding the expression 'purify your hearts' (ἁγνίσατε

---

1. R. Meyer, 'καθαρός', *TDNT*, III (1965), 418-22.
2. F. Hauck, 'καθαρός', *TDNT*, III (1965), 425.

καρδίας). In the context of James the reference to pure hands would refer to the good deeds that one performs, while the pure hearts would denote total personal commitment to God.[1]

The similarities in James and Matthew lie not just in the use of the words καθαρίσατε (καθαροί) and καρδία, but more especially in the actual thought engendered by the very context of these words. Once again one can argue for a similarity in content and vocabulary between James and the beatitudes, in particular the group of beatitudes that originated from an expanded Q within the Matthean community.

2.1.6 *Those who hunger (Jas 2.15-16; Lk. 6.21 = Mt. 5.6)*

Jas 2.15-16

ἐὰν ἀδελφὸς ἢ ἀδελφὴ γυμνοὶ ὑπάρχωσιν καὶ λειπόμενοι τῆς ἐφημέρου τροφῆς, εἴπῃ δέ τις αὐτοῖς ἐξ ὑμῶν· ὑπάγετε ἐν εἰρήνῃ, θερμαίνεσθε καὶ χορτάζεσθε, μὴ δῶτε δὲ αὐτοῖς τὰ ἐπιτήδεια τοῦ σώματος, τί τὸ ὄφελος;

Q 6.21[2]

μακάριοι οἱ πεινῶντες ὅτι αὐτοὶ χορτασθήσονται.

Q promises to those who are hungry that they will be filled (from the verb χορτάζω). James simply makes the statement,

---

1. Davids, *The Epistle of James,* 167.

2. The notable difference between Matthew and Luke lies in the expression καὶ διψῶντες τὴν δικαιοσύνην in Matthew which appear to be an addition to the common source. McEleney ('The Beatitudes', 8 n. 35) presents the arguments in favour of the simple πεινῶντες when he says that 'διψῶντες breaks the π alliteration in these various categories of the blessed: πτωχοί, πενθοῦντες, πεινῶντες, and this seems to argue for a single participle here... Further, while χορτάζειν in the second half of the verse can be used in connection with thirst, its basic reference is to eating solid food. The addition of ποτίζειν would be expected with thirst.' Consequently, the Q form of the beatitude (which was originally the second beatitude) would read as follows: μακάριοι οἱ πεινῶντες, ὅτι αὐτοὶ χορτασθήσονται. Polag (*Fragmenta Q,* 32) as well as Worden ('The Q Sermon on the Mount/Plain', 469) agree basically with this reconstruction, although they omit the word αὐτοί from the second part of the verse. Luz ('Sermon on the Mount/Plain', 474) also upholds this reading as belonging to Q^Mt and Q^Lk, where again αὐτοί is seen to be restricted to the use in Q^Mt.

'Go in peace, be warmed and filled' (from the verb χορτάζω). The same verb (χορτάζω) is used, while those who are in need are referred to by means of a synonymous expression: οἱ πεινῶντες (Q); λειπόμενοι τῆς ἐφημέρου τροφῆς (James). James has introduced an example, or perhaps parable would be better,[1] of what faith is like without works. In constructing the example, it appears that James is using the Jesus tradition and in particular the beatitude from the Q source in order to shock his readers into action.[2]

2.1.7 *Those who are reviled (Jas 1.2; 5.10; Mt. 5.11-12; Lk. 6.22-23)*

So far three of the beatitudes in Q and all those expanded within the community of Matthew (namely seven in all) find their reflection within the Epistle of James. No connection is seen with the eighth beatitude in Matthew, namely blessings invoked on 'those who are persecuted for righteousness' sake'. This is a construction of Matthew himself,[3] and this indicates

---

1.   J. Ropes, *A Critical and Exegetical Commentary on the Epistle of St. James* (Edinburgh: T. & T. Clark, 1916), 206.
2.   Davids, *The Epistle of James*, 121.
3.   μακάριοι οἱ δεδιωγμένοι ἕνεκεν δικαιοσύνης, ὅτι αὐτῶν ἐστιν ἡ βασιλεία τῶν οὐρανῶν. This is the only beatitude which appears to have been composed completely by Matthew. His intention was to unify all the beatitudes and to lock them together into a well-developed unit (Guelich, 'The Matthean Beatitudes', 431). This saying looks back to the very first beatitude with which it forms a parallel: each ends with a promise to possess 'the kingdom of heaven'. The reference to 'those who are persecuted' is intended to make a connection with the final beatitude (Mt. 5.11-12) which deals in detail with the persecuted. At the same time the reference back to the first beatitude shows that those who are 'poor in spirit' are in fact those who have been persecuted. In addition the importance given to 'righteousness' helps to unify the entirety of the beatitudes. The first reference to righteousness occurs at the end of the first section of four beatitudes, whereas the second reference to righteousness takes place here at the end of the next four beatitudes. The evangelist composed this beatitude himself in order to unify the diverse beatitudes and to focus attention on the main thrusts of the entire group. McEleney ('The Beatitudes', 11) comes to a similar conclusion when he says: 'To lock in these shorter beatitudes and also to make a point, Matthew composed an entirely new beatitude (Mt. 5.10) on the pattern of the longest beatitude and ended this new beatitude with the promise found in the first beatitude. ὅτι αὐτῶν ἐστιν ἡ βασιλεία

that the Epistle of James is not familiar with the final redaction of the beatitudes by the evangelist.

The only other beatitude remaining which has not been discussed is the one that belongs to the Q common list of beatitudes found in both Matthew and Luke.[1] In the chart drawn

τῶν οὐρανῶν now become an inclusory formula drawing all the shorter beatitudes into a tightly-knit unit.' Structurally, the unifying position of this eighth beatitude may be illustrated in this way:

```
......3   μακάριοι οἱ πτωχοὶ τῷ πνεύματι,
          ὅτι αὐτῶν ἐστιν ἡ βασιλεία τῶν οὐρανῶν...
  +6      μακάριοι οἱ πεινῶντες καὶ διψῶντες τὴν δικαιοσύνην,
          ὅτι αὐτοὶ χορτασθήσονται...
  +10     μακάριοι οἱ δεδιωγμένοι ἕνεκεν δικαιοσύνης,
          ὅτι αὐτῶν ἐστιν ἡ βασιλεία τῶν οὐρανῶν.
    11    μακάριοί ἐστε
          ὅταν ὀνειδίσωσιν ὑμᾶς καὶ διώξωσιν...
```

1. The fourth and last of the beatitudes common to Matthew and Luke is expressed in a very similar way in both. Because of the tremendous similarities, the exact wording of Q is difficult to ascertain. Polag (*Fragmenta Q*, 32) constructs the Q form tentatively in this way:

μακάριοί ἐστε ὅταν μισήσωσιν ὑμᾶς (οἱ ἄνθρωποι)
καὶ ἀφορίσωσιν καὶ ὀνειδίσωσιν ὑμᾶς
καὶ εἴπωσιν πονηρὸν καθ' ὑμῶν
ἕνεκα τοῦ υἱοῦ τοῦ ἀνθρώπου.
χαίρετε καὶ ἀγαλλιᾶσθε
ὅτι ὁ μισθὸς ὑμῶν πολὺς ἐν τῷ οὐρανῷ
κατὰ τὰ αὐτὰ γὰρ ἐποίουν τοῖς προφήταις οἱ πατέρες αὐτῶν.

The underlined parts of the above text indicate what is firmly agreed as belonging to Q, while the rest indicates what is generally agreed to be Q material. Originally three beatitudes came into being in the ministry of Jesus with this fourth and final beatitude emerging later in the context of the Christian community. Although the form was developed by the Q community and placed in this context, this does not mean that the thought was invented by the community. As Fitzmyer (*The Gospel according to Luke [1-9]*, 635) argues: 'However, though the formulation of the four outrages differs in Matthew and Luke, the point made by them—persecution of the disciples because of Jesus—may well be an idea that is to be traced back to Jesus himself'. His sayings were preserved because they had a particular reference to the audience who transmitted them (Havener, *Q: The Sayings of Jesus*, 91). A study of the sayings of Q reveals something about the people who handed them on. An important theme of the Q community is that just as Jesus is a prophet, so too his followers are to view themselves as prophets. Since Jesus stood in the line of the prophets of Israel, so too his community

up at the beginning of this chapter, two correspondences were observed between James and Q in this connection, namely, in Jas 1.2 referring to joy under persecution (no. 1) and then in Jas 5.10 referring to the persecution of the prophets (no. 23).

The Epistle of James opens with a call to rejoice amidst sufferings and trials. 'Count it all joy, my brethren, when you meet various trials, for you know that the testing of your faith produces steadfastness' (Jas 1.2-3). The trials that James has in mind are those arising from adherence to the Christian faith. Terminologically and contentwise, there is a close connection between Jas 1.2 and the Q beatitude on suffering trials. In both a call is issued to rejoice (Jas 1.2 πᾶσαν χαράν; Mt. 5.12 χαίρετε καὶ ἀγαλλιᾶσθε; Lk. 6.23 χάρητε) and this call is followed by the reference to the trials which are endured. Both consider that trials and sufferings come from outside sources. In no way are they sought, but when they are experienced they are to be accepted with joy because they bring with them an eschatological reward. Both James and Q call upon their hearers to see their sufferings in an eschatological light. From an early period the Christian Church began to experience trials of a social, economic and even physical nature (for example, the stoning of Stephen at a very early stage in its history). Suffering is a part of salvation history and the proper Christian response to it is that of joy. 'It is this perspective that Jesus gave the church in the Sermon on the Mount.'[1]

The theme of suffering and trials occurs again towards the end of the Epistle of James: 'As an example of suffering and patience, brethren, take the prophets who spoke in the name of the Lord. Behold, we call those happy who were steadfast...' (5.10-11). The same theme of joy amidst trials occurs here

was to be seen to exercise a prophetic role. As Havener (*Q: The Sayings of Jesus*, 95) says: 'The prophetic figure of Jesus, who stands himself in line with the prophets of Israel and who is understood to be the prophet par excellence by the Q community, is emulated by the Q prophets who continue to speak his words of the past as well as his words in the present, for they believed that Jesus was present in their message and speaking through them'. An imitation of Jesus, the prophet, in the life of the Q prophets meant that they should also be prepared to accept the possibility of rejection and suffering, as presented in the final beatitude of Q.

1. Davids, *The Epistle of James*, 68.

that was evident in Jas 1.2 and Mt. 5.11-12. A further connection with the Q beatitude is observable in the use of the verb μακαρίζομεν (Jas 5.11), reminiscent of the term μακάριοι which opens the beatitude. At the same time both James and Q refer to the prophets as blessed in their suffering. The theme of enduring sufferings as the prophets did was important for the Q community who saw themselves as a community of prophets charged with imitating the life of Jesus, the true prophet. This explicit reference in Jas 5.10-11 to the prophets as examples of endurance amidst suffering again betrays a connection between James and the Q community. Their blessedness comes not simply because they have experienced trials, but rather because they have endured patiently. As Jas 5.10 indicates, this suffering has been endured because they spoke in the name of the Lord: 'their suffering came from their service to God'.[1]

The closeness of James to the Jesus tradition emerges once again. This similarity lies not simply in the terminology that is common to James and the Q tradition, but especially in the thought-content common to both. Suffering on account of allegiance to the Gospel brings with it the promise of eschatological reward.

2.1.8 Conclusion

The Epistle of James has illustrated contact with the first two stages of the tradition history of the beatitudes: it shows a knowledge of all the beatitudes belonging to the original Q source, as well as of the way in which they were further developed within the Matthean community. The similarities between James and the beatitudes are located in the period prior to the final redaction of the evangelist Matthew. James shows no affinity with the final stage of development whereby the beatitudes were changed by Matthew through the influence of Isa. 61.1-3. James, for example, refers to 'the poor' in unqualified terms and not in the way in which the redactor Matthew has transformed it into 'the poor in spirit'. This demonstrates that the Epistle of James was composed prior to the composition of the Gospel of Matthew.

---

1. *Ibid.*, 186.

The question still remains: Is there any relationship between James and the Lucan woes?[1] Two noticeable connections are

1. In the Gospel of Luke four woes follow the group of four beatitudes. Whether these woes actually belonged to the original Q sermon has been much discussed. Polag (*Fragmenta Q*, 84-85), who incorporates them under his first section of uncertain texts, notes that the majority of scholars reject them as not belonging to Q. However, there are a few scholars of repute who see these woes as having either an origin in Q or at least a pre-Lucan origin. For example, R. Bultmann (*The History of the Synoptic Tradition* [trans. J. Marsh from the 2nd German edn, 1931; rev. edn, Oxford; Basil Blackwell, 1972], 111-12); T.W. Manson (*The Sayings of Jesus: As Recorded in the Gospels according to St. Matthew and St. Luke, Arranged with Introduction and Commentary* [London: SCM, (1937) 1971], 49); V. Taylor ('The Original Order of Q', *New Testament Essays: Studies in Memory of T.W. Manson 1893–1958* [ed. A.J.B. Higgins; Manchester: Manchester University Press, 1959], 267); H. Schürmann (*Das Lukasevangelium*, 339); H. Frankemölle ('Die Makarismen [Mt. 5,1-12; Lk. 6,20-23]: Motive und Umfang der redaktionelle Komposition', *BZ* 15 [1971], 64). If the woes originally formed part of the Q-source known to both Matthew and Luke, then arguments have to be given to explain why they were omitted by Matthew. The supporters of such a view are not able to adduce convincing reasons to justify their contention. For example, the arguments put forward by Frankemölle ('Die Makarismen, Mt. 5,1-12; Lk. 6,20-23', 64) and Schürmann (*Das Lukasevangelium*, 336-41) are not convincing. They propose changes to the beatitudes on the basis that Matthew altered them through the influence of the woes. In fact the influence operated in the opposite direction, as has been shown in the previous discussion. It has also been argued that the beatitudes were originally followed by the section on 'love of enemies'; the final beatitude provided the bridge between the beatitudes and the section on 'love of enemies'. This is a formidable argument and militates against the woes being originally inserted into Q after the beatitudes.

A solution to this much-discussed topic is to view the woes developing in a way analogous to the development of the beatitudes in the context of the community of Matthew. The woes represent a further specification and development of the common beatitudes of Q within the context of the community of Luke. Instead of developing the beatitudes as such, as happened in the Matthean community, the beatitudes were expressed in an antithetical way in order to emphasize their message. Again, this development did not happen independently of Q. In Matthew's community Q material went to make up the 'non-parallel' beatitudes; so too in the community of Luke the woes developed from existing Q material. Bultmann (*The History of the Synoptic Tradition*, 111) drew attention to this view, but it seems to have been ignored in the subsequent debate: 'Apart from v. 26 which is formally an antithesis to vv. 22f., I do not think these woes are a Lucan formulation, even if they

evident between them. The first is between the third woe ('woe to you that laugh now, for you shall mourn and weep', Lk. 6.25) and Jas 4.9 where the similarities rest upon content and not form. This indicates that both James and Luke are using a traditional saying of Jesus remembered in the Q community. Each has taken it over in his own way and developed it within his own tradition.

A second connection emerges between the first woe (Lk. 6.24) and Jas 5.1-6 which concerns the condemnation addressed to the rich. Luke expressed it by means of a woe: οὐαὶ ὑμῖν τοῖς πλουσίοις; Jas 5.1 in a somewhat different way: Ἄγε νῦν οἱ πλούσιοι, κλαύσατε ὀλολύζοντες ἐπὶ ταῖς ταλαιπωρίαις ὑμῶν ταῖς ἐπερχομέναις. In both the rich are addressed directly in strong language that is reminiscent of the prophets and in both the expression is tantamount to that of a woe. James stresses further that the rich have already received their reward (ἐτρυφήσατε ἐπὶ τῆς γῆς καὶ ἐσπαταλήσατε, Jas 5.5), while the Lucan woe also refers to the rich as having been rewarded (ὅτι ἀπέχετε τὴν παράκλησιν ὑμῶν, Lk. 6.24). The thought-content of the Lucan woe appears to be expressed in a developed way in this pericope of James. The contact between James and this woe lies not in the fact that James is actually utilizing the Lucan woe, but that they both are operating with a familiar saying of Jesus belonging to the Q community, which has developed in different ways in the Lucan formula-

seem not to have appeared at this point in Q...' That this form of speech is already present in Q can be illustrated by the woes which appear elsewhere in the Gospels of Matthew and Luke (Mt. 23.4-29; Lk. 11.43-47).

Just as one can speak of a Q^{Mt} version of the Sermon on the Mount used by Matthew, so too can one see a Q^{Lk} version of the sermon used by Luke. The terms Q^{Mt} and Q^{Lk} are not postulated simply because of differences between Matthew and Luke which cannot be explained. They are used in order to show the development of Q within the Matthean or Lucan communities. This development, however, was not the work of the evangelist or the redactor of the Gospel. A threefold development of the Q tradition must be distinguished: first, there is the common Q source; secondly, this source undergoes a distinct development in both the Matthean and Lucan communities, producing Q^{Mt} or Q^{Lk}; and finally, there is the hand of the evangelist himself who transforms and develops the material he has received and incorporates it into his Gospel.

tion of Q and in the expression of James. In Luke sayings from the Jesus tradition developed into Q[Lk] to become a set of woes parallel to the beatitudes. In James, on the other hand, sayings of the Jesus tradition were incorporated within the style of his letter to form part of the instruction without quoting them directly. No direct dependence is to be established between the Lucan woes and James; the contact comes indirectly through the way in which Q has developed in the respective traditions and communities.

2.2 *James and further aspects of the Q Sermon on the Mount*
The investigation is now pressed further to see whether the relationship is limited to this small section, or whether it extends throughout the block of material known as the Sermon on the Mount.

2.2.1 *Love of one's enemies (Lk. 6.27-33; Mt. 5.40-47)*
In the original Q sermon this pericope on loving one's enemies follows the final beatitude on being reviled which forms the bridge between the beatitudes as such and the instruction to love one's enemies.[1] Seen in this perspective, Luke comes closest to preserving the order of the original sermon: only the woes have been introduced between the two sections. On the other hand, between the beatitudes and the command to love (Mt. 5.13-42), Matthew has introduced an extensive section on the spirit in which the commandments are to be obeyed.

Noteworthy in the Epistle of James is the attention given to the law of love of neighbour which is called the kingly law. 'If you really fulfil the royal law according to the scripture, "You shall love your neighbour as yourself", you do well' (Jas 2.8). In the synoptic tradition this law is central, appearing not just in Q but also in the tradition going back to Mark which records the importance given to these commandments: 'There is no other commandment greater than these' (Mk 12.31). This corresponds to James's thought where it is exalted as the kingly commandment.[2]

---

1. According to Guelich ('The Matthean Beatitudes', 421).
2. Rom. 13.9 shows how this tradition also flourished in Paul's circle and was seen to encompass all the comandments: 'The command-

In Matthew's Sermon on the Mount a number of antitheses occur between the beatitudes (5.3-12) and the command to love one's neighbour (5.43). These antitheses, formed from the traditions within the Matthean community, deal with various topics such as murder and adultery (5.21-30). James also makes reference to the breaking of the law by quoting the examples of adultery and murder, but in the reverse order. I am not arguing for a dependence of James on Matthew, but what I think this does illustrate once again is James's awareness of the Q tradition within the Matthean community. This is supported particularly by his reference to the violation of the command not to kill. When James warns his readers not to kill, he has in mind not simply a physical action, but the more comprehensive attitude of hating another. He shows an interpretation of the Lord's command not to kill that has been handed on by the tradition behind Matthew's Gospel.[1] Noteworthy here are James's references to the two examples of adultery and murder which also appear in the tradition of the Lord's words handed on by the Matthean community. This interpretation of the influence of Jesus' words on James is helpful as well in interpreting the difficult passage of Jas 4.2. The image of war is used to describe the arguments and strife within the community. But how can one accuse the community of actual murder?[2] The difficulty resolves itself if one

ments, "You shall not commit adultery, You shall not kill, You shall not steal, You shall not covet", and any other commandment, are summed up in this sentence, "You shall love your neighbour as yourself". Paul shows himself dependent on the tradition of the Lord's words, which is quite evident in Romans 12 and 13 (Kittel, 'Der geschichtliche Ort', 87). Jas 2.11 shows how the violation of just one command is a violation of the entire law (of love) (Davids, *The Epistle of James*, 115): ὁ γὰρ εἰπών μὴ μοιχεύσῃς, εἶπεν καί, μὴ φονεύσῃς· εἰ δὲ οὐ μοιχεύεις φονεύεις δέ, γέγονας παραβάτης νόμου. James illustrates how one transgresses this law of love through the violation of just one commandment by giving two examples of the transgression of the commands of adultery and murder.

1. Kittel, 'Der geschichtliche Ort', 87.
2. Because of the difficulty of attributing to the community the idea of actual murder (φονεύετε), Erasmus conjectured that the verb was an error of a copyist and that the verb φθονεῖτε (you envy) should be read instead (Dibelius, *James*, 217). There is, however, no manuscript evidence whatsoever for this reading (Davids, *James*, 158).

understands once again (as with 2.11) the verb φονεύετε in the context of the words of Jesus, namely as including the actual hatred in the heart of the person under the commandment not to kill.[1]

The reference in Jas 2.11 to adultery should also be seen in this light of the wider sense of Mt. 5.27-30. Reference is made not simply to the physical act of adultery, but to the very heart of the person. Jas 4.4 contains a further allusion to adultery which follows on the previous description of strife within the community (φονεύετε used in its widest sense). Now the community is described in terms of its being an adulterous generation (μοιχαλίδες). This phrase also occurs in Mt. 12.39 (γενεὰ πονηρὰ καὶ μοιχαλίς), coming from the wider synoptic tradition of Mark. In line with what has been illustrated elsewhere, James' usage is certainly influenced by this tradition handed on by Matthew. In the context of Jas 4.4 people are adulterous because they are being lured away by the lust for wealth.

I should like to draw together what has been examined here. James shows a knowledge of the words of the Lord in so far as they interpret the commandments against adultery and murder. Since only the tradition of Matthew hands this on, James shows once again a familiarity with the way in which the words of the Lord are interpreted and handed on within the Matthean community. At the same time James has demonstrated an understanding of the importance given to the command of Jesus to love. The Q Sermon on the Mount had highlighted this basic teaching by issuing the instruction to love one's enemies. The Q^{Mt} Sermon on the Mount developed this further through illustrations on how to implement this command. A similar development is evident in James. Whereas for James the basic teaching of Jesus on loving one's neighbour is emphasized as the kingly law, he too illustrates how it must be observed in terms of avoiding whatever causes harm to one's brother (2.11; 4.1, 11). In James and the Mat-

---

1. As Kittel ('Der geschichtliche Ort', 88) says: 'Ihr streitet und scheltet und versündigt euch gegen das Fünfte Gebot, wie es euch der Herr ausgelegt hat'.

thean community there is a similarity in the way in which the kingly law of Jesus is applied and understood.

2.2.2 *Be merciful and do not judge*

In the pericope following on the command to love, two important sayings occur: the command to be merciful, and the command not to judge. The reconstruction by Polag[1] of the Q text follows closely that of Luke.

Attention has already been given (§2.1.3) to the connection between James and the Q tradition with regard to the command to be merciful (Lk. 6.36). Jas 5.11 and Lk. 6.36 both use the same term οἰκτίρμων to refer to the mercifulness of God. Since Lk. 6.36 reflects the original Q sermon, both James and Q witness to a common understanding related to the definition of God as the merciful one.

The teaching of the synoptic tradition shows the centrality of the theme of judgment.[2] The message of Jesus' call to repent is inspired by the firm conviction of the impending judgment which stands over every person. The Q tradition stresses that since God alone is the judge, no one has the right to usurp this function.[3] In different ways both Matthew and Luke (Mt. 7.1; Lk. 6.37) emphasize this command not to judge. In reconstructing the original Q form of this saying, Polag[4] follows the expression as it appears in Luke. This saying about not judging another has had a decided influence upon James. In fact he appears to be influenced by it on three different occasions where he has inserted it carefully into the context of his writing.

(a) Jas 4.11 considers the question of speaking evil against another. To slander and judge another are viewed as equivalent to slandering and judging the law. The law that is referred to is the command: 'You shall love your neighbour as yourself' (2.8). The implication given is that one sets oneself up as judge

---

1. Polag, *Fragmenta Q*, 34-37.
2. F. Büchsel, 'κρίνω', *TDNT*, III (1965), 936.
3. As Büchsel ('κρίνω', 939) says: 'From the fact that God's judgment threatens man it is often deduced that no man has the right to judge another, Mt. 7.1f.; Jn 4.11...'
4. Polag, *Fragmenta Q*, 34-36.

over another, as judge over the law. In this way the person usurps the authority and power of God.[1]

(b) Jas 5.6. A further influence of the Jesus teaching on not judging another appears in this text. Jas 5.6 refers to the condemnation of the innocent: κατεδικάσατε, ἐφονεύσατε τὸν δίκαιον, οὐκ ἀντιτάσσεται ὑμῖν. The same verb καταδικάζω occurs in the reconstructed form of Q given in Lk. 6.37.[2] Again, this points to the possibility that the same Q saying of Lk. 6.37 lies behind this use in Jas 5.6.

(c) Jas 5.9 appears to be an illustration of the antithesis expressed in Lk. 6.37 (Mt. 7.1). To this admonition is added the reason for its implementation: 'the judge is standing at the doors' (πρὸ τῶν θυρῶν). This saying resembles Mt. 24.33 which refers to the fact that the Son of man 'is near, at the very gates' (ἐπὶ θύραις).[3] This image is found in the Jesus tradition coming from Mk 13.29 (γινώσκετε ὅτι ἐγγύς ἐστιν ἐπὶ θύραις) and expressed in an identical way in Mt. 24.33. The nearness of the eschatological day of judgment is a common theme of the synoptic Gospels and also forms part of Paul's proclamation. In the context of James the nearness of this day requires the hearers to look into their own conduct so that when the Lord does come they will not be condemned.[4]

This command not to judge influences the thought of James on three occasions. To this he adds the reason for the urgency of abiding by this rule: the judge is fast approaching (Jas 5.9). This belief in the near advent of the Lord is a further indication of the early dating of James. It shows familiarity with the early eschatological views of the Christian communities before the problem of the delay of the coming of the Lord had become a major concern (as in 2 Peter). James uses this Jesus tradition

1. As Dibelius (*James,* 228) emphasizes: 'Slander is not a transgression of merely one commandment, but a transgression against the authority of the law in general, and therefore against God—this is the thought here. It is expressed by the rhetorical use of the same words in the two halves of the verse: He who speaks against his brother or makes himself his brother's judge speaks against the law and makes himself judge of the law'.
2. Kittel ('Der geschichtliche Ort', 90) also draws attention to the similar use of this verb καταδικάζω in both texts.
3. *Ibid.*
4. Davids, *The Epistle of James,* 185.

handed on in Q and applies it in his own way within his own teaching. He shows an awareness of the sources of the Jesus sayings as transmitted in the Q tradition. At the same time James shows an awareness of a saying coming from the Markan tradition, but inserted into the Matthean tradition. Once again these arguments support our claim about James's knowledge of the Q tradition of the Sermon on the Mount as well as those traditions developing within the wider scope of the Matthean community.

2.2.3 *The fruit of good works (Jas 3.12; Mt. 7.16-18; Lk. 6.43-44)*

A further connection that can be observed between James and the Q sermon is that related to the fruit of good works. Following on the command not to judge, the Q sermon[1] contains three brief sections which do not find a parallel in James, namely the sayings related to the golden rule (Lk. 6.31; Mt. 7.12); the blind guide and the disciple–master relationship (Lk. 6.39-40; Mt. 15.14 and Mt. 10.24-25); and the log-splinter in the eye (Lk. 6.41-42; Mt. 7.3-5). Then follows the Q saying on the fruit of good works. The Q form, as reconstructed by Polag,[2] is very close to the way it is expressed in Lk. 6.43-45. Matthew presents the same thoughts, but they occur in a number of different contexts even outside of this sermon (7.16; 7.18; 7.21; 12.33-35). Terminologically and linguistically the texts of Jas 3.12 and Q 6.43-44 do not appear to be derived from each other. Instead, the similarities lie in the actual thought-content being presented. Both Q and James present a rhetorical question, which expects the answer: 'That is impossible!' While the images used are not entirely exact in each tradition, a similar thought does appear: just as a tree only produces good or bad fruit according to its nature, so with persons: they will produce good or evil deeds according to their own nature.[3] Once again a connection is noted between James and the Q tradition incorporated in the Q sermon.

---

1. As indicated in the reconstruction of Polag, *Fragmenta Q*, 23.
2. *Ibid.*, 36-39.
3. Davids, *The Epistle of James*, 148.

2.2.4 Doers of the word (Jas 1.22; Mt. 7.24-27; Lk. 6.47-49)
The parable of the house built upon rock which draws the Q
sermon to a close is introduced by the saying on being a doer of
the word. One of the major aims of the Epistle of James as a
wisdom writing is to provide instructions on conduct which
have been derived from the words of the Lord that James's
readers have heard proclaimed. Jas 1.22 shows a close association with the Q saying introducing the parable about the
house built upon rock.

Jas 1.22	Q (Lk. 6.47-49; Mt. 7.24-27)
Γίνεσθε δὲ ποιηταὶ λόγου καὶ μὴ μόνον ἀκροαταὶ παραλογιζόμενοι ἑαυτούς	Πᾶς ὅστις ἀκούει μου τοὺς λόγους καὶ ποιεῖ αὐτούς... καὶ πᾶς ὁ ἀκούων μου τοὺς λόγους... καὶ μὴ ποιῶν αὐτοὺς...

The Q form follows closely the text of Matthew. James and Q
each show concern for being a *doer of the word* and not just a
hearer of the word. James expresses the thought in terms of
an imperative, whereas Q places it in a reversed negative way
in which it belongs to the context of introducing a parable
which illustrates the thought.

The phrase 'to do the word' corresponds largely to the Jewish concept of 'to do the law' (Deut. 28.58; 29.29).[1] In the LXX
the phrase is found in writings such as 1 Macc. 2.16 and Sir.
19.20. As Davids[2] observes: 'Thus all strands of Jewish teaching witness to the idea that one must do the law, not just hear
it'. In both Matthew and Luke the saying occurs in the context
of the Sermon on the Mount/Plain and forms part of the original Q sermon. In the context to 'do the words' refers to the
words of Jesus in the sermon. Consequently, it can be seen as
an expression for carrying out the law of Jesus in one's life.

James's expression 'to do the word' corresponds to the above
explanation in that it also refers to obeying the commands of
Jesus. When James refers elsewhere to the law as the 'perfect
law, the law of liberty' (Jas 1.25), 'the royal law' (Jas 2.8), he

1. S. Laws, *A Commentary on the Epistle of James* (London: Black, 1980), 85.
2. Davids, *The Epistle of James*, 97.

has in mind not the stipulations of the Jewish law, but rather the new law as taught and expressed by Jesus. The follower of Jesus is instructed in both James and Q to put the teaching of Jesus into practice. As Davids[1] says: '[F]or it is the word, the gospel message, one is to do, not the law. The hearing would parallel the listening to the law in the synagogue reading, but would in fact mean the learning of the traditions of Christ, both as they were recited and explained in the church and as one had opportunity to learn privately.'

2.3 *Conclusion*

Remarkable similarities between James and the Q sermon have emerged. While the beatitudes in particular demonstrated a similarity in terminology and thought-content, correspondences were observed not just in this one aspect of the sermon, but in most of the content of the sermon. The question obviously arises: How does one account for these similarities? One solution would be to argue that both James and the Q sermon are dependent upon a common tradition, each using that tradition within the framework of his own work. But this explanation fails to do justice to the noticeable similarities that have been highlighted through this chapter as well as the location of these similarities within a block of Q tradition, namely the Q Sermon on the Mount.

Bauckham[2] draws attention to an important insight, namely that when investigating connections between the Jesus tradition and other traditions in the New Testament, the possibility should not be limited to that of correspondences between Q and a particular New Testament writing. One should also see whether the similarities are to be found within blocks of Q tradition. In the case of James this hypothesis is well illustrated, in that the vast majority of the sayings contained in the Q sermon find a correspondence in the Epistle of James.

While James shows a knowledge of the Q tradition as expressed in the original Q sermon, he also bears witness to how this block of tradition developed within the context of the

---

1. *Ibid.*
2. Bauckham, 'The Study of Gospel Traditions', 378-80.

Matthean community. As argued, his knowledge of this development did not extend to the final redaction of the Q sermon by the evangelist Matthew. James also shows a certain knowledge of Q traditions which formed part of the Lucan sermon (in particular the woes), but the relationship between James and Luke in these instances remains at the level at which James and Luke use common Q material in their own individual ways. This means that James does not show a knowledge of how the Q sermon developed within the Lucan tradition.

Chapter 6

JAMES AND THE JESUS TRADITION:
A COMPARATIVE EXAMINATION OF SOME FURTHER
SPECIFIC TEXTS

The investigation undertaken in the preceding chapter continues now with the examination of further connections
between James and the Jesus traditions (namely, Q, M and L)
as illustrated in the chart in Chapter 5, §1. Attention will be
given first of all to any other contacts between James and the Q
source. While the connections already investigated were with
that block of tradition containing the Q Sermon on the Mount,
the remaining similarities are scattered throughout the rest of
the Q source, in different blocks of material. Finally,
consideration will be devoted to contacts of James with other
Jesus traditions such as the Matthean, Lucan and Markan
traditions.

1. James and Further Contact with Q

1.1 *Asking (Jas 1.5-8; 4.3; Lk. 11.9-13; Mt. 7.7-11)*
On two occasions in the Epistle of James the theme of asking is
prominent (Jas 1.5-8 and 4.3). Both texts have a relationship to
the Q saying on asking in Lk. 11.9-13 and Mt. 7.7-11. The
order differs in Matthew and Luke: whereas Matthew places
the logion in the context of the Sermon on the Mount, Luke
has it later in connection with sayings on prayer. The reconstructed order of Q follows the position of Luke in which the
saying forms part of a block of Q tradition dealing with
prayer:[1] it follows Jesus' instruction on how to pray when

1. According to A. Polag (*Fragmenta Q: Textheft zur Logienquelle*
[Neukirchen-Vluyn: Neukirchener Verlag, 1979], 24), this section

Jesus gives the example of the Our Father to his followers (Lk. 11.2-4).

1.1.1 *Jas 1.5 and 17; Lk. 11.9-13/Mt. 7.7-11*

James 1.5 and 17	Q (Lk. 11.9-13; Mt. 7.7-11)[1]
Εἰ δέ τις ὑμῶν λείπεται σοφίας, αἰτείτω παρὰ τοῦ διδόντος θεοῦ πᾶσιν ἁπλῶς... καὶ δοθήσεται αὐτῷ.	αἰτεῖτε καὶ δοθήσεται ὑμῖν ζητεῖτε καὶ εὑρήσετε κρούετε καὶ ἀνοιγήσεται ὑμῖν... εἰ οὖν ὑμεῖς πονηροὶ ὄντες οἴδατε δόματα ἀγαθὰ διδόναι τοῖς τέκνοις ὑμῶν,
πᾶσα δόσις ἀγαθή... ἄνωθέν ἐστιν καταβαῖνον ἀπὸ τοῦ πατρὸς τῶν φώτων	πόσῳ μᾶλλον ὁ πατὴρ ὁ ἐξ οὐρανοῦ δώσει ἀγαθὰ τοῖς αἰτοῦσιν αὐτόν

In this reconstruction of Q the versions of Matthew and Luke are very close. In comparing James and this Q text, a number of interesting correspondences appear. Both texts are concerned with giving a directive to those who are in need: in such circumstances one is instructed to ask from God in prayer. In both accounts the verb αἰτέω is in the imperative mood, though the person addressed differs in accordance with the context: in James the verb occurs in the third person, while in Matthew it is in the second person. Both passages express in an identical way the assurance that one will receive: καὶ δοθήσεται and the appropriate pronoun. In his context James goes on to consider what type of faith is needed and the reader is warned against double-mindedness. Finally, in 1.17 James resumes the theme of God the giver and his language is very reminiscent of Q in this context. Both have a reference to the good gifts: δόσις ἀγαθή (Jas 1.17) and δόματα ἀγαθά (Q 11.13). These come from the Father, τοῦ πατρὸς τῶν φώτων) (Jas 1.17), and ὁ πατὴρ ὁ ἐξ οὐρανοῦ (Q 11.13). This shows that James,

---

forms the fifth block of Q material (which he terms E), dealing specifically with prayer.

1. *Ibid.*, 48-51.

Matthew and Luke were all aware of the Q formulation of this Jesus saying on asking and each adapted it to his context. In the adaptation of James the emphasis was placed on the role of God as the true giver of wisdom.[1]

One noteworthy difference occurs in the formulation of this saying in Matthew and Luke. Matthew refers to the Father who gives good things (ἀγαθά) to those who ask (Mt. 7.11), while Luke says that the Father gives the Holy Spirit (πνεῦμα ἅγιον) to those who ask him (Lk. 11.13). In the reconstruction of the Q text, Polag[2] judges that Matthew remains closer to the original version of Q with his reference to ἀγαθά. I, however, disagree with this reconstruction of Polag and I would argue for Luke's reference to the Holy Spirit (πνεῦμα ἅγιον) as the more original Q reading. An examination of the context in Matthew shows that the saying occurs in general terms related to one's request. Matthew immediately concludes his reference to asking for 'good things' with 'So whatever you wish that men would do to you...' His context supports the assumption of a more general reference to asking for all good things. Seen in this light, it is more understandable to see Matthew inserting the saying into his context by reading ἀγαθά in place of πνεῦμα ἅγιον.

Further support for Luke's reading of πνεῦμα ἅγιον as the more original Q reading comes from the transmission of the saying within the Epistle of James. Attention has previously been drawn to the relationship between spirit and wisdom in James. What other traditions of the early Church express in reference to the Spirit and its effects, James expresses in reference to the gift of wisdom. In the context of Jas 1.17 the greatest gift that comes from above is the gift of wisdom. This gift

---

1. This view is supported by R. Hoppe (*Der theologische Hintergrund des Jakobusbriefes* [Würzburg: Echter, 1977], 40): 'Die Wahrscheinlichkeit, dass unser Vers auf eine auch von Mt. und Lk. aufgenommene Q-Überlieferung zurückgeht und unser Autor dieser Tradition unter den Gesichtspunkt der Weisheit gestellt hat, lässt vermuten, dass der ganze Zusammenhang nicht nur "die Art des rechten Gebetes hervorheben will", sondern sich auf die Bitte um die verborgene Weisheit richtet und damit die weitere Feststellung von P. Hauck: "Ein Gegenstand des Gebetes wird nicht genannt. Noch an die σοφία zu denken, liegt nicht nahe", unzutreffend ist'.

2. Polag, *Fragmenta Q*, 50-51.

results in the Christian receiving the word of truth (λόγος ἀληθείας, 1.18) and rebirth as the first fruits of God's creatures (1.18). The gift of wisdom from above in James produces an ethical way of life, as well as a rebirth to new salvation.[1] This concept of wisdom conforms to the notion of the gift of the Spirit and its effects as expressed in both the Pauline and Johannine traditions.[2]

That wisdom and the Spirit fulfil analogous roles appears clearly in the text of Hermas, *Mandates* 11.8, which bears a very close resemblance to Jas 3.17. James speaks about the wisdom from above which effects certain virtues in the Christian, while Hermas speaks about the Spirit effecting very similar virtues. In the tradition of the early church it was common to hand on lists of virtues in a similar way. The tradition of James attributes these virtues to the gift of wisdom which comes from above, while another tradition, that of Hermas attributes them to the Spirit which comes from above.

The theme of asking from the Lord and the certainty that one would receive emerges as an important teaching. This is evident from the numerous forms in which it has appeared in the Gospels and James. Each has accepted the tradition and incorporated it within his own context and tradition. The Epistle of James has emphasized the gift of wisdom, while the Q tradition has stressed the gift of the Holy Spirit.

1.1.2 *James 4.2-3*

This is a further reference in James to the theme of asking which reflects again the above mentioned Q saying (Lk. 11.9-13; Mt. 7.7-11). However, the saying appears in a different context. In ch. 4 James considers the problem of inordinate desires; not only do they lead to strife in the community, but in the context of asking and praying the community makes wrong requests in order to pamper their desires.

---

1. P.H. Davids, *The Epistle of James: A Commentary on the Greek Text* (Exeter: Paternoster, 1982), 89.
2. This use of wisdom in place of Spirit in James was discussed earlier (Chapter 3, §§3.2(b) and 4).

James 4.2-3
...οὐκ ἔχετε διὰ τὸ μὴ αἰτεῖσθαι
ὑμᾶς, αἰτεῖτε καὶ οὐ λαμβάνετε
διότι κακῶς αἰτεῖσθε, ἵνα ἐν
ταῖς ἡδοναῖς ὑμῶν δαπανήσητε.

Q 11.9
αἰτεῖτε καὶ
δοθήσεται ὑμῖν.

James considers the problem that not every prayer receives its answer. The Jesus tradition of asking has been put to the test and it has emerged that there are certain requests which are contrary to the spirit of the Gospel and the teaching of Jesus. The reason given for the failure to receive comes from their wrong requests (κακῶς αἰτεῖσθε, 4.3). From experience Christian tradition always noted qualifications to the unequivocal command of asking: 'And this is the confidence which we have in him, that if we ask anything according to his will he hears us' (1 Jn 5.14). Later Christian tradition also developed the emphasis on asking in the correct way: 'Every request needs humility: fast therefore and you shall receive what you ask from the Lord' (Hermas, *Vis.* 3.10.6). 'Therefore purify your hearts from all the vanities of this world, and from the words which were spoken to you beforehand, and ask from the Lord, and you shall receive all things, and shall not fail to obtain any of your petitions, if you ask from the Lord without doubting' (Hermas, *Mand.* 9.4). This latter reference shows affinity with Jas 1.6 where reference is made to asking God in faith without doubting. In Jas 1.5-8 the reference is to asking for wisdom, whereas in Hermas it refers to making requests in general. The two types of teaching which James records and to which Christian tradition bears witness are in no sense contradictory. The first type calls upon the Christian to ask for needs in an unequivocal way: it places the emphasis upon putting trust and confidence entirely in God. The second type of teaching based upon experience gives instruction to the Christian on how to pray and how to avoid praying in the wrong way.

In assessing the dependence of James on the Q tradition, the use of the verb αἰτέω is worth noting. In Jas 4.2 it occurs as αἰτεῖσθαι in the middle voice, and in Jas 4.3 it appears twice: once as αἰτεῖτε in the active voice, and then it shifts back to αἰτεῖσθε, the middle voice. Kittel[1] argues that the active form betrays the background to James's saying, namely it shows James switching consciously from the middle to the active voice, because he remains true to the words of Jesus which were rendered by the active voice when translated from Aramaic to the Greek. This lends weight to the argument advanced earlier that James is dependent upon the tradition of Jesus. By using αἰτεῖτε he shows a close association with the words of Jesus as recorded in Q (Lk. 11.9-10; Mt. 7.7-8).

This Q saying on asking belongs to that block of traditions in Q which deals with prayer.[2] The only other element relating to prayer which belongs to that block is the prayer of Jesus, the Our Father. Although James does not refer explicitly to this prayer, there is a clear illustration that he does know it. The Q form of the Our Father ends with the petition: καὶ μὴ εἰσενέγκῃς ἡμᾶς εἰς πειρασμόν (Q 11.4). Whereas this petition of the Our Father refers expressly to the eschatological test and not especially to temptations of each day,[3] it is possible (in the Greek form in which it has been translated from the Aramaic) to understand it as referring to everyday temptations.[4] Consequently, as Jeremias proposed,[5] James could have had this

1. G. Kittel ('Der geschichtliche Ort des Jakobusbriefes', *ZNW* 41 [1942], 89). This change from middle to active and back to middle is not seen to have any significance by M. Dibelius (*James: A Commentary on the Epistle of James* (trans. from the German *Der Brief des Jakobus*, 11th rev. edn prepared by H. Greeven, 1964; English trans. by M.A. Williams; ed. H. Koester for Hermeneia; Philadelphia: Fortress, 1975], 219 n. 63) who gives support from 1 Jn 5.15; Jn 16.24, 26, etc. to illustrate this vacillation on Greek moods. This contention of Kittel is supported by F. Mussner (*Der Jakobusbrief: Auslegung* [4th edn; Freiburg: Herder, 1981], 179): 'Auffällig ist der Wechsel im Modus (einmal Aktiv αἰτεῖν, zweimal das Medium αἰτεῖσθαι); sollte er wirklich "darin seinen Grund haben…, dass der Verfasser zwar im allgemeinen das Medium gebraucht, dass aber in der ihm vertrauten griechischen Übersetzung des Jesuswortes die aktivische Form gegeben war", wie G. Kittel meint? Vielleicht (vgl. aber einen ähnlichen Wechsel in 1 Joh 5, 15!).'
2. Polag (*Fragmenta Q*, 25) identifies this block of tradition on prayer as section E.
3. Davids, *The Epistle of James*, 81.
4. Mussner, *Der Jakobusbrief*, 86.
5. J. Jeremias, *The Prayers of Jesus* (London: SCM, 1967), 104.

prayer in mind when he argued that God was not to be blamed for evil and temptations: 'Let no one say when he is tempted, "I am tempted by the Lord"; for God cannot be tempted with evil and he himself tempts no one; but each person is tempted when he is lured and enticed by his own desire' (Jas 1.13-14).

From this investigation it is clear that James shows a number of close associations with the Q tradition's block of material on prayer. In two instances James gives a direction to Q sayings that could possibly be misunderstood, namely the issue of asking and not receiving, and the issue of God tempting. Although the structure and form of this block of material cannot be illustrated within the Epistle of James, nevertheless it does indicate that James has a knowledge of this Q block of tradition. Previously, it was argued that James was familiar with the way in which the Sermon on the Mount tended to develop in Matthew's Gospel. It is difficult to answer the question whether James is utilizing the Sermon on the Mount as it is developing within the Matthean community (Q^{Mt}), or whether he has in mind the original Q tradition where the theme of prayer is treated in a block. From the above examination which shows that James develops the reference to the Holy Spirit in the direction of wisdom, it seems reasonable to conclude in favour of the use of the original Q tradition, and not just that which developed within the Matthean community.

1.2 *Treasure in heaven (Jas 5.2-3; Lk. 12.33-34; Mt. 6.19-21)*
The saying in Matthew and Luke goes back to the same tradition (Q), but is expressed differently in each text. In reconstructing this text in Q, Polag[1] opts for a closer dependency on the text of Matthew as more representative of the Q form.

Μὴ ποιήσατε ὑμῖν θησαυροὺς ἐπὶ τῆς γῆς,
ὅπου σὴς καὶ βρῶσις ἀφανίζει,
καὶ ὅπου κλέπται διορύσσουσιν καὶ κλέπτουσιν·
ποιήσατε δὲ ὑμῖν θησαυροὺς ἐν οὐρανῷ,
ὅπου οὔτε σὴς οὔτε βρῶσις ἀφανίζει,
καὶ ὅπου κλέπται οὐ διορύσσουσιν οὐδὲ κλέπτουσιν·

---

1. Polag, *Fragmenta Q*, 62-63.

ὅπου γάρ ἐστιν ὁ θησαυρὸς ὑμῶν,
ἐκεῖ καὶ ἡ καρδία ὑμῶν ἔσται.

A comparison with Jas 5.2-3 is quite revealing:

ὁ πλοῦτος ὑμῶν σέσηπεν καὶ τὰ ἱμάτια ὑμῶν σητόβρωτα
γέγονεν,
ὁ χρυσὸς ὑμῶν καὶ ὁ ἄργυρος κατίωται καὶ ὁ ἰὸς αὐτῶν εἰς
μαρτύριον ὑμῖν ἔσται καὶ φάγεται τὰς σάρκας ὑμῶν ὡς
πῦρ.
ἐθησαυρίσατε ἐν ἐσχάταις ἡμέραις.

The following similarities are observable:

(a) Both passages have a similar reference to wealth. Q
refers to moths and rust (σὴς καὶ βρῶσις) and their ability to
destroy things by consuming them. James also refers to riches
rotting and the garments being moth-eaten (σητόβρωτα), a
form in which the two words in Q are now combined.

(b) Both passages look beyond the present possession of
earthly wealth to the hope of attaining heavenly wealth.

The similarities in thought and vocabulary support the contention that James is operating in a world which is aware of
the Q tradition of the sayings of Jesus. James is not quoting the
Q tradition directly, but is using it according to his usual
method of working it into his argument. In fact, one can say
that this passage in James is a commentary upon the Q saying,
reflecting upon it and showing its further implications. The
wisdom tradition is aware of similar thoughts and expressions:
the image of moth-eaten garments is known (Sir. 42.13); and
the image of wealth and money rusting was also part of the
common wisdom heritage (Sir. 29.9-12). James shows again
his twofold roots in the wisdom tradition as well as Q.

Matthew and Luke have also reworked the Q tradition.
Luke has remained faithful to the original order of the saying,
but has nevertheless abbreviated the saying and represented it
in his own way. Matthew in his turn appears to have
remained closest to the original wording of the Q saying, but
has inserted it within the developing Sermon on the Mount
which has incorporated sayings from the Q source appearing
originally in different contexts. Previously, it was argued that
James was aware of both the Q tradition as well as the way in

which it developed within the Matthean Sermon on the Mount. The use that James makes of this saying (which is virtually the same in both Matthew and Q) can be attributed to both of these sources. On the one hand it would show James's familiarity with one saying belonging to the Q block of tradition identified by Polag[1] as block H: on proper concerns. On the other hand it would lend further support to our suggestion about James's awareness of the development of the Q Sermon on the Mount in the Matthean community.

1.3 *Conversion of the sinful brother (Jas 5.19-20; Lk. 17.3; Mt. 18.15)*
Here the similarity between James and the Q source (as represented in Matthew and Luke) lies chiefly in thought rather than any form of verbal similarity. All the traditions have in mind a person within the community who is leading a reprehensible life and is disregarding certain of its moral norms. He is in need of someone within the community who will lead him to realize the error of his ways and bring him back to observe again the moral norms of the community.

On its own this similarity is not striking, since it is a common theme both in the Old and New Testament traditions (for example Lev. 19.17; Ps. 51.13; Ezek. 3.17-21; 33.7-9; Sir. 28.2-3; Gal. 6.1; 1 Thess. 5.14; 1 Jn 5.16).[2] However, taken together with the previous examinations of correspondences between James and the Q tradition, it becomes a further example of similarity in thought. According to Polag,[3] Luke is a better witness to the original Q formulation of the saying because Matthew's Gospel has tended to develop the saying within the context of a narrative. James, in fact, concludes his epistle with this specific counsel and in doing so confirms the straightforward advice to strive positively to draw a sinner back from the error of his ways. The connection between James and the Jesus tradition lies in the thought content as expressed in Q and not as it developed further in the Gospel of Matthew. This particular saying occurs in Q as part of that block of Q mate-

1. *Ibid.*, 25.
2. See Davids, *The Epistle of James,* 199.
3. Polag, *Fragmenta Q,* 76-77.

rial identified by Polag[1] as block K: on the responsibility of disciples. The wider context of this saying is that one should not be a stumbling-block to others (Q 17.1-6).

1.4 *Obligation to keep the whole law (Jas 2.10; Lk. 16.17; Mt. 5.18-19)*

James 2.10	Q 16.17[2]
ὅστις γὰρ ὅλον τὸν νόμον	Ἀμὴν λέγω ὑμῖν,
τηρήσῃ, πταίσῃ δὲ ἐν ἑνί,	ἕως ἂν παρέλθῃ ὁ οὐρανὸς
	καὶ ἡ γῆ,
γέγονεν πάντων ἔνοχος.	μία κεραία οὐ μὴ παρέλθῃ
	ἀπὸ τοῦ νόμου.

The Q form of this Jesus saying is handed on differently by the Gospels of Luke and Matthew. Lk. 16.17 presents the essence of the saying without any form of commentary. Mt. 5.18 incorporates the saying within the context of the Sermon on the Mount, and specifies it further with the saying: 'Whoever then relaxes one of the least of these commandments and teaches men so, shall be called least in the kingdom of heaven; but he who does them and teaches them shall be called great in the kingdom of heaven' (Mt. 5.19). In reconstructing the Q text, Polag[3] placed Mt. 5.19 within the list of texts he referred to as 'texts possibly pertaining to Q' in the first appendix to the text. This means that from a very early stage the Jesus saying on keeping the whole law was handed on with an explanation and elaboration.

Jas 2.10 fits within this tradition of using the Q saying in its own way, and elaborating and emphasizing it. In a graphic illustration of how one is guilty of the entire law by breaking one law, Jas 2.11 refers to the commands against adultery and murder (in that order). The Matthean Sermon on the Mount also gives an illustration of how one is to abide by the whole law by providing developed illustrations on the breaking of the various commandments such as murder and adultery (in that order).

---

1. *Ibid.*, 74.
2. *Ibid.*
3. *Ibid.*, 86-87.

The argument of James and of Matthew is each presented in a different way and the reference to the commandments shows a difference in sequence. Our examination argues that the Jesus tradition did not simply hand on the isolated saying on keeping the whole law, but that it was combined with an explanation as well. This again supports the closeness of James to the Q tradition. The material referred to here in Q is that found in the section Polag refers to as block I: parables.[1] This is an inappropriate heading, for the contents are more than simply parables: they contain much wider sayings of a general nature. Using the terminology of Kloppenborg,[2] it would be better to refer to it as one of the speeches of Q. What is noteworthy is the use that James makes of material from another block of Q material. While most of the similarities between James and Q have been in the Q Sermon on the Mount, James also shows a use of Q from other blocks of tradition, as is evident in this section.

1.5 *Serving two masters (Jas 4.4; Lk. 16.13; Mt. 6.24)*

Jas 4.4 contains two distinct connections with the Jesus tradition. The first occurs in the address 'unfaithful creatures' (μοιχαλίδες). The phrase appears in the Markan tradition (Mk 8.38) and is continued within the Matthean community (Mt. 12.39; 16.4). In this manner of address Jesus had adopted the prophetic accusation levelled against God's people for deserting him.[3] James addresses his readers in a similar vein. Because of its common use in the Jesus tradition, it would be logical to presume that James took it over from the tradition being handed on within the Matthean community. This description does not come to James via Q, but rather from his connection with the Matthean community.

---

1. *Ibid.*, 25-26.
2. J.S. Kloppenborg, 'The Formation of Q and Antique Instructional Genres', *JBL* 105 (1986), 456.
3. As Davids (*The Epistle of James,* 160-61) says: 'This tradition was picked up by Jesus, calling the Jews "an adulterous generation" (Mk 8.38; Mt. 12.39; 16.4—γενεὰ πονηρὰ καὶ μοιχαλίς). In each case in both Testaments the concept is applied only to Jews, never gentiles, for only those who have had a claim to have a covenant relationship with Yahweh can be included in such a condemnation.'

The second point of contact between Jas 4.4 and the Jesus tradition lies in the thought that friendship with the world brings enmity with God. In some ways this comes as a further explanation of the previous condemnation by which Jesus' generation is called 'adulterous'.[1] To abandon God for the love of the world is indeed adultery. This division in allegiance between God and something else occurs in the Q tradition in Lk. 16.13 and Mt. 6.24 where the form is practically identical:[2]

Οὐδεὶς δύναται δυσὶ κυρίοις δουλεύειν· ἢ γὰρ τὸν ἕνα μισήσει καὶ τὸν ἕτερον ἀγαπήσει, ἢ ἑνὸς ἀνθέξεται καὶ τοῦ ἑτέρου καταφρονήσει. οὐ δύνασθε Θεῷ δουλεύειν καὶ μαμωνᾷ.

Jesus makes the point here (Q 16.13) that there is no possibility of compromise: one is either a servant of God or a servant of his enemy, the world, with its love and attraction of wealth. 'Love for God and love for the world are mutually exclusive.'[3] Exactly the same point is made by Jas 4.4: one cannot be a friend of God and a friend of the world—there is no possibility of holding a middle position.[4] Although there is no question of a verbal connection between James and Q, both are undoubtedly reproducing the same teaching of Jesus. This text does not prove a direct connection between James and Q, but taken together with all the previous illustrations, it does tend to support a further connection. In the Q tradition this saying on serving two masters follows the sayings on the obligation to keep the whole law (Q 16.17) and draws the whole block of material (I) on parables to a fitting conclusion. This is the second illustration of a saying in James that is similar to material in this block.

1. Dibelius, *James*, 220.
2. Polag, *Fragmenta Q*, 74-75.
3. Dibelius, *James*, 220.
4. The same idea is presented by James on other occasions. For example, in 1.27 he defines religion in this way: 'Religion that is pure and undefiled before God and the Father is this: to visit orphans and widows in their affliction, and to keep oneself unstained from the world'. Both James and Q show the viewpoint that friendship with the world and friendship with God cannot be harmonized. The two attitudes are in fact mutually contradictory and the traditions of James and Q witness to a similar emphasis and reflection on this theme.

1.6 Humility and exaltation (Jas 4.10; Mt. 23.12; Lk. 14.11; 18.14)

James 4.10	Q (Lk. 14.11/18.14; Mt. 23.12)[1]
ταπεινώθητε ἐνώπιον κυρίου	πᾶς ὁ ὑψῶν ἑαυτὸν ταπεινωθήσεται,
καὶ ὑψώσει ὑμᾶς.	καὶ ὁ ταπεινῶν ἑαυτὸν ὑψωθήσεται.

In Mt. 23.12 and Lk. 14.11/18.14 the saying occurs in completely different contexts. Because of the close similarity of the saying in Matthew and Luke, I would argue that it belongs to Q, but that each writer has used it differently and inserted it into a different context. Polag[2] places this among the disputed Q sayings, and the form he gives for Q is closer to the Lucan formulation. Matthew and Luke differ in their expression only in a grammatical way, while the thought remains identical.

Jas 4.10 preserves the same antithesis with the verbs ταπεινόω and ὑψόω, but expresses the thought in a much more concise way. This thought also occurs elsewhere in James, for example in 1.9-10: 'Let the lowly (ταπεινός) brother boast in his exaltation (ὕψει) and the rich in his humiliation (ταπεινώσει)'; and again in 4.6, 'God opposes the proud (ὑπερηφάνοις), but gives grace to the humble (ταπεινοῖς)'. This theme of humiliation–exaltation is quite familiar in the writings of the Hebrew Bible (Job 5.11; 22.29; Ps. 149.4; Prov. 3.34) as well as in the deuterocanonical literature such as Sir. 2.17: 'Those who fear the Lord will prepare their hearts, and will humble themselves before him'. This theme is evident as well in other literature such as *T. Jos.* 10.3; 18.1.[3] However, it is more probable that the Jesus saying forms the immediate background to the saying in James. Just as this saying of Jesus, handed on in Q, found its way into the Gospels of Matthew and Luke in many and different contexts, so too is this saying used by James in a number of different contexts. Once again one may argue for the dependence of James on the Jesus tradition preserved in Q

---

1. Polag, *Fragmenta Q*, 86.
2. *Ibid.*, 86-87.
3. Davids, *The Epistle of James*, 168.

because of the linguistic similarities in the words used and the antithesis that has been expressed by them.

1.7 *Conclusion*

These are the most striking similarities to be observed between James and the Q tradition outside of the block of material identified as the Sermon on the Mount. Only two possible explanations can be given for these similarities. Either both James and Q are dependent upon a common tradition which is reflected in these examples; or James is dependent directly on the Q tradition. The argument of this investigation supports the direct dependence of James on Q. The main reason for opting for this second possibility arises from the closeness of the language used. While no one example is capable of proving the point conclusively, all these examples taken together provide an argument from convergence. If one were to opt for the first possibility whereby James and Q are independent of each other, yet dependent upon a common tradition, one would in fact have to postulate a common tradition very similar to Q. One would simply be multiplying literary sources unnecessarily, a point that Kloppenborg warns against quite forcibly in his thesis: 'Litterae non sunt multiplicandae praeter necessitatem!'[1]

In examining the major blocks of material into which Q has been divided,[2] one notes connections between James and certain of these blocks of material. The most notable are with Block B: the Sermon on the Mount; and block E: on prayer. At the same time some sayings occur in the following blocks of tradition which bear resemblance to certain sayings in James: block H: on proper concerns; block K: on the responsibility of the disciples; and block I: on parables.

Out of the eleven blocks of material that Polag[3] identified in Q, there are connections in James with virtually half, while two blocks emerge prominently in James's use of them. From this evidence a number of conclusions emerge. First, James's

1. J.S. Kloppenborg, 'The Literary Genre of the Synoptic Sayings Source' (PhD thesis, University of St Michael's College, Toronto School of Theology, 1984), 86.
2. Polag, *Fragmenta Q*, 23-26.
3. *Ibid.*, 23-26.

knowledge of Q is not limited to one block of tradition, but does show a familiarity and use of material from different unrelated blocks of Q material. Bauckham[1] argues that to demonstrate a writer's dependence upon Q one would have to show that he depends not 'on only one or two particular blocks of Q material', but that there should be 'allusions to a wide range of Q material'. This has indeed been shown in the previous investigation. Secondly, the material that James uses conforms to the nature of his writing. He incorporates wisdom-paraenetical advice which supports and illustrates the particular teachings which he is concerned to communicate. This accounts for the selection that he has made, and provides the reason why he has tended to focus attention more on certain blocks of tradition than on others. Thirdly, the parallels in James to Q material that are independent of the Gospels of Matthew and Luke are of significance in actually bearing witness to the existence of the Q source. One has in fact an independent witness to the existence of such a document as the Q source. Bauckham[2] issued a warning that 'a general impression of dependence on Q is sometimes given without a sufficiently careful examination of each possible parallel to Gospel traditions'. Attention has been focused in the preceding on all the possible parallels between James and Q. Now it is necessary to investigate the parallels between James and the other Jesus traditions in order to arrive at a firm conclusion on the possible relationship to and position of James within the Jesus tradition.

2. *James and Further Contact with the Matthean Community Traditions*

An argument that would limit James's knowledge of Q to a dependence upon Matthew's Gospel or to Q^{Mt} is too simplistic an approach. The preceding investigation has shown that James is aware of both Q and Q^{Mt}. This section will examine

1. R. Bauckham, 'The Study of Gospel Traditions outside the Canonical Gospels: Problems and Prospects', *Gospel Perspectives*, vol. 5: *The Jesus Tradition outside the Gospels* (ed. D. Wenham; Sheffield: JSOT, 1985), 379.
2. *Ibid.*

further connections between James and the development of traditions within the Matthean community. In this latter regard Bauckham[1] has made a vital observation: 'In my opinion, of all the putative sources of the Synoptic Gospels, the one for which there is the best evidence outside the Synoptic Gospels is not Q, but Matthew's special source, though that evidence has been little enough recognized and studied'. There are indeed a couple of striking parallels between material in James and Matthew's special source which lend support to Bauckham's contention.

2.1 *The oath (Jas 5.12; Mt. 5.33-37)*

The saying on the taking of an oath presents the clearest association between James and the words of the Lord.

Matthew 5.33-37	James 5.12
Πάλιν ἠκούσατε ὅτι ἐρρέθη τοῖς ἀρχαίοις· οὐκ ἐπιορκήσεις, ἀποδώσεις δὲ τῷ κυρίῳ τοὺς ὅρκους σου. ἐγὼ δὲ λέγω ὑμῖν μὴ ὀμόσαι ὅλως·	
μήτε ἐν τῷ οὐρανῷ ὅτι θρόνος ἐστὶν τοῦ θεοῦ,	ἀδελφοί μου, μὴ ὀμνύετε μήτε τὸν οὐρανὸν
μήτε ἐν τῇ γῇ ὅτι ὑποπόδιόν ἐστιν τῶν ποδῶν αὐτοῦ,	μήτε τὴν γῆν
μήτε εἰς Ἱεροσόλυμα, ὅτι πόλις ἐστὶν τοῦ μεγάλου βασιλέως, μήτε ἐν τῇ κεφαλῇ σου ὀμόσῃς, ὅτι οὐ δύνασαι μίαν τρίχα λευκὴν ποιῆσαι ἢ μέλαιναν.	μήτε ἄλλον τινα ὅρκον·
ἔστω δὲ ὁ λόγος ὑμῶν ναὶ ναί, οὒ οὔ· τὸ δὲ περισσὸν τούτων ἐκ τοῦ πονηροῦ ἐστιν.	ἤτω δὲ ὑμῶν τὸ ναὶ ναὶ καὶ τὸ οὒ οὔ, ἵνα μὴ ὑπὸ κρίσιν πέσητε.

Of concern here are the literary or textual relationships between James and Matthew. James is not a paraphrase of

---

1. *Ibid.*, 380.

the saying in Matthew[1] and early Christian writings seem to bear witness to the fact that the saying has been handed on in two distinct forms. In the New Testament these two texts are the only ones that forbid categorically the taking of oaths. In Matthew these words occur in the context of the Sermon on the Mount where Jesus illustrates how he has come to establish a new order. He contrasts what was said in the past with an emphasis on the central aspect of the law: 'You have heard, that it was said... but I say to you...' He teaches that in the new order of life of those who belong to the kingdom, there is no more place for the taking of the oath.[2] Jesus, therefore, replaces this custom by means of a simple Yes or No. There are a number of striking similarities between the way in which this saying of the Lord is reported in Matthew and James:[3]

Matthew		James	
1	Direct prohibition of all oaths	1	Direct prohibition of all oaths
2	*Examples*: (a) by heaven, for it... (b) or by earth, for it... (c) or by Jerusalem, for it... (d) or by your head, for you...	2	*Examples*: (a) by heaven (b) or by earth (c) or with any other oath
3	Call for absolute truthfulness 'Let what you say be simply "Yes" or "No"...	3	Call for absolute truthfulness 'Let your yes be yes and your no be no'.
4	*Reason*: Anything more than this comes from evil	4	*Reason*: that you may not fall under condemnation.

James's stylistic expression seems to be closer to that of classical Greek than the more Hellenistic form of Matthew. For example, in the negative prohibitions James uses the

1. Dibelius, *James*, 250.
2. J. Schneider, 'ὀμνύω', *TDNT*, V (1967), 178.
3. Dibelius, *James*, 250.

classical Greek construction of ὀμνύω μήτε + accusative, whereas Matthew opts for the more familiar expression in Hellenistic Greek of ἐν + the dative.[1] The form in James appears to be much simpler than that in Matthew: the prohibition is presented in general terms and concludes with a personal threat. Matthew, on the other hand, shows an enlargement of the saying.[2]

It is not necessary to argue for a direct linear connection between James and Matthew. Although James appears to be the earlier form, this is not to say that Matthew simply borrowed from James. It is far more likely that Matthew and James represent the way the saying of Jesus came to expression in the course of time. James is the earlier formulation, while Matthew betrays deeper reflection on and expansion of the saying. The question has been discussed as to whether this saying is to be traced back to Jesus, or whether it is the simple adoption of a saying that belonged to the general ethical wisdom teaching of the time. Laws[3] sums up the argument well: 'As the unqualified prohibition of oaths seems to have no precedent before the Christian tradition, and as it would be an extraordinary stand to take in the Jewish context, given the OT background, it seems most probable that it derives from Jesus himself'. Given that the saying is attributable to Jesus, Matthew and James have handed it on in their own way.

One is dealing here with a saying of the Lord which only James and Matthew have preserved—which means that it was not part of the original Q tradition. However, being a saying of the Lord and containing such close relationships, some connection between James's expression and that of Matthew is to be observed. The relationship can be envisaged in this way: James shows an earlier knowledge of the saying as it is being handed on within the Matthean community, while Matthew's form demonstrates how it has been further

1. Davids, *The Epistle of James,* 190.
2. From the examination of the form in both Matthew and James, Dibelius (*James,* 251) concludes: 'The simpler, more unified and ethically purer form of the saying in James must be considered the earlier form'.
3. S. Laws, *A Commentary on the Epistle of James* (London: Black, 1980), 224.

developed or expressed by the Matthean community and the
evangelist himself when it was inserted within the context of
the Sermon on the Mount. This conclusion will agree with that
emerging from other connections observed between James
and Matthew in what follows. None of the subsequent
correspondences is as striking either textually or linguistically
as this one; if each was taken on its own, it would be
insignificant. However, when they are all viewed together
then the correspondences appear to be impressive.

2.2 *Care of the needy (Jas 2.15-16; Mt. 25.34-35; Lk. 3.11)*
Jas 2.15-16 introduced an example, rather like a parable,[1] to
illustrate what faith without works is like. In this context
James is commenting upon the need to fulfil the royal law
(2.8), 'You shall love your neighbour as yourself.' From the
example cited one concludes that this particular act of charity
is not being implemented in the community. Both Matthew
and Luke show a similar concern for providing clothing and
food for the needy. However, they do so in different contexts
and with texts that are not parallel. Lk. 3.11 presents the
teaching of John the Baptist in which the Baptist calls on his
hearers to share their coats and food with those who do not
have any. (James also mentions these two needs in his
passage.) Mt. 25.31-46 contains the eschatological parable
which teaches that the disciples are rewarded or condemned
according to the way in which they have responded to the
needs of others. Among the needs listed are again those of
feeding the hungry and clothing the naked—but other needs
are also mentioned.

The text of James does not have a direct dependence upon
either of the above two texts. However, it does show that the
teaching related to caring for the needs of others was an
important theme in the early Christian tradition. In emphasizing the importance that this has for one's salvation, James
in fact shows a closer similarity with the tradition handed on
in Matthew's Gospel, in that the eschatological judgment
depends upon the way in which one has cared for the needs of

---

1. J. Ropes, *A Critical and Exegetical Commentary on the Epistle of
St. James* (Edinburgh: T. & T. Clark, 1916), 206.

others (in particular the feeding of the hungry and clothing the naked).

2.3 *Conclusion*

In addition to the above there are some smaller similarities that can be observed between James and Matthew's Special Source (M). Jas 2.20 uses the adjective κενέ to amplify the address ὦ ἄνθρωπε. This implies much the same as the adjective used to describe faith without works: namely ἀργή (barren, empty). Oepke[1] sees the expression ὦ ἄνθρωπε κενέ as 'linguistically comparable with the ῥακά of Mt. 5.22'. There ῥακά has the meaning of 'empty simpleton'.[2] This is in direct opposition to the wise man who receives from God the gift of wisdom which enables him to act in a specific way.

In examining the relationship between James and Matthew what emerges quite clearly is James's awareness of both the Q tradition which developed within the Matthean comunity as well as the source that was special to the Matthean community (M). As has been noted, most of the parallels occur in material found in the Q[Mt] Sermon on the Mount. This is not surprising because James's perspective is to give moral and paraenetical instruction on how to lead one's life, which is also the goal of the Q[Mt] Sermon on the Mount. The relationship between Matthew and James lies not in the fact that the one tradition used the other's completed works—this cannot be shown because there are no close and consistent verbal dependencies. Instead, the relationship appears in the area of the development of the Q tradition, especially the Sermon on the Mount, within the Matthean community. James shows an awareness of this developing tradition and incorporates it within his own instruction, adopting it to his own perspective and context.

3. *James and Contact with the Gospel of Luke*

In examining contact between James and the Q source, particularly in regard to the Q Sermon on the Mount, many simi-

---

1. A. Oepke, 'κενός', *TDNT*, III (1965), 660.
2. *Ibid.*

larities were noticed between James and Luke. Because Luke represents at times a closer witness to the Q source, these similarities were important for illustrating James's contact with the Q source. For example, a point of connection was noted between James and the Lucan woes in Jas 4.9 and Lk. 6.25. This contact, however, was not such as to allow us to argue for a dependence of one upon the other. Rather, they both (James and Luke) show how each has developed the words of Jesus within his own tradition. Within the Lucan community the Q beatitudes were developed by contrasting them to four woes which were composed as antitheses to the beatitudes. But in no way can it be argued that James is aware of the Gospel of Luke. Their relationship rests solely upon the fact that both James and Luke are making use of a common source, Q. In fact, where James and Luke demonstrate some form of similarity, it is a further argument, independent of the synoptic Gospels, for the existence of the Q source.

Attention has been given to all the possible relationships between James and Luke as indicated in the chart of correspondences between James and the synoptic tradition given at the beginning of Chapter 4. The only one not yet considered is that of the Elijah example. Both Jas (5.17) and Lk. (4.25) refer to the incident where Elijah was responsible for the absence of rain in Israel for three years and six months. The point of similarity is in the specific length of time. Apart from this, the comparison falters because each uses the example of Elijah in a decidedly different way. Davids[1] argues that the length of time is really a symbolic figure which was quite popular in legendary material circulating about Elijah. Consequently, no direct connection between James and Luke can be established here.

In his list of similarities between James and the synoptic tradition, Davids[2] notes three other possible similarities which have not been included in this examination (namely, Jas 1.21 and Lk. 8.8; Jas 2.6 and Lk. 18.3; Jas 4.17 and Lk. 12.47). Looking at these three examples, it is very hard to see how they can be termed similarities. There is hardly any point of

1. Davids, *The Epistle of James,* 197.
2. *Ibid.,* 47-48.

contact that can be established among them. Even to say that
they are a reflection of a common tradition would be to stretch
the argument. For example, with reference to Jas 2.6, 'But you
have dishonoured the poor man. Is it not the rich who oppress
you, is it not they who drag you into court?', Davids[1] sees this as
bearing a possible similarity to Lk. 18.3, 'And there was a
widow in that city who kept coming to him and saying,
"Vindicate me against my adversary"'. The only remote
points of contact here are the court, and a widow—poor man.
To my mind it is carrying the argument too far to see any
form of contact between these two texts. James is referring to a
practical example and problem within the Christian
community to which he is writing; Luke is reporting an actual
parable of Jesus. The one is an actuality; the other a story.

The analysis has shown that James is aware of the Q tradition and its development within the Matthean community, but
not with its development within the Lucan community. This is
contrary to the view expressed by Davids[2] who argues that
James is closer to the Lucan sermon than to that of Matthew
in three ways. The arguments advanced by Davids in support,
however, are not too convincing. His first argument concerns
statistics with regard to the similarities in vocabulary between
James and Luke, but these are not substantiated by specific
examples.[3] He has argued for a closer similarity between
James and the Lucan sermon (than between James and the
Matthean sermon), yet in doing so the evidence he advances is
that of words found only in James and in the whole of Luke–
Acts. He immediately jumps from the Lucan sermon to the
entire work Luke–Acts to establish a connection with James.
The examination undertaken in this and the previous chapter
does not support Davids's contention. The connections that do
exist between Luke and James are best explained as going
back to their origins in Q. They must take into account the fact
that Luke is a better witness to the order of the original Q sermon. From the verbal similarities between James and Luke–

1. Davids, *The Epistle of James*, 47.
2. *Ibid.*, 49.
3. Davids is relying upon a doctoral thesis by J.B. Adamson, *An Inductive Approach to the Epistle of James* (PhD thesis, Cambridge University, 1954), 293-95.

Acts, Davids[1] concludes that 'in itself this datum means only that James has a grasp of Greek similar to Luke's... but it is suggestive of a further relationship between the two traditions'. I would argue that the relationship remains on the level of the common Q source which they both use in their own way.

His other two arguments on the similar nature of eschatology and the social outlook of James and the Lucan tradition also do not establish a direct connection between the two. The similarities are better explained through their fidelity to the common source Q. For example, James has been shown to be closer to the expression of the form of the beatitude, 'Blessed are the poor', rather than 'poor in spirit'. It has been argued that the original form of the beatitude in Q referred to the undeveloped form 'Blessed are the poor'. Consequently, when James shows a support for the material poor, it is not because he is relying upon the Lucan tradition, but because he is remaining faithful to the original Q form (as Luke did).

Davids does not argue for a direct dependence of James on Luke or vice versa. He himself says: 'The result of this examination is not to say that James knew Luke or came from his community, but simply to argue for similarity'.[2] He concludes that the similarity lies in the fact that James has used 'the unwritten Jesus tradition freely'.[3] Again this is a generalized statement. Our entire examination has shown that the matter is more significant than this. James has used the Jesus tradition as it has been handed on in Q, and also as it has been developed further within the Matthean community. He has certainly adapted it in his own way to suit his context and his own teaching. The similarity between James and Luke rests ultimately in their common origin in Q.

4. *More General Parallels between James and the Jesus Tradition*

All the correspondences listed at the beginning of Chapter 5 between James and the Q, M and L traditions have been

---

1. Davids, *The Epistle of James*, 49.
2. *Ibid.*
3. *Ibid.*

examined in detail. In some passages the similarities amount to merely an echo in the language used. In other cases the thought expressed was judged to be very close. In still others there was a close degree of verbal and thought correspondence. In essence, then, the similarities extend above all to the Q source and to the intermediate stage within the Matthean community between Q and the final redaction of the Gospel of Matthew. This conclusion differs from the view expressed by Davids[1] who opts for a dependence of James upon a version of the Q source that is different from that used by Matthew and Luke. This would amount to postulating, besides Q^{Lk} and Q^{Mt}, a Q^{Jas}. In the examination undertaken above, I do not think that it is necessary to propose yet another version of Q on which James is dependent. I think that, as far as has been argued, James is aware of the traditionally accepted version of Q as well as the way in which it tends to develop within the Matthean community. Nevertheless, I fully endorse the conclusion that Davids reaches: 'Thus James witnesses to a third community for which the ethical teaching of Jesus was important'.[2]

In the chart of correspondences between James and the synoptic tradition a few connections were noted with the Markan tradition of the sayings of Jesus. A close analysis, however, indicates that these sayings do not come to James directly from Mark, but rather via the Matthean community. This can be seen in two specific instances. Jas 1.6 states: αἰτείτω δὲ ἐν πίστει μηδὲν διακρινόμενος while Mt. 21.21 expressed a very similar thought when he says: ἀμὴν λέγω ὑμῖν, ἐὰν ἔχητε πίστιν καὶ μὴ διακριθῆτε... The origin of this saying in Matthew is that of Mk 11.23f.: καὶ μὴ διακριθῇ ἐν τῇ καρδίᾳ αὐτοῦ ἀλλὰ πιστεύῃ... Given the association already indicated between James and the Matthean community, the saying of Jas 1.6 would seem to owe its origin to the Matthean community.

A similar example occurs in Jas 5.9 in reference to the judge standing at the doors: ἰδοὺ ὁ κριτὴς πρὸ τῶν θυρῶν ἔστηκεν. Mt. 24.33 and Mk 13.29 express it in a similar way: γινώσκετε ὅτι ἐγγύς ἐστιν ἐπὶ θύραις. Once again the parallel between James

1. *Ibid.*, 68.
2. *Ibid.*

and the Markan tradition comes via the Matthean community; there is no reason to postulate a direct dependence of James on Mark in this instance.

Mussner[1] makes mention of a further connection with Markan material. Jas 5.7 calls for patience as one awaits the parousia and compares this to the image of the farmer who waits for the harvest with patience until the rains come. Mk 4.26-29 gives a parable of Jesus referring to the seed which grows by itself whereas Mt. 13.24-30 shows a development of this parable which goes on to speak about the farmer letting the weeds and the wheat grow side by side until harvest time when they will be separated. It is difficult to show direct dependence of James upon either Matthew or Mark. Obviously one is dealing with similarities of thought. While Mussner sees a parallel between James and Mark in this connection, I think that he fails to note the direction the parable has taken in the Matthean community. The emphasis has been placed upon the patient waiting for the harvest time when the good and bad will be separated. James, too, speaks of a patient waiting for the harvest. The similarity is indeed closer between James and Matthew in this instance, than between James and Mark. This is a further illustration of how James echoes material found in the Matthean community which originally had an origin in the Markan tradition. All the connections are in fact explained by the way the Markan tradition has been absorbed within the Matthean community.

Davids[2] indicates further some 'more general parallels in thought' between James and the Jesus tradition. A few of these parallels have already been discussed in the course of this examination. They are really nothing more than echoes of similar thoughts and do not add anything new to the discussion. They simply add more support to the argument that has been advanced throughout this examination. Attention will be given to three of the more important 'general parallels' that Davids[3] notes.

1. Mussner, *Der Jakobusbrief*, 50.
2. Davids, *The Epistle of James*, 48.
3. *Ibid.*

(a) Jas 1.9-10; 4.10; Mt. 18.4; 23.12; Lk. 9.48;[1] 14.11; 22.26. All these references are illustrations of the saying that has already been discussed, namely: 'Whoever exalts himself will be humbled, and whoever humbles himself will be exalted'. The wealth of references to this theme shows the importance it assumed in the early Church traditions. It was argued previously that this was a saying that possibly belonged to the Q tradition, and was adopted by the various traditions and inserted into their different contexts. Here, then, Matthew, Luke and James all depend upon this original Q saying of the Lord.

(b) Jas 1.26-27; 2.14-26; Mt. 7.21-23. These all concern the general theme of action as expressive of one's faith. In these instances both James and Matthew echo once again a common theme and illustrate the importance given to the role that actions must play in illustrating one's faith.

(c) Jas 3.1-12; Mt. 12.36-37. Here echoes occur of a similar thought related to the control of speech. All that can be said of these similarities is that they bear witness to a common thought on the need to take care with regard to what one says. No direct connection can be established at all, but taken in conjunction with what has already been indicated, they do show that both James and the Matthean community gave importance to the control that should be exercised over one's speech.

No example or detail on its own is conclusive. All such examples are to be judged not as individual items, but on the basis of coherence. James is steeped in the tradition of the sayings of Jesus, and in all the similarities discussed the connections operate on the level of the words of Jesus. Although James does not present them as sayings of the Lord, nevertheless these words operate for him as that law which is meant to direct all action.

---

1. Davids (*The Epistle of James,* 48) gives this as Lk. 9.40, whereas in fact it is Lk. 9.48.

Chapter 7

THE WISDOM THEME OF PERFECTION IN JAMES AND THE
JESUS TRADITIONS

The connections between James and Q have shown that both
traditions continue wisdom themes by reflecting upon the
nature of wisdom as well as by emphasizing the practical ethical dimension of wisdom. In discussing the relationship
between James and Q, attention also focused upon textual
similarities involving linguistic comparisons and certain
common conceptual approaches. This chapter aims at bringing together the examination already undertaken whereby
James and Q were shown to reflect both a common perception
of wisdom, and close textual similarities. It is especially in the
wisdom theme of perfection that James and Q^{Mt} show this
common perception of wisdom as well as certain textual similarities. This investigation adds further support to the hypothesis of a connection between James and the Q source as well as
its development within the Matthean community.

1. *The Call to Perfection (Jas 1.4; Mt. 5.48)*

While attention has already been devoted to a number of similarities between James and Q^{Mt}, one very noticeable parallel
between the two lies in the relationship between perfection,
suffering and eschatological glory. The Epistle of James operates as a call to enable steadfast endurance amidst trials and
sufferings to come to its full effect, namely the acquiring of
perfection. In all this James illustrates an eschatological direction and argues that perfection is really only attainable in the

eschatological age.[1] Jas 1.2-4 shows that this theme of the
testing of faith through suffering leads to perfection. This discussion aims to establish how the same connection is upheld in
the Q Sermon on the Mount as it is handed on in the Matthean
community.

James 1.4	Matthew 5.48
ἡ δὲ ὑπομονὴ ἔργον τέλειον ἐχέτω,	ἔσεσθε οὖν ὑμεῖς τέλειοι
ἵνα ἦτε τέλειοι καὶ ὁλόκληροι ἐν μηδενὶ λειπόμενοι.	ὡς ὁ πατὴρ ὑμῶν ὁ οὐράνιος τέλειός ἐστιν.

1.1 The context of the call to perfection in Matthew 5.48
In the original Q form of the sermon the four beatitudes were
immediately followed by sayings dealing with the command to
love one's enemies.[2] As has been indicated previously,[3] the
Matthean tradition separated these two entities by means of a
long discourse dealing with the antitheses related to the Jewish
law.[4] On the other hand the Lucan tradition inserted at this
point the fourfold woes as antitheses to the beatitudes. The final
beatitude shows a close harmony in thought and terminology
with the section on the love of one's enemies, which immediately followed it in the Q sermon. The original sequence in Q
was probably as follows:

> 'Blessed are you when men hate you, and when they exclude
> you...' (Q 6.22f.).
> 'But I say to you that hear, Love your enemies, do good to those
> who hate you...' (Q 6.27f.).

As argued previously,[5] Luke has followed more closely the
original sequence and terminology. Matthew, on the other
hand, has introduced changes which bring the section into

1. 'Der "Perfektionismus" des Jakobus ist ein eschatologischer!' (F.
Mussner, *Der Jakobusbrief: Auslegung* (4th edn; Freiburg: Herder,
1981], 67).
2. A. Polag, *Fragmenta Q: Textheft zur Logienquelle* (Neukirchen-
Vluyn: Neukirchener Verlag, 1979), 23, 32-34.
3. See Chapter 5, §2.2.1.
4. W.D. Davies, *The Setting of the Sermon on the Mount* (Cambridge:
Cambridge University Press, 1964), 301.
5. See Chapter 5, §2.2.1.

harmony with the beatitudes. In particular the agreements
are with features that are evident in the earliest strata of the
beatitudes, particularly the first two stages before the final
redaction of Matthew. This would favour the view that the
changes made to Q in this section (Mt. 5.44-48) took place
prior to the final redaction of Matthew. One such change that
has been observed is the reference in the final beatitude to persecution (διώξωσιν). This is absent from the Q source and the
form handed on in Luke. Mt. 5.44 introduces the verb
(διωκόντων) at the opening of the section dealing with love of
one's enemies and praying for those who persecute you,
whereas Lk. 6.28 makes the request to pray for those who
abuse you (ἐπηρεαζόντων). The same verb διώκω is used in Mt.
5.11 (in the future) and in Mt. 5.44 (participle).

The Matthean community believed that by showing love for
their enemies and for their persecutors they would be considered 'sons of [their] Father' (5.45). At the same time the
Matthean beatitude, 'Blessed are the peacemakers, for they
shall be called sons of God' (5.9), is brought into harmony with
this promise. The beatitude makes a direct connection to the
section on love of enemies through the reference to divine sonship.[1] In the beatitudes divine sonship is promised to those who
bring about peace, but in the command to love those who hate
one the same divine sonship is promised. Showing love for
one's enemies and persecutors is a concrete demonstration of
one's desire to bring about peace. In the context, the promise of
divine sonship is united closely to the theme introduced by the
beatitudes. Since the beatitude on the peacemakers belongs to
that group introduced into the wider context of the Matthean
community, it is plausible to accept these changes as having
occurred at the stage prior to the final redaction of Matthew.

The culmination of this section is expressed differently by
Matthew and Luke:

Γίνεσθε οἰκτίρμονες καθὼς (καὶ) ὁ πατὴρ ὑμῶν οἰκτίρμων ἐστίν (Lk.
6.36).
ἔσεσθε οὖν ὑμεῖς τέλειοι ὡς ὁ πατὴρ ὑμῶν ὁ οὐράνιος τέλειός ἐστιν
(Mt. 5.48).

---

1. R. Hoppe, *Der theologische Hintergrund des Jakobusbriefes*
(Würzburg: Echter, 1977), 134.

The positions these sayings presently hold in Matthew and Luke exercise decidedly different functions. In Matthew the sentence brings to an end the section of sayings, whereas in Luke it operates as a transition to another section dealing with judgment.[1] For Luke the disciple is called upon to imitate the mercy of God, whereas for Matthew the quality of perfection is all-important. In support of Luke's originality one can quote Fitzmyer's observation: 'Since Matthew uses *teleios* elsewhere (19:21), he may have redacted the "Q" saying; Luke never uses this adjective and has *oiktirmōn*, "merciful", only here'.[2] Hoppe[3] argues that the question is open as to whether the word τέλειος actually belongs to the work of the evangelist himself (that is, to the final stage of the redaction of the Sermon on the Mount) or whether it belongs to a change introduced into the wider tradition of the Q-source in the Matthean community. I have already argued[4] that this is certainly not the case. Contrary to Fitzmyer and Hoppe, it is my contention that the change from 'merciful' to 'perfect' took place in that intermediate stage when the Q beatitudes had developed further within the Matthean community (Q^Mt), but before the final stage of their redaction by the final author Matthew. I see the change as taking place at the same stage as when the original four beatitudes were expanded to incorporate a further four beatitudes. The construction of these further beatitudes took place on the basis of Q material being used from elsewhere. Noticeable among those beatitudes so constructed is one which specifically deals with the question of mercy: 'Blessed are the merciful, for they shall obtain mercy'.

In constructing such a beatitude, a change took place in the section on the love of enemies: the focus changed from that of the mercy of God to that of his perfection. God is the one to be imitated in so far as he is perfect. The context shows how this is to be understood. God pours out his blessings in an undivided way on good and evil alike: 'for he makes his sun rise on the

---

1. J.A. Fitzmyer, *The Gospel according to Luke (1–9): Introduction, Translation and Notes* (The Anchor Bible; Garden City: Doubleday, 2nd edn, 1983), 641.
2. *Ibid.*, 640.
3. Hoppe, *Der theologische Hintergrund*, 137.
4. See Chapter 5, §2.1.3.

evil and the good, and sends rain on the just and on the unjust' (Mt. 5.45). God shows his goodness towards all no matter how they themselves act with regard to him. The perfection that is referred to is a perfection with regard to a way of action[1] and in this sense God is totally undivided in his action with regard to humanity. Just as God is total in his love for humanity, so too the disciple is meant to be total and undivided in love for others. This incorporates love even for enemies, and in particular for those who persecute the disciple.[2] In this way Jesus is calling on his followers not to be content 'with half measures in respect of human relationships'.[3] Love of others must have its basis in love of God, and this love incorporates all, even those who persecute one.

This same interpretation of perfection is evident in Mt. 19.21 where the notion occurs again. 'Jesus said to him, "If you would be perfect, go, sell what you possess and give to the poor, and you will have treasure in heaven; and come, follow me".' Jesus calls upon the rich man to be total in his allegiance to God; he, however, shows that he is divided in his allegiance.[4] Although the call to perfection in Mt. 5.48 replaces the call to be merciful in Q, it is indeed representative of the fundamental teaching of Jesus, as seen in Mt. 19.21. At the same time this call unifies the theme that has developed in the Q^{Mt} Sermon on the Mount stressing the total allegiance to God which is demonstrated through love of all, even one's persecutors. The use of the term 'perfect' on both occasions in Matthew is quite consistent. The word denotes a total, undivided allegiance to God which demonstrates itself in a love for others which also knows no boundaries.[5] Mt. 5.48 becomes the climax of what has been said previously. Love of one's enemies makes a radical demand: it knows no limits and incorporates those who persecute others. As God's perfection entails his total love for

---

1. P.J. Du Plessis, 'ΤΕΛΕΙΟΣ: The Idea of Perfection in the New Testament' (Proefschrift ter verkrijging van de graad van Doctor in de Godgeleerdheid; Kampen: J.H. Kok, 1959), 171.
2. G. Delling, 'τέλειος', *TDNT*, VIII (1972), 74.
3. Du Plessis, 'ΤΕΛΕΙΟΣ', 170.
4. As Delling ('τέλειος', 74) says: '[T]o be undivided in relation to God includes detaching oneself from that which separates from God'.
5. Du Plessis, 'ΤΕΛΕΙΟΣ', 172-73.

humanity, so too the disciple's love must embrace all. This total love is observed especially in love toward one's persecutors.

1.2 *The context of the call to perfection in Jas 1.4*

Jas 1.2-4 presents a connection between persecution and perfection. In this section the theme of perfection emerges as the climax[1] since through testing and suffering one is led to patient endurance and finally brought to perfection. The purpose of the whole development has been ἵνα ἦτε τέλειοι καὶ ὁλόκληροι.

What does James actually understand by perfection? The concept τέλειος is quite important for him: the adjective τέλειος occurs twice in 1.4, as well as in 1.17, 1.25, and 3.2; the verb τελέω occurs in 2.8; and the verb τελειόω occurs in 2.22. Altogether this is more than in any other New Testament writing. In the LXX τέλειος usually translates the Hebrew words שָׁלֵם and תָּמִים which meant 'unblemished, undivided, complete, whole'.[2] τέλειος is generally connected with the noun καρδία, referring to the heart which is undivided in its loyalty and devotion to God.[3] The word also acquired an ethical dimension when it is used in Deut. 18.13 of the people whose lives serve God: τέλειος ἔσῃ ἐναντίον κυρίου.[4] The idea in the foreground of the Hebrew writings is that one gives one's heart to God in an unconditional way; that excludes completely any idolatry or devotion to other gods.[5]

---

1. See Chapter 3, §1.1.3.
2. Delling, 'τέλειος', 72.
3. *Ibid.*
4. *Ibid.*
5. In the Qumran Scrolls the use of the word תָּמִים is extremely common. 1QS uses the word תָּמִים eighteen times (P.H. Davids, *The Epistle of James: A Commentary on the Greek Text* [Exeter: Paternoster, 1982], 70). It is often used to refer to the path that the follower of the law pursues. One is only able to follow a blameless path if one follows the instructions of the community, which are inspired by the Torah. 1QS 8.17f. says that the person who is part of the community but does not walk in the 'fullness' of the path cannot take part 'in the fellowship of the pure' (Delling, 'τέλειος', 73). Consequently, to walk perfectly means simply for the adherents of Qumran that they abide by the fullness of the stipulations of the community. The contexts in which תָּמִים appears in the Qumran writings show clearly that the reference is to total ful-

In Jas 1.4 the meaning of τέλειος is 'total' or 'complete', meaning that the person who remains steadfast is total or complete because total allegiance is given to God. For James the meaning of τέλειος in 1.4 shows a twofold direction. First, it implies a total dedication to God, which is not undermined by trials and sufferings. Secondly, this total faith produces a style of life which is dedicated to a total action which demonstrates this allegiance.

Viewed in this context the thoughts of James and Matthew show very close connections. They both concern the situation of disciples facing trials and persecutions. Disciples are urged not to be deflected from their true purpose, namely that of total dedication and allegiance to God. This total adherence illustrates itself in a total work (James), a specific action which shows unconditional love (Matthew) for one's enemies, in particular for those who are one's persecutors.

1.3 The relationship between James and Q^{Mt} on the call to perfection through suffering
Perfection in the traditions of both James and Matthew's Sermon on the Mount is the main goal of the Christian life. In both traditions the same concept of perfection is operative and refers to that mode of action by which one gives total allegiance to God. This gives rise to a single-minded devotion to actions. The theme of suffering occurs as well in both traditions: despite the sufferings brought by trials and persecutions one does not deviate from the total commitment of showing love for God in action.

Do both traditions emanate from a common process of tradition or are they independent of each other? The similarity of the concept of perfection together with its connection to the thought of suffering and persecution leads one to argue for a connection in the two processes of tradition. For Hoppe[1] the evangelist Matthew was responsible for the introduction of the theme of the 'perfect' (τέλειος) into the Sermon on the Mount, by which he changed the meaning of the original Q source (as

filment of God's will, keeping all the rules of the community' (Delling, 'τέλειος', 73).
1. Hoppe, *Der theologische Hintergrund*, 137.

in Luke) to that of τέλειος. Contrary to this view, I have argued that it is more plausible that the change occurred within the context of the Matthean community itself at the same time as the original Q beatitudes underwent expansion. One beatitude to emerge was 'Blessed are the merciful...', which was based on the Q saying found in Lk. 6.36: 'Be merciful, even as your Father is merciful'. The change from 'Be merciful...' to 'Be perfect...' occurred at that stage when the beatitude of mercy was composed. This took place within the Matthean community in the course of its own reflection upon and transformation of the Q material.

The Epistle of James bears a very close relationship to this stage of the Q material. Once again the affinities between James and Q occur at that period when the Q tradition was developing within the context of the Matthean community. This was clearly evident in connection with the beatitudes and their relationship to James. Now, in the matter of the theme of perfection through suffering and persecution, both James and Q^{Mt} are seen to be very close. James commenced his writing by focusing upon the central idea of perfection which is illustrated when the disciple encounters suffering, trials and persecution. The same sequence appears in the Q^{Mt} Sermon on the Mount in which perfection is attained amidst persecution.

Also of marked significance for the traditions of James and Matthew is that they both illustrate the promise of reward for those who endure faithfully in the midst of suffering and persecution. Not only does it lead to perfection, but this perfection is attained in the future gift of eternal life. The wisdom and apocalyptic traditions speak about the 'crown of life' which is the reward of those who remain faithful under persecutions and trials. James (1.12-18) promises those who endure patiently in time of trial the reward of eternal life in the eschatological age. The same thought occurs in the final beatitude 'Rejoice and be glad, for *your reward is great in heaven*' (Mt. 5.12; Lk. 6.23). In this sense James and the Q^{Mt} beatitudes come very close. They show a common development of the wisdom theme of a reward of life for patient endurance under persecution. They transfer this hope from the present world order to the future life in the eschatological age to come.

James and Q^{Mt} belong to the same thought-world which handed on and reflected upon the Jesus tradition in a very similar way. Although it may not be possible to demonstrate a linguistic and verbal dependence of one text on the other, what the investigation does demonstrate is that the development of the Q tradition within the Matthean community is reflected as well in the Epistle of James. This similar and parallel way of expressing the same thoughts belongs to the period prior to the final redaction of the Gospel of Matthew.

2. *Perfection and the Law of Love*

James and Matthew are both concerned with the importance of illustrating faith by means of actions, by the works that one performs. 'Let your light so shine before men, that they may see your good works and give glory to your Father who is in heaven' (Mt. 5.16). This leads Matthew on to speak about the necessity of fulfilling all the stipulations of the law (Mt. 5.17-20). At the same time one of the major themes of the Epistle of James is that one must not simply be a hearer of the word, but a doer as well: 'But be doers of the word, and not hearers only, deceiving yourselves' (Jas 1.22). The law in this context is 'the perfect law, the law of liberty' (1.25), which is referred to elsewhere as the 'royal law' (2.8), the 'law of love' (2.8).

Both James and Matthew urge the necessity of carrying out the full stipulations of the law: 'For whoever keeps the whole law but fails in one point has become guilty of all of it' (Jas 2.10). In a somewhat similar vein Matthew has 'For truly, I say to you, till heaven and earth pass away, not an iota, not a dot, will pass from the law until all is accomplished' (Mt. 5.18).

2.1 *The development of Matthew 5.17-19*
The origin of this Q saying, as well as James's relationship to it, has already been investigated.[1] Polag[2] has illustrated how the Q text of Mt. 5.18 was developed by Mt. 5.19 and that the latter belongs to 'texts possibly pertaining to Q'. The importance of this observation lies in suggesting that the command to keep

---

1. See Chapter 6, §1.4.
2. Polag, *Fragmenta Q*, 86-87.

the entire law was handed on in the beginning with some form of explanation. The text of Mt. 5.17-19 has undergone a complicated development around Mt. 5.18 which is the core of this passage. The saying comes from Q and the Gospel of Luke (16.17) also demonstrates a knowledge of the saying. A further expansion of this saying occurred within the Q community, as Polag argued, finding its way also into the Matthean community (Mt. 5.19). Finally, the evangelist Matthew was responsible for v. 17 which unified the whole section.[1] Even though the final construction appears as that of the evangelist, the ideas are rooted in tradition history within the framework of the Matthean community. The whole passage Mt. 5.17-19 reflects a development from Q by way of expansion and achieves finally a redaction at the hand of the evangelist Matthew. The thought corresponds in essence to that of the Palestinian Jewish-Christian Church in which the emphasis is placed upon the fulfilment of the law. Every disciple is called upon to do and to fulfil the law in the way in which Jesus himself carried it out. The promise of beatitude and reward in the future kingdom of heaven (Mt. 5.19) depends upon the way in which the disciple has imitated Jesus and has endeavoured to fulfil the law in the sense that the disciple has done the whole law.

2.2. *Perfection comes through the law of love*
Mt. 5.19 and Jas 2.10 show a common thought process[2] in that they are concerned with putting the law into practice, and carrying it out fully in one's actions. Mt. 5.19 considers the relaxation of the law in its least important commandment as a non-observance of the law in its totality. Jas 2.10 equates breaking the law in one point with breaking the entire law. The thought in both traditions amounts to exactly the same thing: the entire law in all its parts is to be fulfilled. Since Mt. 5.19 has been shown to belong to Q^{Mt}, the connection between these traditions of Matthew and James must belong to that period of time. James has taken Q^{Mt}, used it and applied it

---

1. Hoppe, *Der theologische Hintergrund*, 126.
2. Both these texts have been examined in relationship to each other (see Chapter 6, §1.4).

within his own context. The specification of the law as the law of love is not something unique to the Epistle of James, but is basic to almost all the streams of tradition emanating from the person of Jesus. Found many times in the synoptic Gospels, it is also in evidence in the Pauline (Rom. 13.9) as well as Johannine theology. Here, again, James shows himself to be at home in the heart of the Jesus tradition.

The Q^{Mt} tradition makes a connection between the fulfilment of the law in all its essentials and the fact that Jesus himself has fulfilled the law. The Epistle of James forges a similar connection with the person of Jesus. With reference to fulfilling the law of love, James instructs his readers to show no distinctions (2.9) for this goes against the very essence of the law of love. James initiated this section (2.1) with a call to his readers to show no partiality for that would be contrary to their faith in Jesus Christ (2.1). In this way the fulfilment of the law of love is connected with the person of Jesus who is the reference point in both traditions for the way in which all law is interpreted.[1] The law of love in both traditions receives its direction and meaning through the influence of the person of Jesus.

The traditions of James and Q^{Mt} both see the fulfilment of the law as a path to perfection. They show themselves to be within the framework of the wisdom tradition in which law, perfection, wisdom all come together.[2] The theological horizons of the traditions of wisdom, James and Q^{Mt} blend together in their perception of the fulfilment of the law as the path to perfection. Once again the position of James has been illustrated in its relationship to the Q tradition and wisdom not simply by its linguistic usages, but more specifically through its theological concepts. At the same time James has developed both the wisdom and Q traditions by identifying the law that is referred to as the law of love. The law is the path to follow in acquiring

1. As Hoppe (*Der theologische Hintergrund*, 129) notes.
2. For example, the Book of Wisdom shows how perfection comes through the carrying out of laws which have been inspired by wisdom (Wis. 6.5-10; 6.18-20). The law comes from God and as such it is perfect, while its observance leads to wisdom. In a similar vein the traditions of Matthew and James also emphasize that the law comes from Jesus and its observance is the path one is to follow in attaining perfection.

wisdom and perfection, but the law that James has in mind is
the law of love which in all the synoptic traditions (cf. Mt.
22.34-40) is presented as the basis for all law. James argues
that it is in the fulfilment of the law of love, the true law of liberty, that perfection is attained.

3. Perfection Comes through the Gift of God's Wisdom

A further theological connection to be investigated in the traditions of James and Q is the theme of perfection which comes
through the wisdom given by God. This divine wisdom is in
direct opposition to all human efforts geared towards the
attainment of human wisdom. Attention is given to the connection between this thought as expressed in James and in the
synoptic Jesus tradition of Q^{Mt}.

3.1 *The wisdom from above (Mt. 11.25-27; Lk. 10.21-22; Jas 3.13-18)*

In Q (Lk. 10.21-22; Mt. 11.25-27)[1] wisdom is first communicated to Jesus, who in turn communicates it to the νήπιοι. Two
meanings are evident in this use of νήπιοι:[2] on one level the
νήπιοι are those who are weak in the eyes of the world. On the
other level it refers to those to whom God shows a special care,
to whom his revelation and his wisdom are communicated. By
a free choice on the part of the Son this communication is
made to them. These νήπιοι are those who are the truly wise
because they have been chosen by God as the bearers of his
revelation.

This choice of those who are νήπιοι according to human
standards is identical with the choice of those who are poor,
according to human standards. To such a choice Jas 2.5 refers:

1. Previously, the Q form of this text was examined (see Chapter 4, §4)
in illustrating the nature of wisdom and the different perspectives evident in Q, Matthew and Luke.
2. 'In the LXX, then, νήπιος bears a twofold sense. On the one hand it
denotes the weak and innocent child who is helplessly implicated in
the world's misfortune. On the other hand it denotes the righteous who
are simply as the world sees it. The two meanings flow together in the
emphatic use of the word in the Gospel of Jesus' (G. Bertram, 'νήπιος',
TDNT, IV [1967], 917).

'Listen, my beloved brethren. Has not God chosen those who are poor in the world to be rich in faith and heirs of the kingdom which he has promised to those who love him?' In this sense the poor belong to the group who are despised by the world (just as the νήπιοι are despised by the world). The νήπιοι are the same as the πτωχοί to whom James makes the promise of a kingdom, as do Matthew and Luke in the beatitudes. God shows a special concern for those who are despised and rejected by society, whether they are the simple children or the poor.

3.2 *The development of this saying within the Matthean community (Mt. 11.28-30)*

3.2.1 *The person of Jesus and wisdom*
The Gospel of Matthew contains a further saying connected to the above which is not found in Luke, and hence does not belong to the Q source. This addition is of great significance for it shows how Jesus' relationship to wisdom is transformed in the Gospel of Matthew. The previous passage in Q saw Jesus exercising a privileged position with regard to wisdom. He was wisdom's envoy entrusted with the unique task of communicating that wisdom to others, to the νήπιοι. Now Jesus speaks in the manner of wisdom herself. This is quite familiar in the wisdom writings such as Sir. 51.26-27, which seems to lie behind its usage here. The saying, taken from the mouth of wisdom, is used by Jesus to speak in the manner of wisdom incarnate.[1] It is a clear development of the thought contained in Q (and Luke) where Jesus remains in the role of the revealer of wisdom. In the context of Matthew this passage presents the Son as identified with wisdom. This development took place over time within the confines of the Matthean community.

3.2.2 ὅτι πραΰς εἰμι *(Mt. 11.29)*
Jesus speaks as wisdom personified and in doing so characterizes himself as gentle or meek. The word πραΰς in the beatitudes of Matthew (5.5) in fact is a parallel term for πτωχός.

---

1. See Chapter 4, §4 where this was investigated.

Both Greek terms translate the Hebrew words עָנָו and עָנִי,[1] which refer to those who are rejected by the world. By designating himself by this term, Jesus shows his solidarity with this group of people. As wisdom incarnate he still belongs to the group of those who are weak, poor and looked down upon by society.

In the Gospels the term πραΰς only occurs in Matthew (three times, in 5.5; 11.29; 21.5),[2] which shows that it is a term popular with the Matthean community. In James it occurs twice, in 1.21 and 3.13. Terminology that is not common in the New Testament is found to be quite noticeably common in the Matthean tradition and James. In 3.13 James says: 'By his good life let him show his works in the meekness of wisdom'. Here the disciple is called upon to show signs of being 'meek' (πραΰς) in life; meekness is a virtue which is inspired by the wisdom from above. As wisdom incarnate Jesus is the truly meek person who calls his followers to meekness (Mt. 11.28-30). In both traditions one is dealing with an association between wisdom and meekness. This lends support to the view that both traditions emerge from a similar worldview and similar traditions.

3.2.3 ἄρατε τὸν ζυγόν μου ἐφ' ὑμᾶς *(Mt. 11.29)*

Sir. 51.26-27 refers to the yoke (ζυγός) in the sense of the Law, the Torah. As has been indicated, this passage lies behind Mt. 11.28-30. As wisdom incarnate, Jesus is making a further identification between the Torah and himself: he is the Torah by which his followers must abide. Jesus is not proposing an alternative law, but he is asking his followers to put the law into practice in their lives.[3] In like manner Jas 3.13 calls upon the person who has received the wisdom from above to show wisdom by the type of life that is led (δειξάτω ἐκ τῆς καλῆς ἀναστροφῆς τὰ ἔργα αὐτοῦ...). Once again the association of ideas connecting wisdom with a way of life illustrates the same thought-world. Together with the other illustrations given it

---

1. F. Hauck & S. Schulz, 'πραΰς', *TDNT*, VI (1968), 647; and E. Bammel, 'πτωχός', *TDNT*, VI (1968), 888.

2. Hauck & Schulz, 'πραΰς', 649.

3. Suggs, *Wisdom*, 106.

shows that the traditions of Matthew and James are very close.

3.2.4 καὶ εὑρήσετε ἀνάπαυσιν ταῖς ψυχαῖς ὑμῶν *(Mt. 11.29)*

Jesus gives a promise to those who turn to him as the source of wisdom and meekness, and follow his law in their lives. This promise entails the eschatological hope that they 'will find rest for their souls'. An examination of Jas 3.17[1] showed that the gift of wisdom from above brought with it many virtues. In particular it brought about a transformation of the life of the recipient. The same idea was expressed earlier in that the receiver was reborn by the word of truth (1.18) and the implanted word (1.21). The wisdom from above brings with it two important results: a rebirth to a life of salvation and to a moral ethical way of life. Jas 3.18 emphasizes the first of these consequences, namely the rebirth to a life of salvation where the promise is made of 'a harvest of righteousness'. The greatest result that this wisdom from above brings is the promise of the eschatological gift of righteousness. In the receiver the wisdom from above works rebirth and that in turn is illustrated through action. The traditions of Matthew and James each in its own way offer a similar promise. The eschatological gifts of 'rest' (Matthew) or 'rebirth and righteousness' (James) are given to those who receive the wisdom from above. Consequently, perfection is a possibility which comes from the gift of God's wisdom and is not attained independently by one's own efforts.

3.3 *Mt. 11.25-30 and Jas 3.13-18 betray evidence of coming from a common tradition*

A comparison of Mt. 11.25-30 and Jas 3.13-18 has illustrated the similarities in the thought-world of both traditions. The argument is not for the actual textual dependence of James upon Matthew or vice versa; this cannot be demonstrated. What, however, we have shown is that the similarities between the two traditions rest upon the same thought-world and that indicates a common development and common emphasis.

---

1. See Chapter 3, §3.3.

Both traditions lay emphasis upon wisdom, which is the greatest gift of God. The receivers of this wisdom are those who are despised by society: the νήπιοι (Matthew) or the πτωχοί (James). The role which Jesus plays in relation to wisdom receives a different emphasis in Matthew and James. In fact the reflection upon this relationship shows that Matthew and James lie in the same line of development, as has been argued previously. In the different traditions Jesus is presented as:

REVEALER OF WISDOM	ESCHATOLOGICAL WISDOM	WISDOM INCARNATE
(Q)	(JAMES)	(MATTHEW)

4. The Ethical Lifestyle of the One Seeking Perfection

The entire Epistle of James is concerned with offering advice to the reader on how best to lead a Christian life. An examination of Jas 3.17 has shown that the gift of wisdom from above has certain ethical consequences for the way of life of the receiver. 'But the wisdom from above is first pure, then peaceable, gentle, open to reason, full of mercy and good fruits, without uncertainty or insincerity.' Four of these adjectives, namely, pure, peaceable, gentle and full of mercy correspond in thought to the beatitudes, particularly those which developed into Q^{Mt}.

	Matthean Community Beatitudes		James 3.17
MEEK	μακάριοι οἱ πραεῖς...	(5.5)	ἐπιεικής
MERCIFUL	μακάριοι οἱ ἐλεήμονες...	(5.7)	ἐλέους
PURE	μακάριοι οἱ καθαροὶ τῇ καρδίᾳ...	(5.8)	ἁγνή
PEACEMAKERS	μακάριοι οἱ εἰρηνοποιοί...	(5.9)	εἰρηνική

Although the words used do differ, the same basic thought underlies these beatitudes and the virtues produced by wisdom in James. In the Q^{Mt} beatitudes the emphasis is placed upon the values and virtues which a follower of Jesus is to implement in life in order to inherit the kingdom and be 'a son of God'. James emphasizes that these are the virtues and values which will be exercised by the one who has received the gift of wisdom from above. In both traditions the same ethical way of life is stressed. In the Christian way of life perfection is to be aimed at, but it can only be achieved through God's help, through the communication of His wisdom.

The practical wisdom teaching of both James and Q centres upon the view that faith must be illustrated by means of actions. James shows that faith has to be imbued with the wisdom from above if it is to be expressed correctly in action. Wisdom holds faith and action together and produces a faith that saves (2.14). Perfection is the goal of a life of faith that illustrates itself in action. In this James is again very close to the teaching of the Sermon on the Mount whose aim is to outline the type of life that the disciple is to lead. In the original Q Sermon there was a simple saying which expressed this basic teaching: 'Why do you call me "Lord, Lord", and not do what I tell you?' (Q 6.46; Mt. 7.21). While Luke and Matthew do differ in their actual presentation of this saying, the important thing is the thought to which they both bear witness. A profession of faith in God with one's lips is not sufficient. This faith must be demonstrated by a lifestyle led in conformity with God's will. James and Q unite in upholding the central tenet of wisdom teaching: all wisdom's practical advice has aimed at providing directions for a lifestyle that aims at perfection. Although perfection is only fully attainable in the age to come, it is something for which one constantly strives in all that one does. At the same time these thoughts must be kept in harmony with what has been said before, namely that wisdom itself is a gift which comes from God and enables the believer to lead the life that God wants.

5. Conclusion

The Jesus traditions evident in Q and the development of Q within the Matthean community form the basis for all James's instructions. Throughout the entire epistle these sayings are in James's mind and he uses them in many different ways to communicate his teaching. The epistle is permeated by the thought and sayings of Jesus—more so than any other

New Testament writing outside the Gospels, as Kittel[1] has noted.

A question has been raised in this connection: If James is so steeped in the Jesus tradition and is imbued with the words of the Lord, why did he not quote these words directly? Kittel[2] has, I suggest, provided an answer which indeed solves this problem. In his investigations he has shown that in the beginning the attitude adopted to the words of the Lord was not to treat them as though they had been 'written' and to quote them as words of the Lord. Instead, as examples from the writings of Paul as well as the first part of the *Didache* show, the early preaching and teaching was actually steeped in the teachings of the Lord. They imbibed this teaching totally and used it in their writings without expressly quoting it as the words of Jesus. James operates in much the same way. The words of the Lord permeate his entire writing; in fact the writing breathes the sayings of the Lord without actually quoting them.[3]

This again points to the early nature of the Epistle of James. It belongs to that period of time when the early community was steeped in the tradition of the words of Jesus, but prior to the period in which it was necessary to treat them as γραφή, which occurred in the period of the written Gospels. From many different directions one sees everything pointing towards the same focus of viewing James as an early writing which is steeped in the tradition of the words of the Lord reflected in Q, as well as their development within the Matthean community. All this occurred prior to the actual composition of the Gospel of Matthew.

The awareness which James has of the Jesus tradition in the different developments of the Q sayings is extremely impor-

1. G. Kittel, 'Der geschichtliche Ort des Jakobusbriefes', *ZNW* 41 (1942), 84.
2. *Ibid.*, 91-94.
3. As Kittel ('Der geschichtliche Ort', 94) concludes: 'Sind aber diese Beobachtungen und Erwägungen richtig, dann wäre weiter zu fragen, ob nicht vielleicht unser Jakobusbrief ein besonders anschauliches und echtes Beispiel dieser frühen Form sein könnte, wie die Menschen der Apostolischen Zeit in und mit dem lebten, was sie von ihrem Herrn empfangen hatten'.

tant because it means that with the emergence of the New Testament writings the witness to the oral tradition did not cease. Once Q was put in writing it continued to develop in different centres such as those around Luke and Matthew. Ultimately, the development it underwent in the Matthean community had an influence on the Epistle of James. The implications of this perspective will be drawn out in the next chapter which will attempt to situate James within the context of the early Christian Church, both chronologically and geographically.

PART III

RECONSTRUCTION

Chapter 8

A VISION OF THE EMERGENCE OF JAMES WITHIN THE
EARLY CHRISTIAN COMMUNITY

This examination of James's relationship to the early Christian traditions concludes with an attempt to situate the epistle
within the context of the early Christian community both
chronologically and geographically. The aim is to construct a
working hypothesis by which one brings the available evidence
into a unified perspective. Much of what is presented remains
of necessity conjectural for the information is rather limited.
This perspective is constructed by means of drawing together
recent research that has focused attention on the early Christian churches and the insights drawn from the investigation
in this study into the relationship between James and Q. A
picture of the Q community will first of all be sketched and
from this a concept of the Matthean community will emerge.
Finally, the situation of the Epistle of James will be discussed in
order to harmonize this setting with what is known about the
churches of Q and Matthew.

1. *The Q Community*

The sayings which belong to the Q-source owe their origin and
preservation to a specific environment. For their preservation
it is necessary to postulate people who proclaimed them, as
well as people who heard them. The origin of the community
responsible for handing on the Q material is to be traced back
to the historical ministry of Jesus with its proclamation to
repent and believe in the kingdom of God.[1] The Q community

1. H. Schürmann, 'Die vorösterlichen Anfänge der Logientradition:
Versuch eines formgeschichtlichen Zugangs zum Leben Jesu', *Der*

arose, not after the death and resurrection of Jesus, but rather
during his actual ministry when he sent out his followers to
preach his message on the kingdom (Lk. 10.1). Since no names
of the actual disciples of Jesus occur in Q, this group is probably
distinct from the Twelve.[1] The death and resurrection of Jesus
undoubtedly influenced these preachers to expect the return of
the apocalyptic Son of man at the end of time because this hope
became an important feature of their proclamation.

Galilee was the area where the historical Jesus exercised
most of his preaching ministry, so it is logical to presume that
it was here that the origin of the Q community is to be located.
Havener[2] offers three rather important arguments for cen-
tering the activity of the Q community and its proclamation in
Galilee, northern Palestine and western Syria. First, a large
amount of Christian tradition is in evidence in Syria and Antioch associated with the traditions around the Gospel of
Matthew. This would account for the knowledge Matthew
has of Q because it emanates from the same region and vicin-
ity.

Secondly, Luke demonstrates contact with Antioch[3] because
his work, the Acts of the Apostles, shows knowledge of many
Antiochene traditions. Probably Luke was familiar with the Q
source as a consequence of his association with Antioch and he
would have taken it with him to Achaia where tradition has
him writing his Gospel.[4] Here this tradition could develop in its
own right, while the Q tradition at Antioch would undergo a

---

historische Jesus und der kerygmatische Christus (ed. H. Ristow and
K. Matthiae: Berlin: Evangelische Verlagsanstalt, 3rd edn, 1964), 193-
210.

1. I. Havener, *Q: The Sayings of Jesus: With a Reconstruction of Q by
Athanasius Polag* (Wilmington: Michael Glazier, 1987), 42.

2. *Ibid.*, 43.

3. The earliest testimony to the authorship of the Gospel of Luke is
from the anti-Marcionite prologue: 'Luke is a Syrian of Antioch, a doctor by profession, who was a disciple of the apostles, and later followed
Paul until his martyrdom' (J.L. Price, *Interpreting the New Testament* [New York: Holt, Rinehart & Winston, 1971], 100). By associating
Luke with Antioch, this tradition supports the view that Luke was
familiar with the traditions circulating in Antioch, among them the Q
tradition.

4. *Ibid.*, 225.

development of its own within the Matthean tradition. To my
mind this would explain why the order of Q^{Lk} is probably more
faithful to the original Q than that of Q^{Mt}. Luke is the historian
who, according to his prologue, has investigated many sources.
The Q source, which he had earlier accepted from Antioch,
would have undergone less change in his hands than it did in
the community of Matthew where it continued to grow and
develop. Thirdly, in eastern Syria traditions developed around
the person of Thomas[1] such as the *Gospel of Thomas*, itself a
sayings collection. Some of the L material is similar to that
contained in the *Gospel of Thomas*.[2] This shows Luke's
awareness of traditions belonging to eastern Syria.

In an important study on the nature of oral transmission
Kelber[3] has used the insights gained from studies on the relationship between orality and textuality[4] to show the orality
inherent in the Q community's transmission of the sayings of
Jesus. He has combined this with research done by Boring[5]
and Theissen[6] to give some insight into the social context out of
which the Q community developed. It is to these studies that
this presentation is indebted.

The earliest of the Q sayings originated in the ministry of the
historical Jesus and those destined to be remembered were the
ones that affected the lives of their audience.[7] Kelber[8] has
noted that that the preservation and handing on of oral words
does not occur passively, but depends to a large extent on 'their

---

1. H. Koester, 'Gnomai Diaphoroi: The Origin and Nature of Diversification in the History of Early Christianity', *Trajectories through
Early Christianity* (ed. J.M. Robinson & H. Koester; Philadelphia:
Fortress, 1971), 127-36.
2. Havener, *Q: The Sayings of Jesus*, 44-45.
3. W. Kelber, *The Oral and Written Gospel: The Hermeneutics of
Speaking and Writing in the Synoptic Tradition, Mark, Paul and Q*
(Philadelphia: Fortress, 1983).
4. Such as W.J. Ong, *Orality and Literacy: The Technologizing of the
Word* (New York: Methuen, 1982).
5. M.E. Boring, *Sayings of the Risen Jesus: Christian Prophecy in the
Synoptic Tradition* (Cambridge: Cambridge University Press, 1982).
6. G. Theissen, *Sociology of Early Palestinian Christianity* (Philadelphia: Fortress, 1978).
7. Havener, *Q: The Sayings of Jesus*, 91.
8. Kelber, *The Oral and Written Gospel*, 24.

social relevancy and acceptability'. He terms this 'the law of social identification' of the hearers with the message.[1]

A number of sayings within Q concern antisocial behaviour and most of these occur in the block of Q tradition referred to by Polag as 'Mission of the Disciples' (Q 9.57–10.24).[2] These sayings call into question basic values such as the importance of family life and the ownership of possessions; in their place they advocate 'hatred' for members of one's family (Q 14.26), as well as homelessness (Q 9.57-60). The follower of Jesus is also instructed: 'Carry no purse, no bag, no sandals; and salute no one on the road' (Q 10.4). Clearly, the picture that emerges is that of a group of people wandering from place to place, who have no money since they do not carry a purse, and who have no extra clothes since they carry no bag with them.

According to Kelber's 'law of social identification',[3] the members of the Q community preserved these sayings because they in fact mirrored their existence, style of life and outlook on the world. They were a group of people who lived 'as outsiders'[4] and had embraced the wandering style of life reminiscent of the very life of Jesus himself. In doing so, they also took to heart the sayings of Jesus on a life entailing homelessness, rejection of family ties, poverty and a vagrant lifestyle.[5] Consequently, those who handed on these sayings were characterized as wandering prophets or charismatics 'who considered themselves the loyal followers of Jesus'.[6] In this manner they so identified themselves with Jesus that they regarded him as speaking through their own voices. 'He who hears you hears me, and he who rejects you rejects me, and he who rejects me rejects him who sent me' (Q 10.16). In this sense, no clear distinction is drawn between the earthly Jesus and the Risen Lord speaking through them.

Jesus was situated within the long line of the prophets of Israel whose lot it was to endure suffering for the message that

---

1. *Ibid.*
2. A. Polag, *Fragmenta Q: Textheft zur Logienquelle* (Neukirchen-Vluyn: Neukirchener Verlag, 1979), 24.
3. Kelber, *The Oral and Written Gospel*, 24.
4. Theissen, *Sociology of Early Palestinian Christianity*, 15.
5. *Ibid.*, 10-16.
6. Kelber, *The Oral and Written Gospel*, 24.

they proclaimed. As all prophets are destined to suffer, the Q
prophets envisaged sharing in the same lot (Q 6.22-23). The Q
prophets were convinced that the Risen Lord was speaking
through them and they awaited with keen expectation his
return at the end of time, which they considered to be imminent.

The Q proclamation tended to undergo both development
and transformation. These factors witness to a message that
was vital, and not something static and passive. At first the
message was directed to a Jewish audience who rejected it.
Then its proclaimers turned to the Gentiles. This accounts for
many of the sayings which praise the faith of the Gentiles. The
parable of the banquet is a good illustration of this change from
the Jews to the Gentiles: those originally invited to the wedding
reject the invitation, so people from the highways and byways
are invited in their place (Q 14.16-24). This mission to the
Gentiles was different from the Pauline mission to the Gentiles. Throughout its existence the Q community was a group
of Christian Jews, who still adhered to the practices of Judaism. As Havener states: '[T]herefore, for a Gentile convert to
become a member of the Q community probably meant
becoming, in effect, a Christian-Jew, following the Jewish law
and customs like the rest of the community. It is precisely this
kind of Gentile mission that Paul was adamantly opposed to
but one which the Q community could hardly have conceived
of in any other way.'[1]

So far, reference has been made to a Q community; but such
terminology actually runs counter to the 'anti-social' tendencies characterizing the Q prophets. Community is quite contrary to the lifestyle outlined above of such wandering, charis-
matic prophets. Other forces were at work enabling the emergence of such a community. Kelber[2] notes that 'Experience
teaches us that one can well remember and reproduce information without living out its content in one's personal life. By
the same token, members of the more settled classes could
identify with these sayings as a matter of principle, and still
not apply them in actuality.' This would give rise to hearers

---

1. Havener, *Q: The Sayings of Jesus,* 103.
2. Kelber, *The Oral and Written Gospel,* 25.

who would accept the Q prophets' message and sayings without actually changing their lifestyles, but remaining members
of the settled classes.

One can imagine the emergence of the written composition
of Q from such a settled audience. From this point onwards I
part company with Kelber. He attributes the passage from
orality to textuality within the early Christian community to
Mark.[1] In arguing in this way, Kelber has glossed over the
significant passage within the Q tradition from orality to textuality. That Q did not exist solely as an oral tradition, but had
passed from orality into textuality has been discussed previously.[2] When Q was put into writing, the oral traditions did not
cease to exist: they continued side by side and enabled the
written Q source to undergo different stages of development,
thus showing that Q did not remain a static entity.

In writing about the passage from orality to textuality in the
Gospel tradition with particular reference to Mark, Kelber[3]
has tended to overemphasize the new dimension that is introduced in this transition. 'The text, while asserting itself out of
dominant oral traditions and activities, has brought about a
freezing of oral life into textual still life. In short, the oral
legacy has been transplanted into a linguistic construct that
has lost touch with the living, oral matrix.'[4] The insights of
Kelber may be true with regard to the Gospel of Mark, but
they certainly do not apply to Q in its emergence as a written
source. Q retained contact with its oral source, which continued to have an influence on it. Within the communities of
Matthew and Luke, the form of Q also tended to undergo
development through the influence of other oral traditions,
thus producing Q^{Mt} and Q^{Lk} within the respective communities before they became part of the Gospels of Matthew and
Luke.

---

1. As Kelber (*The Oral and Written Gospel*, 95) says: 'If, in other
words, the thesis of predominant synoptic orality is valid, then Mark,
the writer of the text, must have had to assume a critical viewpoint
over and even against his oral heritage'.
2. See Chapter 2, §1.
3. Kelber, *The Oral and Written Gospel*, 90-131.
4. *Ibid.*, 91.

As a written document Q appeared originally in Greek, but behind it lay Aramaic origins going back to the preaching of Jesus and the Q prophets.[1] With the location of the proclamation of the Q prophets being in the Galilee region, northern Palestine and western Syria, and with this proclamation directed no longer to Jews but to Gentiles, the use of Greek would have become a natural phenomenon within the Q community. This is the place of origin for the emergence of the written Q source. Although an exact date is difficult to determine, a date around 50 AD would seem to be the most accept-

1. Since the time of Schleiermacher the view that Q was originally written in Aramaic has consistently found its supporters (P. Vassiliadis, 'The Nature and Extent of the Q-Document', *NT* 20 [1978], 55). For example, T.W. Manson ('Some Outstanding New Testament Problems. XII. The Problem of Aramaic Sources in the Gospels', *ET* 47 [1935/36], 10) championed the Aramaic nature of Q: 'The only case in which one can feel fairly confident that a written Aramaic source lies behind the Gospels is that of the document Q'. F. Bussby, writing in a later volume of the *Expository Times* ('Is Q an Aramaic Document?', 65 [1953/54], 272-75), proceeded to illustrate this point on the basis chiefly of the names that appear in Q. Above all M. Black (*An Aramaic Approach to the Gospels and Acts* [3rd edn; Oxford: Clarendon, 1967], 191) became a forceful supporter of the Aramaic elements of the Gospels.

N. Turner ('Q in Recent Thought', *ET* 80 [1968/69], 324-28) has given a detailed analysis of the hypothesis that Q was originally written in Aramaic. For him the strongest argument in favour of an Aramaic original would be if one could provide indications of mistranslations into Greek from the Gospels of Matthew and Luke (p. 326). Turner, however, finds little evidence of this. In fact, an examination of the language of Q shows it to be greatly different from the typical language of a translation. '[T]he characteristically free Greek μὲν ... δέ construction (unusual in translated books) occurs relatively often in Q: Mt. 9.37; 10.13; 13.22; 16.3; (22.5, 8); 23.27, 28; (25.15). Another instance of idiomatic free Greek is the frequent occurrence of the genitive absolute' (p. 326). All the elements of the style of non-translational Greek are present in Q, according to Turner (p. 326). For example: (i) the use of coordinating participles in the second position in a clause, (ii) the word order sequence of subject–object–verb, (iii) the infrequent use of καί, and δέ betrays good Greek style, (iv) the insertion of other words between the noun and the article. From this examination Turner rightly concludes: 'So far, all the indications are against the translation hypothesis. The language of Q is typical of the Biblical Greek which has no Semitic Vorlage' (p. 327).

able period for the written Q source to emerge and that would make it one of the first Christian writings to appear.

2. *The Matthean Community*

2.1 *Different groups of Jewish-Gentile Christianity*
A very interesting discussion on the church of Antioch is presented by Meier[1] in *Antioch and Rome*, to which attention will be given here. In the introduction to this work Brown[2] gives a very useful overview of the different Jewish-Christian/Gentile groups within the early Christian communities. Although the distinctions he makes may be oversimplified, they show that the approach to the admission of Gentiles into the early church differed greatly. In general four main groups can be distinguished which evince clear differences from one another.

(a) Group One[3] would comprise Jewish Christians together with Gentiles who had been converted to Christianity. They continued to abide by all the stipulations of the Jewish law and demanded circumcision for the Gentile converts. Originally some Jewish Christians in Jerusalem would have belonged to this group, which Acts refers to as 'the circumcision party' (Acts 11.2). Without doubt this group had also embarked on missionary activity among the Gentiles, which brought it into sharp conflict with Paul. The letter to the Galatians shows Paul combatted the influences they were having among his own converts. Phil. 3.2 also shows Paul's fear that this group might unsettle his most loyal church.[4] I would argue that the Q community originally belonged to this particular group because the mission of Q prophets to the Gentiles was of the type which envisaged the Gentile becoming a Christian Jew.

1. J.P. Meier, 'Antioch', in R.E. Brown and J.P. Meier, *Antioch and Rome* (New York: Paulist, 1983), 11-86.
2. R.E. Brown, 'Introduction', in R.E. Brown & J.P. Meier, *Antioch and Rome* (New York: Paulist, 1983), 1-9.
3. For what occurs here and in what follows I am reliant upon the views of Brown ('Introduction', 1-9).
4. As Brown ('Introduction', 3) says: 'Therefore, we must speak of *a mission* to the Gentiles that was quite antagonistic to Paul and resulted in the existence of a Jewish/Gentile Christianity of the strictest Law observance, not only in Palestine but in some of the cities of Asia Minor and Greece at least'.

This was the only way in which the Q community could perceive things. With the passage of time the Q-source was adopted by the communities of Matthew and Luke who used it according to their respective outlooks on the relationship of Gentile Christians to the Jewish law. Consequently, Q would soon transcend the narrow confines of this group.

(b) Group Two represents a more moderate approach. Circumcision was not required of those Gentiles embracing Christianity; but certain Jewish practices were still demanded. Acts 15.20 contains the decision of the Council of Jerusalem (AD 49)[1] which presents the mediating view expressed by James, namely that Gentile converts still had to observe certain food laws. This type of Jewish-Gentile Christianity also had a missionary dimension in that James sent out a letter after the Council of Jerusalem outlining the decision (Acts 15.23). At the same time 'certain men came from James' (Gal. 2.12) to Antioch and caused a great dissension within the community. They criticized Peter for eating with Gentiles, which implied that Peter was not abiding by the dietary laws. Peter accepted their position under duress (Gal. 2.12). To this type of Jewish-Gentile Christianity James and Peter would belong. It liberated the Christians from the necessity of circumcision, yet it upheld certain practices belonging to Judaism.

(c) Group Three is that group championed by the views of Paul. Neither circumcision nor any Jewish dietary laws were demanded for converts from the Gentiles. This was probably the most widespread Jewish-Gentile Christianity in the early communities.

(d) Group Four is a more radical group than Paul's. Not only did they reject circumcision and the Jewish food laws (as Paul did), but they also saw no relevance or meaning in the Jewish worship and festivals. Among these one may count the

---

1. Although numerous arguments surround the exact relationship between the Council of Jerusalem and Paul's information in Galatians and although it is difficult to harmonize these positions, I follow the position adopted by Brown and Meier (*Antioch and Rome*). To my mind their conciliatory picture does the best justice to the facts at hand.

Hellenists of Acts 6.1-6.[1] The traditions of the beloved disciple in the Gospel of John are also in line with this more radical approach whereby the feasts of the Jews are to be replaced.[2] Even the Temple is to be superseded by the worship centred on Christ's body (Jn 2.19-21).

2.2 *The church at Antioch*

There was, then, no monolithic Jewish-Gentile Christianity. The different views and approaches, outlined above, all had an influence upon the world that was being christianized. Consequently, within the city of Antioch (with which this study is concerned) one might observe house-churches in which the different approaches or groups would have their adherents. All the different approaches would not be reflected in each house-church but in different house-churches. Acts 11.19-20 speaks of the origin of the church at Antioch following the death of Stephen. Those Christians who fled to Antioch belonged to the Hellenists (or Group Four above). Soon they made many converts and the Jerusalem church sent Barnabas (Acts 11.22-24) in an attempt to keep control of the church of Antioch. Haenchen[3] presents Barnabas as having come to Antioch on his own initiative and not as an emissary of the church of Jerusalem. I, however, agree with Meier who argues that '[h]is submission to the Jerusalem authorities and his abandonment of Paul at such a critical juncture are more easily explained if Barnabas' activity at Antioch was from the beginning dependent on those same Jerusalem authorities'.[4]

Although it is very difficult to harmonize the details regarding the Council of Jersualem in Acts 15 and the account of Gal. 2.1-10, as well as what exactly occurred in the clash between

---

1. As Brown ('Introduction', 7) indicates: 'Stephen's speech indicates a disdain for the Temple where God does not dwell—an attitude quite unlike that attributed by Acts to Paul who is kept distinct from them'.

2. R.E. Brown, *The Gospel according to John: Introduction, Translation and Notes* (Anchor Bible; London: Chapman, 1971), vol. 1, 201-415.

3. E. Haenchen, *Die Apostelgeschichte* (16th edn; Göttingen: Vandenhoeck & Ruprecht, 1977), 350-58.

4. Meier, *Antioch*, 34.

Peter and Paul at Antioch in Gal. 2.11-14, a number of important points do emerge from these accounts:[1]

(a) A decision was reached, agreed upon by all, that circumcision was not to be imposed on Gentiles.
(b) Both Luke and Paul attribute to James the decision to
impose dietary laws on Gentiles.
(c) Shortly after 'the Jerusalem Council' Paul, Peter and
Barnabas had a serious disagreement over the dietary
observances. The pressure exerted by emissaries from
James sent to Antioch from Jerusalem forced Peter to
stop sharing meals with Gentile Christians. This was
because they did not abide by the dietary laws. Barnabas
sides with Peter and a rift occurs among the leaders.
(d) No details are given as regards what exactly occurred
thereafter, but Paul set out on his second missionary
journey leaving Barnabas behind. I agree with Meier[2]
who infers from all this that Paul actually lost the dis-
pute. He realized that he did not have support at Antioch
and so he left Antioch, which he visited only very briefly
once more in his life (Acts 18.22) and which he never
referred to again in the course of his correspondence.
(e) All these events support the view that the Jerusalem
church exercised authority over the church of Antioch.
'Up to and including the Apostolic Council and the Antioch incident Paul has to receive authoritative words
from the leadership of the Jerusalem church, which
enjoys undisputed superiority of status.'[3]

The above picture suggests that all the groups of Jewish-
Gentile Christianity are in evidence in the church of Antioch.
One could understand house-churches in existence with par-
ticular emphases belonging to the respective groups. With the
departure of Paul, the approach of James and Peter (Group
Two) would become the more dominant approach within the
Christian community. As time went on a much closer unity

1. For what occurs here I am indebted to the picture drawn by Meier
(*Antioch*, 36-39).
2. Meier, *Antioch*, 39.
3. B. Holmberg, *Paul and Power* (Philadelphia: Fortress, 1980), 35.

would be built among believers in Antioch. The compromise of allowing Christians to share in meals together, provided they observed the dietary regulations laid down in Acts 15.20, 'meant that for some time Jewish and Gentile Christians had been able to enjoy once again the full fellowship they had had in the church's earliest days'.[1]

2.3 *Traditions within the Antiochene church*
During the three decades (AD 50–80) extending from the time of the crisis between Paul and Peter to the emergence of the Gospel of Matthew, one can trace three major streams of tradition within the Antiochene church. All these traditions would have a marked influence upon the Gospel of Matthew. One can see these traditions as having a varied influence upon the different groups mentioned above within the Antiochene church.

2.3.1 *The Gospel of Mark*
Without doubt Mark formed the kernel or heart of the Gospel of Matthew. A date prior to AD 70 is usually assigned to the Gospel of Mark.[2] If one adopts the traditional location for its origin in Rome, its acceptance by the church of Antioch would occur within a very short space of time. Antioch was the capital of the Roman province of Syria, and once the mother city of Jerusalem had been destroyed, it would be natural for Antioch now to turn her allegiance 'towards the church in the capital of the Empire, where the two significant figures of Antioch's early days, Peter and Paul, had both died martyrs'.[3] Further support for this comes from the tradition connecting Mark and Peter. The apostle Peter, who had an important role within the Antiochene church, had left behind a record of his preaching and thought in the Gospel of Mark. This would have been an added incentive in Antioch to take over the Gospel of Mark and use it in teaching, preaching and in the liturgy.

1. Meier, *Antioch*, 50.
2. *Ibid.*, 51.
3. *Ibid.*, 52.

2.3.2 *The Q source*

Without doubt the wandering lifestyle of the itinerant Q prophets enabled the views, teaching and sayings of Jesus to spread, especially from Jerusalem to Antioch. Very soon after its appearance in writing the Q document would have found its way to Jerusalem as well as to Antioch, the two main churches in the area and the mother churches of the different branches of Jewish-Gentile Christianity. Although it had appeared in writing, many of the sayings of Jesus still continued to circulate and influence the Q document.[1]

2.3.3 *The M material*

The siglum M designates that material which does not belong to Mark or to Q, but which was used by Matthew in the construction of his Gospel. M is not to be viewed as a document in its own right, alongside that of Q or Mark. Instead, it incorporated the different and at times even conflicting viewpoints of the different groups within the Antiochene community.[2]

---

1. Meier (*Antioch*, 53) notes that 'the eclectic nature of the Q collection would have facilitated its acceptance at Antioch: various groups could find in the words of Jesus something to bolster their position'.

2. One can note, as Meier (*Antioch*, 53-57) does, the following tendencies contributing towards the M material:

(a) The Judaizers of Group One still uphold their rejection of admitting Gentiles without circumcision. The Q sayings, 'But it is easier for heaven and earth to pass away, than for one dot of the law to become void' (Q 16.17), would have been endorsed by this particular group. A number of sayings in the Gospel of Matthew tend to emphasize the exclusive approach: 'Go nowhere among the Gentiles, and enter no town of the Samaritans, but go rather to the lost sheep of the house of Israel' (Mt. 10.5-6). And again, in the ministry of Jesus, he states: 'I was sent only to the lost sheep of the house of Israel' (Mt. 15.24).

(b) Group Two gave its allegiance to James and Peter. The attitude of the Christian towards the Mosaic Law was indeed the centre of concern as can be seen in the Sermon on the Mount. 'You have heard that it was said... but I say to you...' (Mt. 5.21) indicates the approach adopted.

(c) There were also traditions stemming from Group Four which favoured a Gentile mission. In particular the Hellenists would have developed traditions of their own. The final command of Jesus to his disciples in Mt. 28.18-19 would represent this outlook. The Magi from the east came to accept the child Jesus, while the Jewish leaders were intent on his annihilation (Mt. 2.1-23). This is a good commentary on

These traditions of Mark, Q and M did not live in total isolation from one another. They frequently cross-pollinated within the activities of the church. Meier[1] expresses the situation well when he says: 'M was the living sea of oral tradition in which Mark and Q floated and were steeped'. M would exert an influence upon Mark and Q before Matthew began the writing of his Gospel. I have argued consistently that the Q source, once accepted into the Matthean community, underwent a development through the incorporation of other Q sayings as well as the insertion of M material. This was evident in the development of the Sermon on the Mount and, in particular, in the growth of the Beatitudes. Ultimately a written form of Q, which we term Q^{Mt}, emerged within the Matthean community and was used by Matthew in the construction of his Gospel.

3. *The Epistle of James in the Context of the Early Christian Communities*

The investigation of the relationship between James and Q can help to give us some understanding of the development of the Epistle of James and its destination. The indications coming from the epistle will be used as a starting-point and the attempt will be made to harmonize these with what has already been established in the examination of the relationship of James and Q.

the favourable attitude adopted towards the Gentiles, and a negative assessment of the Jews. The attitude adopted towards the Mosaic Law was far more liberating, but at the same time it could be far more demanding. For example, the revocation of oaths frees them from the legalism of the Mosaic Law, but in its turn places a new requirement on the Christian: namely, not to take any oaths.
(d) The concern of Group Two (the James group) as well as Group Four (the Hellenists) was to give direction and instruction to believers on how to lead their lives. With more and more Gentiles accepting the teachings of Christianity, urgent necessity demanded clear guidance on how they were to lead their lives. Consequently, these traditions developed an ethical instruction or catechesis to give guidance for these new converts.

1. *Ibid.*, 55.

3.1 *A probable Sitz im Leben for the epistle*

Some scholars argue that it is impossible to give an exact local-ization for this epistle, 'for paraenesis is not interested in locale'.[1] The epistle itself contains no historical allusions, nor is there any reference to a crisis which was the immediate cause of writing as was the case with most of Paul's letters. Never-theless, one may attempt to offer a probable scenario for the epistle based upon a close examination of it.

3.1.1 *Community leadership*

The picture that emerges from this writing suggests that one is dealing with a very early form of church leadership. The only church officers, if they can be called that, who are men-tioned, are the 'elders' (5.14) and 'teachers' (3.1). This refer-ence may be important in that other officers who became important at a later stage are not mentioned in the epistle. It is almost self-evident that were these other officers in existence at the time of this writing, James would have referred to them, particularly when he mentions calling in the elders of the Church to pray over the sick person (5.14). This argues for an early date for this epistle.

3.1.2 *The Jewish-Christian connection*

In addition to the wisdom heritage, on which James undoubt-edly draws, the epistle shows many other similarities with the thought-world of Judaism. The concept of God is in close har-mony with that of the Old Testament: God is one (2.19, in reference to the Shema); he is creator of all (1.17); he is holy (1.13) and he bestows all good gifts on humans (1.5, 17); he is also the Lord of hosts (Yahweh Sebaoth, 5.4). The phrase, 'the Lord of glory', applied in 2.1 to Jesus Christ, is a biblical way of speaking, referring to the Shekinah of the Old Testament. The term used for the place of worship in Judaism, 'the syna-gogue', is now applied to the Christian centres of worship

---

1. M. Dibelius, *James: A Commentary on the Epistle of James* (trans. from the German *Der Brief des Jakobus*; 11th rev. edn prepared by H. Greeven, 1964; English trans. M.A. Williams; ed. H. Koester for Hermeneia; Philadelphia: Fortress, 1975), 47.

(2.2).[1] This shows that the writing emerges from a world of Jewish Christianity that has maintained its roots in Judaism.

Although rooted in the Jewish tradition and heritage, James is not a purely Jewish document as some (such as Massebieau, Spitta and A. Meyer) have tried to argue. Our investigation has demonstrated the knowledge James has of the Q source, as well as the way this had developed in the Matthean community. As such James is a Jewish-Christian writing familiar with the traditions of Jesus circulating throughout Palestine and western Syria, in particular the city of Antioch.

3.1.3 *The social situation of the readers*

An examination of the epistle from the viewpoint of the information it gives about the readers tends to support both an early date as well as a distinctly Jewish-Christian audience.

We notice first the address of the apostle, '*to the twelve tribes in the dispersion*'. This designation refers to the Jewish-Christian communities living in the Diaspora. This does not necessarily entail a vast area—because of various specific references in the writing it is perhaps best to see it as addressed to Syria and the northern and north-western areas with the city

---

1. Later writings such as the letters of Ignatius still continue to refer to the Christian community gathering for worship as a synagogue (συναγωγή). In Ignatius's letter to Polycarp (4.2) he uses the following phrase: πυκνότερον συναγωγαὶ γινέσθωσαν: 'let the meetings be more numerous' (K. Lake [trans.], *The Apostolic Fathers*, vol. 2 [London: Heinemann, 1970], 273). Dibelius gives a number of other references from the early Christian writers to illustrate this use of the term συναγωγαί for the early Christian assemblies: 'Hermas writes of the cultic assembly: 'Therefore, when a person who has the Divine Spirit comes into a meeting of righteous men' (ὅταν οὖν ἔλθῃ ὁ ἄνθρωπος ὁ ἔχων τὸ πνεῦμα τὸ θεῖον εἰς συναγωγὴν ἀνδρῶν δικαίων *Herm. Mand.* 11.9; similarly 11.14; cf. also 11.13); and Dionysius of Alexandria (Eus., *Hist. eccl.* 7.9.2; 7.11.11, 12, 17) calls someone who takes part in the Christian assemblies τῆς συναγωγῆς μετασχών, and he calls the assemblies themselves συναγωγαί. Also, mention should be made here of Justin, who in *Dial.* 63.5 speaks of "those who believe on Him, who are of one soul and one assembly and one church' (τοῖς εἰς αὐτὸν πιστεύουσιν, ὡς οὖσι μιᾷ ψυχῇ καὶ μιᾷ συναγωγῇ καὶ μιᾷ ἐκκλησίᾳ); and also the compound ἐπισυναγωγή ("assembling") in Heb 10:25...' (Dibelius, *James*, 133-34).

of Antioch as the heart of the region.[1] The Jewish Christians in
the Diaspora are urged to promote the well-being of the world
in which they find themselves.[2] Its specific address to Jewish-
Christian communities is further support for upholding an
early date. By using the phrase 'the Dispersion', the writing is
placing itself in a clearly defined geographical setting. It looks
out from Jerusalem and is written to all those living outside of
Palestine who now constitute the New Israel, the new people
of God. The eschatological hope for the reconstitution of the
people of Israel around the twelve tribes of Israel is in the
process of taking place. Those who have already accepted
belief in Jesus, the Lord of glory, are the 'first fruits' (Jas 1.18).

The polemic on the admission of Gentiles to the community
is not an issue to which the epistle gives attention. Consequently, the clash of Peter and James with Paul in Antioch
(around AD 50) is a thing of the past. Those to whom the letter
is addressed could be seen as Jewish-Gentile Christians who
had endorsed (around the late fifties) the perspective of Group
Two in the classification given to the Jewish-Christian communities in the early Church.

A second type of information about the readers of the epistle
comes from references to poor and rich in the community.
There are three main texts in James which deal with the presence of rich members in the community (1.9-11; 2.2-6; 5.1-6).

1. F. Mussner, *Der Jakobusbrief: Auslegung* (4th edn; Freiburg:
Herder, 1981), 11.
2. A similar message was contained in a previous letter addressed to
exiles in the Dispersion. The first such letter (which could be a
paradigm for the Epistle of James) was addressed by the prophet
Jeremiah in Jerusalem to the exiles in the Diaspora, particularly to
Babylon (Jer. 29). This letter came at a decisive moment in the life and
religion of Israel. It was a time when the nation had been destroyed
and a new pagan power had emerged, to whom the Israelites were
subject. The message of the letter to the exiles is well summed up in
Jer. 29.7: 'But seek the welfare of the city where I have sent you into
exile, and pray to the Lord on its behalf, for in its welfare you will find
your welfare'. This is the calling God has directed to the exiles: they
are to involve themselves in the life of the new city to which they have
been brought. They are to promote the welfare of the city of their exile.
One can apply the same message to that epistle which, in the New Testament, directs its attention to the New Israel which is scattered in the
Dispersion.

The vast majority of the community was poor. On the other hand, the rich are the ones who are responsible for the hardships within the community: 'Is it not the rich who oppress you, is it not they who drag you into court?' (Jas 2.6). The rich referred to here should not be seen as members of the community, but as non-Christian outsiders, probably Jews.[1] The oppressions and persecutions of the early Christians came from the hand of the Jewish leaders, particularly the wealthy Sadducees. They were the ones who arrested Peter and John in Acts 4.1-3. The references here to the social situation reflect not just the situation of the audience, but also that of the author himself.

3.2 *The Epistle of James in the context of early Christianity*
The epistle is attributed to 'James, a servant of God and of the Lord Jesus Christ' without any further designation. The only James that could possibly have been referred to in this manner without needing any further clarification is James, the Just, referred to as 'the brother of the Lord'.[2] Various factors contributed to project James to the position he held in the early church. Probably the departure of Peter and the other apostles from Jerusalem was decisive for James assuming the leadership of the Jerusalem church.

Attention has already been drawn to the fact that the early Christian Church did not consist of a monolithic community in which everyone was united in viewing and presenting the Christian faith in the same way. Different communities became the home or seat for the preservation of the memories of certain apostles or Christian leaders. Although these communities tended to be independent, a certain opposition and

1. J.B. Mayor, *The Epistle of St. James: The Greek Text with Introduction, Notes, Comments and Further Studies in the Epistle of James* (3rd rev. edn; Grand Rapids: Zondervan, [1913] 1954), cxxxviii.
2. 'James the Just' or 'the brother of the Lord' is a common traditional designation for James the leader of the church in Jerusalem. In using the phrases 'brother of the Lord' and 'family of the Lord', it is not my intention to enter into the controversies surrounding their interpretation as this would take one beyond the scope of this thesis. As a Roman Catholic, I understand these terms in their widest possible designation, as referring to the relations of the extended family.

rivalry did develop among them, as is evidenced in the church
of Antioch where various groups differed largely according to
their attitude to the admission of Gentiles.

3.2.1 *The Epistle of James and the Apostle Paul*
The Epistle of James is often cited as an example of opposition
to Paul's doctrine of justification by faith. But is this a valid
conclusion? One can tabulate the passages in which similarity
and opposition are seen to emerge in this way:

James 2.21	Galatians 2.16
Ἀβραὰμ ὁ πατὴρ ἡμῶν οὐκ ἐξ ἔργων ἐδικαιώθη, ἀνενέγκας Ἰσαὰκ τὸν υἱὸν αὐτοῦ ἐπὶ τὸ θυσιαστήριον;	εἰδότες (δὲ) ὅτι οὐ δικαιοῦται ἄνθρωπος ἐξ ἔργων νόμου ἐὰν μὴ διὰ πίστεως Ἰησοῦ Χριστοῦ, καὶ ἡμεῖς εἰς Χριστὸν Ἰησοῦν ἐπιστεύσαμεν, ἵνα δικαιωθῶμεν ἐκ πίστεως Χριστοῦ καὶ οὐκ ἐξ ἔργων νόμου, ὅτι ἐξ ἔργων νόμου οὐ δικαιωθήσεται πᾶσα σάρξ.
James 2.24	Romans 3.28
ὁρᾶτε ὅτι ἐξ ἔργων δικαιοῦται ἄνθρωπος καὶ οὐχ ἐκ πίστεως μόνον.	λογιζόμεθα γὰρ δικαιοῦσθαι πίστει ἄνθρωπον χωρὶς ἔργων νόμου.

The closest similarity in these passages is the use of the word
ἔργα: James uses the word twice, while Paul speaks on four
occasions of ἔργα νόμου. Despite the similarity in the use of this
word, each author has a different thought in mind. The works
to which Paul refers are simply works of the law which he
rejects. Paul has in mind a very restricted and specific meaning. James, on the other hand, has a completely different perspective. The works which he has in mind are the outgrowth
of faith; they are indeed works of faith. Consequently, the conclusion arrived at by Ropes[1] is unfounded, namely, that James
quotes Paul's formula exactly.

Where James and Paul do in fact agree is in their notion of
faith. For James faith, to be truly alive, must always express

1. J. Ropes, *A Critical and Exegetical Commentary on the Epistle of St. James* (Edinburgh: T. & T. Clark, 1916), 35.

itself in action, in works, whereas for Paul faith incorporates within its very notion an action of response. The example to which they both refer, namely Abraham, bears this out. Although they are clearly stressing different aspects, they both converge in their notion of faith as being active—an idea common to first-century Judaism. In accepting this fundamental insight of faith as the starting-point, James wishes to teach that faith is only really true if it demonstrates itself by means of works; it must bear fruit, must show what type of faith it is. Good works are essential and are a result of one's faith: they are works of faith. Paul, on the other hand, is attacking those who say that faith is a result of works of the law. For Paul, faith is a gift from God and no person can demand this gift as a result of producing good works of the law.

Although the Epistle of James was not written as an attack upon Paul's views, one may postulate that it was addressed to the community of Antioch to present an understanding of the relationship between faith and works which, until then, had not been given sufficient importance. While Paul was in Antioch, his teaching would have stressed his customary dimension of freedom from works of the law. With Paul's withdrawal from Antioch and the triumph of the views of James and Peter on the obligation for Gentiles to abide by certain dietary laws, the polemic had ceased. Consequently, there was no need to take up the polemic once more. Instead, James's epistle took the opportunity to develop more fully the teaching on the quality of faith which needs to be illustrated by means of action. The epistle was probably written shortly after the polemic in Antioch had died down.

3.2.2 *The Epistle of James and the Apostolic Churches*
Tensions also developed within the early Christian communities between the churches which were followers of Peter and those who looked to James as their leader. An examination of the Gospels reveals this rivalry and tension.[1] Among certain Jewish Christians the position of James, 'the brother of the

---

1. K.L. Carroll, 'The Place of James in the Early Church', *BJRL* 44 (1961), 56ff., presents this tension very well when he compares the approach of the three synoptic Gospels to the family of Jesus.

Lord', receives more and more importance. James eventually
became what Carroll[1] terms 'the "patron saint" of the Jewish
Christians'. The apostolic churches emphasized the position of
Peter among them, possibly as a reaction to the position
claimed by the Beloved Disciple for his community, and
because of the position attributed to James in certain Jewish-
Christian churches.

One can envisage James writing an epistle to his loyal followers in Antioch, using traditions in free circulation, especially in the Jewish-Gentile form of Christianity that is known
and embraced by his followers. It is catechesis of the finest
form instructing believers on their style of life as Christians.
This study arrives at the conclusion that all the indications
point to a date for the epistle around the second half of the fifth
decade of the first century AD. Its contact with the Q source
and its further development within the Matthean community
of Antioch support this date. The view that it comes from a
time in which the polemic with Paul has resolved itself in
Antioch also supports this period (the fifties).[2]

4. *The Results of this Study*

Over the course of the centuries scholarship has tended to
place the Epistle of James on the periphery of the New Testament. Even in more recent scholarship this still remains true.[3]
This neglect has proved to be a great oversight in New Testament scholarship. James has deep and firm roots both in

---

1. *Ibid.*, 64-65.
2. P.H. Davids (*The Epistle of James: A Commentary on the Greek
Text* [Exeter: Paternoster, 1982], 34) arrived at a similar conclusion
with regard to the dating of this epistle: 'This commentary assumes,
then, that the original traditions appeared during the early part of this
period, i.e. late 40s and early 50s. They were gathered together during
the latter part to solidify the church's position. This work is perhaps
the last picture one has of the Palestinian Church before the storms of
war closed over it.'
3. For example, in two very recent studies on the early Christian
church (Brown & Meier, *Antioch and Rome*, and R.E. Brown, *The
Churches the Apostles Left Behind* [New York: Paulist, 1984]), Brown
hardly mentions this epistle, depite the importance assigned to the
person of James the Just in the early Christian church.

Judaism and in early Christianity. The twofold character of
James as a wisdom writing, as well as being steeped in the
early Christian traditions, especially that of Q and Q^{Mt}, supports both its Jewish and early Christian roots. It is hoped that
this study will give fresh impetus to future scholarship on
James.

4.1 *The theme of wisdom*
James has utilized a form of the Graeco-Roman letter in his
own right and to great ability in order to highlight the essential
themes of the entire epistle. Although previous studies on
James may have mentioned the theme of wisdom, they failed
to note or stress the importance that wisdom has in the overall
structure of this writing. This wisdom perspective is in line
with the development of the wisdom trajectory extending
from the Old Testament through to the New. In this sense
James is clearly the bridge between the two testaments.

4.2 *James's witness to the development in an understanding of Jesus' relationship to wisdom within early Christianity*
No longer is wisdom understood within the world-view of
Judaism and the Hebrew traditions, but it has taken on a
decidedly Christian perspective. Jesus, as the Lord of glory
(2.1), is the wisdom of God. A trajectory, developing reflection
on the relationship of Jesus to wisdom, has been postulated
from Q through James and Matthew and finally ending in the
Gnosticism of the *Gospel of Thomas*. Starting with the Q
source, Jesus is conceived as an emissary or spokesman for
wisdom. Wisdom is personified, and as such she sends forth
her emissaries, chief of whom is Jesus, whose task it is to
instruct humanity on the wisdom direction their lives should
take. In the Epistle of James this line of reflection underwent
an important development. Jesus Christ is no longer the
earthly emissary, but the eschatological Lord of glory. Jesus as
the Risen Lord is now cast as wisdom herself: no distinction is
to be drawn between the heavenly Jesus and heavenly wisdom. In the Gospel of Matthew a further progression took
place whereby the historical, earthly Jesus speaks and acts as
wisdom incarnate. The Gospel of Luke tends to remain outside
this line of development in that it lies closer to the Q conception

of the relationship of Jesus to wisdom. If anything, the Gospel of Luke avoids the idea of a personification of wisdom and presents instead a direct identification of God and wisdom. This trajectory shows that there is a strand of thought which has tended to reflect upon the relationship of Jesus to wisdom. The various documents of Q, James and Matthew are testimony to the various stages through which this thought developed. The intermediate stage to which James bears witness is necessary for the reflections which the Gospel of Matthew would initiate.

4.3 *Wisdom and the Holy Spirit*
What occurs elsewhere in the biblical traditions relating to the effects of the gift of God's Spirit, James expresses by means of the concept of the communication of divine wisdom. As with the gift of the Spirit, the gift of wisdom brings about a moral regeneration within the life of the believer. This will, however, only reach fulfilment in the eschatological age. On the one level, then, Jesus is the wisdom of God. Whereas the Hebrew traditions had reflected more and more upon the personification of wisdom next to God, in James this personification has now reached its culmination in its identification with the person of Jesus Christ, as the Lord of glory. On the other level, wisdom is the greatest of God's gifts communicated to humanity. It is highly significant that this same communication is referred to in other traditions as the gift of God's Spirit. To my mind, this is an illustation of the early nature of the Epistle of James. One may perhaps note here the root of what in other traditions will develop into a fully fledged trinitarian theology. In embryonic form one has reference to the Father, and to the Son, as identified with wisdom, and to the communication of this very essence of divine wisdom, divine life to the believer which works a moral regeneration. This communication of divine wisdom will become in other traditions the communication of God's Spirit, proceeding from the Father and the Son.

4.4 *James as an independent witness to the existence of the Q source*
From a tradition outside of the synoptic Gospels, James bears witness to the Q source. Not only does James show an aware-

ness of the Q tradition, but he is also conscious of the way it developed within the Matthean community. James shows that he has emerged from a world which holds as sacred traditions that are common to the Gospel of Matthew. This perspective again places James in an intermediary position between Q and the Gospel of Matthew. This does not mean that Matthew utilized the Epistle of James or vice versa. The knowledge that James has of the traditions and sources that go into the Gospel of Matthew is such that the epistle situates itself before the codification of these sources took place within the Gospel of Matthew.

4.5 *The transmission of the sayings of Jesus in the early community*

Like Paul, James does not quote the sayings of Jesus verbatim. Instead, he uses them freely, interweaving them into his admonitions and advice. No distinction is drawn between the words of James and the sayings of Jesus. The latter are all deeply embedded in the paraenetical advice offered by James, and indirectly form the very basis and authority for the advice. The epistle comes as a communication from the leader of the church in Jerusalem to the Jewish-Gentile Christians of Antioch who acknowledge his authority and leadership and adopt a particular stance regarding the admission of Gentiles within their community. As the 'first fruits' of the reconstituted people of God they live in the eschatological age. As 'the twelve tribes in the Dispersion' they have a responsibility to the world around them to aim at reconstituting the New Israel.

4.6 *James bears witness to being an early writing*

Its early appearance is evident from its connections with the Jewish wisdom heritage, its early relationships to the Jesus traditions, and its picture of the relationship of Jesus to wisdom. As such James is an important writing for it presents a picture of the early Christian community and the way in which the traditions stemming from Jesus were handed on and developed.

4.7 The whole assessment of the Epistle of James needs to be changed

If the Epistle of James is viewed as one of the earliest writings of the New Testament, as this study contends, its value and importance is inestimable because it provides a link in the chain bringing one closer to the traditions dealing with the sayings of Jesus. A study of James brings one to a clearer and deeper appreciation and understanding of the early Christian church in its attempt to preserve its heritage and at the same time grasp the full understanding of the novelty that the teaching of Jesus brought with it. Through its emphasis on wisdom James shows its firm roots in its Jewish heritage. Through its close affinities with and use of the Q tradition and other Jesus traditions, James affirms its adherence to the very centre of the Christian message. Through its relationship to both wisdom and the Q source, James shows the heritage of Judaism flowering forth into the new world of Christianity. In this sense the Epistle of James becomes 'the first fruits'. It prepares the way for other Christian traditions to put forth in writing their own understanding and witness to the message taught by Jesus.

APPENDIX A

SUMMARY OF THE STRUCTURE OF THE EPISTLE OF JAMES

SECTION 1: OPENING ADDRESS
    Pericope A   Opening formula (1.1)

SECTION 2: INTRODUCTORY FORMULAE EXPRESSING THEMES (1.2-27)
    PART ONE: INTRODUCTORY FORMULA OF JOY (1.2-11)

    Pericope B   Testing of faith produces steadfastness (1.2-4)
    Pericope C   Asking for wisdom in faith (1.5-8)
    Pericope D   Antithesis between the rich and lowly (1.9-11)

    PART TWO: INTRODUCTORY FORMULA OF BLESSEDNESS (1.12-27)

    Pericope E   Endurance under testing (1.12-18)
    Pericope F   A series of sayings (1.19-27)

SECTION 3: BODY OF EPISTLE (2.1–5.6)

    Pericope G   Partiality and distinctions made between rich and poor are excluded by the Christian faith (2.1-13)
    Pericope H   Relationship between faith and works (2.14-26)
    Pericope I   Speech and the tongue (3.1-12)
    Pericope J   The wisdom from above (3.13-18)
    Pericope K   The art of living happily: advice from a wise man (4.1-10)
    Pericope L   To speak evil (4.11-12)
    Pericope M   Do not neglect God in what you do (4.13-17)
    Pericope N   Arrogance of the rich (5.1-6)

SECTION 4: CONCLUSION TO THE EPISTLE (5.7-20)

    Pericope O   Exhortation to patience (5.7-11)
    Pericope P   The oath (5.12)
    Pericope Q   Prayer and concern for others (5.13-18)
    Pericope R   Bringing back a sinner (5.19-20)

APPENDIX B

THE COMPOSITIONAL RELATIONSHIP AMONG THE
PERICOPAE

SECTION 1: OPENING ADDRESS
    Pericope A   Opening formula (1.1)

SECTION 2: INTRODUCTORY FORMULAE EXPRESSING THEMES (1.2-27)
  PART ONE: INTRODUCTORY FORMULA OF JOY (1.2-11)

    Pericope B   Testing–steadfastness (1.2-4) (E)
    Pericope C   Asking for wisdom (1.5-8)   (D)
    Pericope D   Rich–poor (1.9-11)   (A)

  PART TWO: INTRODUCTORY FORMULA OF BLESSEDNESS (1.12-27)

    Pericope E   Endurance–testing (1.12-18) (E)
    Pericope F   Series of sayings (1.19-27)
          (i)   Anger (1.20-21)   (F)
         (ii)   Doers of the word (1.22-25)   (B)
        (iii)   Bridling the tongue (1.26-27) (C)

SECTION 3: BODY OF EPISTLE (2.1–5.6)

    Pericope G   Partiality: rich–poor (2.1-13) (A)
    Pericope H   Faith and works (2.14-26)   (B)
    Pericope I   Speech and tongue (3.1-12)   (C)
    Pericope J   Wisdom from above (3.13-18) (D)
    Pericope K   Advice from the wise (4.1-10) (D) (D) (C) (B) (A)
    Pericope L   To speak evil (4.11-12)   (C)
    Pericope M   Doers of right (4.13-17)   (B)
    Pericope N   Arrogance of rich (5.1-6)   (A)

SECTION 4: CONCLUSION TO THE EPISTLE (5.7-20)

    Pericope O   Exhortation to patience (5.7-11)
    Pericope P   The oath (5.12)
    Pericope Q   Prayer and concern for others (5.13-18)
    Pericope R   Bringing back a sinner (5.19-20)

BIBLIOGRAPHY

Adamson, J.W. 'An Inductive Approach to the Epistle of James'. PhD thesis, Cambridge University, 1954.
—*The Epistle of James*. Grand Rapids: Eerdmans, 1976.
—*James: The Man and his Message*. Grand Rapids: Eerdmans, 1989.
Aland, K. and Black, M. *The Greek New Testament*. 3rd edn corrected. Stuttgart: United Bible Societies, 1983.
Amphoux, C.B. 'Les Manuscrits grecs de l'épître de Jacques', *RHT* 8 (1978) 247-76.
Argyle, A.W. *The Gospel according to Matthew*. Cambridge: Cambridge University Press, 1963.
—'The Methods of the Evangelists and the Q Hypothesis', *Theol.* 67 (1964) 156-57.
Baasland, E. 'Der Jakobusbrief als neutestamentliche Weisheitsschrift', *ST* 36 (1982) 119-39.
Bammel, E. 'πτωχός', *TDNT*, VI (1968) 885-915.
Bartlett, D.L. 'The Epistle of James as a Jewish-Christian Document', *Society of Biblical Literature, Seminar Papers 17* (1979) 173-86.
Bauckham, R. 'The Study of Gospel Traditions outside the Canonical Gospels: Problems and Prospects', in Wenham, *Gospel Perspectives*, vol. 5, 369-419.
Beardslee, W.A. *Literary Criticism of the New Testament*. Guides to Biblical Scholarship. Philadelphia: Fortress, 1969.
—'The Wisdom Tradition and the Synoptic Gospels', *JAAR* 35 (1967) 231-40.
Bentzen, A. *Introduction to the Old Testament*, vol. 1. Copenhagen: G.E.C. Gad, 1948.
Bertram, G. 'νήπιος', *TDNT*, IV (1967) 912-23.
Betz, H.D. 'The Hermeneutical Principles of the Sermon on the Mount (Mt 5.17-20)', *JTSA* 42 (1983) 17-28.
—'Die Makarismen der Bergpredigt (Matthäus 5,3-12): Beobachtungen zur literarischen Form und theologischen Bedeutung', *ZThK* 75 (1978) 3-19.
Biggs, H. 'The Q Debate since 1955', *Themelios* 6/2 (1980/81) 18-28.
Black, M. *An Aramaic Approach to the Gospels and Acts*. 3rd edn. Oxford: Clarendon, 1967.
Blass, F. & Debrunner, A. *A Greek Grammar of the New Testament and Other Early Christian literature*. Trans. from the German by R.W. Funk. Chicago: University of Chicago Press, 1961.
Blondel, J.-L. 'Le Fondement théologique de la parénèse dans l'épître de Jacques', *RThPh* 29 (1979) 141-52.

Boring, M.E. *Sayings of the Risen Jesus: Christian Prophecy in the Synoptic Tradition.* Cambridge: Cambridge University Press, 1982.

Brown, J.P. 'The Form of "Q" Known to Matthew', *NTS* 8 (1961/62) 27-42.

—'Mark as Witness to an Edited Form of Q', *JBL* 80 (1961) 29-44.

—'Synoptic Parallels in the Epistles and Form-History', *NTS* 10 (1963/64) 27-48.

Brown, R.E. *The Churches the Apostles Left Behind.* New York: Paulist, 1984.

—*The Community of the Beloved Disciple.* London: Geoffrey Chapman, 1979.

—*The Gospel according to John: Introduction, Translation and Notes*, vols. 1 and 2. The Anchor Bible. London: Geoffrey Chapman, 1971.

—'Introduction', and 'Rome', in Brown & Meier, *Antioch and Rome*, 1-9 and 87-216.

Brown, R.E., Fitzmyer, J.A. & Murphy, R.E. (eds.), *The Jerome Biblical Commentary*, vol. 1: *The Old Testament*, and vol. 2: *The New Testament.* London: Geoffrey Chapman, 1970.

Brown, R.E. & Meier, J.P. *Antioch and Rome.* New York: Paulist, 1983.

Brueggemann, W. *In Man We Trust: The Neglected Side of Biblical Faith.* Richmond: John Knox, 1972.

Büchsel, F. 'κρίνω', *TDNT*, III (1965), 933-54.

Bultmann, R. 'ἔλεος', *TDNT*, II (1964) 477-87.

—*The History of the Synoptic Tradition*, trans. J. Marsh from the 2nd German edition (1931); rev. edn, Oxford: Basil Blackwell, 1972.

Bussby, F. 'Is Q an Aramaic Document?', *ET* 65 (1953/54) 272-75.

Buttrick, G. (ed.), *The Interpreter's Bible in Twelve Volumes.* New York: Abingdon, 1957.

—*The Interpreter's Dictionary of the Bible. An Illustrated Encyclopedia in Four Volumes.* New York: Abingdon, 1962.

Calvin, J. *Commentaries on the Catholic Epistles*, trans. & ed. by J. Owen. Grand Rapids: Eerdmans, 1959.

Carrington, P. *The Primitive Christian Catechism: A Study in the Epistles.* Cambridge: Cambridge University Press, 1940.

Carroll, K.L. 'The Place of James in the Early Church', *BJRL* 44 (1961) 49-67.

Chaine, J. *L'Épître de Saint Jacques.* 2nd edn. Paris: Gabalda, 1927.

Charlesworth, J.H. (ed.). *The Old Testament Pseudepigrapha.* Vol. 1: *Apocalyptic Literature and Testaments.* Garden City: Doubleday, 1983.

—*The Old Testament Pseudepigrapha.* Vol. 2: *Expansions of the 'Old Testament' and Legends, Wisdom and Philosophical Literature, Prayers, Psalms, and Odes, Fragments of Lost Judeo-Hellenic Works.* London: Darton, Longman & Todd, 1985.

Christ, F. *Jesus Sophia: Die Sophia-Christologie bei den Synoptikern.* Zurich: Zwingli, 1970.

Crenshaw, J.L. *Old Testament Wisdom: an Introduction.* Atlanta: John Knox, 1981.

Crim, K. (ed.). *The Interpreter's Dictionary of the Bible. Supplementary Volume.* Nashville: Abingdon, 1976.

Cullmann, O. 'The Significance of the Qumran Texts for Research into the Beginnings of Christianity', *JBL* 74 (1955) 213-26.

Dahood, M. *Proverbs and Northwest Semitic Philology.* Rome: Pontifical Biblical Institute, 1963.

Davids, P.H. *The Epistle of James: A Commentary on the Greek Text.* Exeter: Paternoster, 1982.

—'James and Jesus', in Wenham, *Gospel Perspectives,* vol. 5, 63-84.

—'The Meaning of ἀπείραστος in Jas 1.13', *NTS* 24 (1978) 386-92.

—'Theological Perspectives on the Epistle of James', *JETS* 23 (1980) 97-103.

—'Tradition and Citation', in Gasque & LaSor, *Scripture, Tradition and Interpretation,* 113-26.

Davies, W.D. *The Setting of the Sermon on the Mount.* Cambridge: Cambridge University Press, 1964.

Delling, G. 'τέλειος', *TDNT,* VIII (1972) 49-87.

Delobel, J. (ed.). *Logia: Les Paroles de Jésus—The Sayings of Jesus: Mémorial Joseph Coppens.* Leuven: Leuven University Press, 1982.

Deutsch, C. *Hidden Wisdom and the Easy Yoke: Wisdom, Torah and Discipleship in Matthew 11.25-30.* Sheffield: JSOT, 1987.

Devisch, M. 'Le Document Q, source de Matthieu: problématique actuelle', in M. Didier (ed.), *L'Évangile selon Matthieu: rédaction et théologie.* Gembloux: Duculot, 1972, 71-98.

Dibelius, M. *Der Brief des Jakobus,* ed. H. Greeven, 6th edn. Göttingen: Vandenhoeck & Ruprecht, 1984.

—*From Tradition to Gospel,* trans. B.L. Woolf. Greenwood: Attic, 1971.

—*James: A Commentary on the Epistle of James.* Trans. M.A. Williams. Philadelphia: Fortress, 1975.

Dillman, C.N. 'A Study of Some Theological and Literary Comparisons of the Gospel of Matthew and the Epistle of James'. PhD thesis, University of Edinburgh, 1978.

Dion, P.E. 'The Aramaic "Family Letter" and Related Epistolary Forms in Other Oriental Languages and in Hellenistic Greek', *Semeia* 22 (1982) 59-76.

Du Plessis, I.J. 'Contextual Aid for an Identity Crisis: An Attempt to Interpret Luke 7.35', in Petzer & Hartin, *A South African Perspective on the New Testament,* 112-27.

—'ΤΕΛΕΙΟΣ: The Idea of Perfection in the New Testament'. Unpublished dissertation, Kampen: J.H. Kok, 1959.

Dupont, J. 'Beati i puri di cuore, perché vedranno dio (Mt 5.8)', *Parole di Vita* 15 (1970) 301-16.

—*Les Béatitudes.* Tome I. *Le Problème littéraire.* Paris: Gabalda, 1969.

—*Les Béatitudes.* Tome II. *La Bonne Nouvelle.* Paris: Gabalda, 1969.

—*Les Béatitudes.* Tome III. *Les Évangélistes.* Paris: Gabalda, 1973.

Du Toit, A.B. 'The Significance of Discourse Analysis for New Testament Interpretation and Translation', *Neotestamentica* 8 (1974) 54-79.

Du Toit, H.C. 'What is a Colon?', *Addendum to Neotestamentica* 11 (1977) 1-10.

Easton, B.S. 'The Epistle of James: Introduction and Exegesis', in Buttrick (ed.), *The Interpreter's Bible,* XII, 1957, 3-74.

Edwards, R.A. 'An Approach to a Theology of Q', *JR* 51 (1971) 247-69.

—*A Concordance to Q.* Missoula: Scholars Press, 1975.

—'The Eschatological Correlative as a Gattung in the New Testament', *ZNW* 60 (1969) 9-20.
—'Matthew's use of Q in Chapter 11', in Delobel, *Logia*, 257-75.
—*A Theology of Q: Eschatology, Prophecy and Wisdom.* Philadelphia: Fortress, 1976.
Exler, F.X.J. *The Form of the Ancient Greek Letter: A Study in Greek Episto-lography.* Washington: Catholic University of America, 1923.
Farmer, W.R. 'A Fresh Approach to Q', in J. Neusner (ed.), *Christianity, Judaism and Other Greco-Roman Cults: Studies for Morton Smith at Sixty.* Leiden: Brill, 1975, 39-50.
—*The Synoptic Problem: A Critical Analysis.* New York: Macmillan, 1964.
Farrar, A.M. 'On Dispensing with Q', in D.E. Nineham (ed.), *Studies in the Gospels: Essays in Memory of R.H. Lightfoot,* Oxford: Basil Blackwell, 1967, 55-88.
Fitzmyer, J.A. *The Gospel according to Luke (1–9).* The Anchor Bible. 2nd edn. Garden City: Doubleday, 1983.
—'New Testament Epistles', in Brown, Fitzmyer & Murphy (eds.), *The Jerome Biblical Commentary,* II, 223-26.
—'The Priority of Mark and the "Q" Source in Luke', *Perspective* 11 (1970), 131-70.
Foerster, W. 'εἰρήνη', *TDNT*, II (1964) 406-20.
Fohrer, G. 'σοφία', *TDNT*, VII (1971) 476-96.
Francis, F. 'The Form and Function of the Opening and Closing Paragraphs of James and 1 John', *ZNW* 61 (1970) 110-26.
Frankemölle, H. 'Die Makarismen (Mt 5,1-12; Lk. 6,20-23): Motive und Umfang der redaktionellen Komposition', *BZ* 15 (1971) 52-75.
Funk, R.W. 'The Form and Structure of II and III John', *JBL* 86 (1967) 424-30.
Gasque, W.W. & LaSor, W.S. (eds.). *Scripture, Tradition and Interpretation. Essays Presented to Everett F. Harrison by his Students and Colleagues in Honor of his Seventy-Fifth Birthday.* Grand Rapids: Eerdmans, 1978.
Goulder, M.D. 'On Putting Q to the Test', *NTS* 24 (1978) 218-34.
Griesbach, J.J. 'Commentatio qua Marci Evangelium totum e Matthaei et Lucae commentariis decerptum esse monstratur', in B. Orchard & T. Longstaff (eds.), *Synoptic and Text-critical Studies 1776–1976,* Cambridge: Cambridge University Press, 1978, 68-135.
Grundmann, W. 'δόκιμος', *TDNT*, II (1964) 255-60.
Guelich, R.A. 'Mt 5.22: Its Meaning and Integrity', *ZNW* 64 (1973) 39-52.
—'The Matthean Beatitudes: "Entrance-Requirements" or Eschatological Blessings?', *JBL* 95 (1976) 415-34.
Guillaumont, A., Peuch, H.-Ch., Quispel, G., Till, W. & Yassah, A. (trans.). *The Gospel according to Thomas: Coptic Text Established and Translated.* San Francisco: Harper & Row, 1959.
Hadas, M. 'Wisdom of Solomon', in Buttrick (ed.), *The Interpreter's Diction-ary of the Bible,* IV, 861-63.
Haenchen, E. *Die Apostelgeschichte.* 16th edn. Göttingen: Vandenhoeck & Ruprecht, 1977.

Hartin, P.J. 'James: A New Testament Wisdom Writing and its Relationship to Q'. DTh thesis, University of South Africa, Pretoria.

—'James and the Sermon on the Mount/Plain', in Lull, D.J. (ed.), *Society of Biblical Literature 1989 Seminar Papers*, Atlanta: Scholars Press, 1989, 440-57.

Hauck, F. 'ἁγνός', *TDNT*, I (1964) 122-24.

—*Der Brief des Jakobus*. Kommentar zum Neuen Testament, ed. T. Zahn. Leipzig: Deichert, 1926.

—*Die Briefe des Jakobus, Petrus, Judas und Johannes*. 8th edn. Göttingen: Vandenhoeck & Ruprecht, 1957.

—'καθαρός', *TDNT*, III (1965) 423-31.

—'μακάριος, μακαρίζω, μακαρισμός', *TDNT*, IV (1967) 362-64, 367-70.

—'ὑπομένω, ὑπομονή', *TDNT*, IV (1967) 581-88.

Hauck, F. & Schulz, S. 'πραΰς', *TDNT*, VI (1968) 645-51.

Havener, I. 'Jesus in the Gospel Sayings', *BiTod* 21 (1983) 77-82.

—*Q: The Sayings of Jesus: With a Reconstruction of Q by Athanasius Polag.* Wilmington: Michael Glazier, 1987.

Higgins, A.J.B. (ed.). *New Testament Essays: Studies in Memory of T.W. Manson (1893-1958)*. Manchester: Manchester University Press, 1959.

Hoffmann, P. *Studien zur Theologie der Logienquelle*. Münster: Aschendorff, 1972.

Holmberg, B. *Paul and Power*. Philadelphia: Fortress, 1980.

Hoppe, R. *Der theologische Hintergrund des Jakobusbriefes*. Würzburg: Echter, 1977.

Jacobson, A.D. 'The Literary Unity of Q', *JBL* 101 (1982) 365-89.

—'Wisdom Christology in Q'. PhD thesis, Claremont Graduate School, 1978.

Johnson, M.D. 'Reflections on a Wisdom Approach to Matthew's Christology', *CBQ* 36 (1974) 44-64.

Kamlah, E. *Die Form der katalogischen Paränese im Neuen Testament*. Tübingen: Mohr, 1964.

Kee, H.C. *Jesus in History: An Approach to the Study of the Gospels*. New York: Harcourt, Brace & World, 1970.

Kelber, W. *The Oral and Written Gospel: The Hermeneutics of Speaking and Writing in the Synoptic Tradition, Mark, Paul and Q*. Philadelphia: Fortress, 1983.

Kirk, J.A. 'The Meaning of Wisdom in James: Examination of a Hypothesis', *NTS* 16 (1969/70) 24-38.

Kittel, G. 'Der geschichtliche Ort des Jakobusbriefes', *ZNW* 41 (1942) 71-105.

—'Der Jakobusbrief und die apostolischen Väter', *ZNW* (1950/51) 54-112.

—review of Martin Dibelius, *Der Brief des Jakobus*, *ThLBl* 44 (1923) 3-7.

Kloppenborg, J.S. 'The Formation of Q and Antique Instructional Genres', *JBL* 105 (1986) 443-62.

—*The Formation of Q: Trajectories in Ancient Wisdom Collections*. Studies in Antiquity and Christianity. Philadelphia: Fortress, 1987.

—'The Literary Genre of the Synoptic Sayings source'. PhD thesis, University of St Michael's College, Toronto School of Theology, 1984.

—'Tradition and Redaction in the Synoptic Sayings Source', *CBQ* 46 (1984) 34-62.

—'Wisdom Christology in Q', *LTP* 34 (1978) 129-47.

Koester, H. 'Gnomai Diaphoroi: The Origin and Nature of Diversification in the History of Early Christianity', in Robinson & Koester, *Trajectories through Early Christianity*, 114-57.

Kümmel, W.G. *Introduction to the New Testament*. London: SCM, rev. edn, 1975.

Lake, K. (trans.). *The Apostolic Fathers*, vol. 1. London: Heinemann, 1965.

— (trans.). *The Apostolic Fathers*, vol. 2. London: Heinemann, 1970.

—'The Date of Q', *Exp.* 7 (1909) 494-507.

Laws, S. *A Commentary on the Epistle of James*. London: Black, 1980.

Lindars, B. & Smalley, S. (eds.). *Christ and Spirit in the New Testament*. Cambridge: Cambridge University Press, 1973.

Louw, J.P. 'Discourse Analysis and the Greek New Testament', *BT* 24 (1973) 101-18.

Lührmann, D. *Die Redaktion der Logienquelle: Anhang: Zur weiteren Überlieferung der Logienquelle*. Neukirchen-Vluyn: Neukirchener Verlag, 1969.

Luther, M. *Luther's Works: Word and Sacrament I*, vol. 35, ed. T. Backmann. Philadelphia: Fortress, 1960.

—*Luther's Works: Table Talk*, vol. 54, ed. and trans. T.G. Tappert. Philadelphia: Fortress, 1967.

Luz, U. 'Sermon on the Mount/Plain: Reconstruction of Q^{Mt} and Q^{Lk}, in Richards (ed.), *Society of Biblical Literature 1983 Seminar Papers*, 473-79.

MacGorman, J.W. 'A Comparison of the Book of James with the Jewish Wisdom Literature'. DTh thesis, Southwestern Baptist Theological Seminary, Forth Worth, 1956.

—'Introducing the Book of James', *SWJT* 12 (1969) 9-22.

Manson, T.W. *The Sayings of Jesus*. London: SCM, [1937] 1971.

—'Some Outstanding New Testament Problems: XII The Problem of Aramaic Sources in the Gospels', *ET* 47 (1935/36) 7-11.

Massebieau, L. 'L'Épître de Jacques est-elle l'oeuvre d'un chrétien?', *RHR* 32 (1895) 249-83.

Mayor, J.B. *The Epistle of St. James: The Greek Text with Introduction, Notes, Comments and Further Studies in the Epistle of St James*. 3rd rev. edn. Grand Rapids: Zondervan, [1913] 1954.

McEleney, N. 'The Beatitudes of the Sermon on the Mount/Plain', *CBQ* 43 (1981) 1-13.

McKenzie, J.L. 'Reflections on Wisdom', *JBL* 86 (1967) 1-9.

Meier, J.P. 'Antioch', in Brown & Meier, *Antioch and Rome*, 11-86.

Metzger, B. *A Textual Commentary on the Greek New Testament*. New York: United Bible Societies, 1971.

Meyer, A. *Das Rätsel des Jacobusbriefes*. Giessen: Töpelmann, 1930.

Meyer, P.D. 'The Community of Q'. PhD thesis, University of Iowa, 1967.

—'The Gentile Mission in Q', *JBL* 89 (1970) 405-17.

Meyer, R. 'καθαρός', *TDNT*, III (1965) 418-23.

Michaelis, C. 'Die π-Alliteration der Subjektsworte der ersten 4 Seligpreisungen in Mt v.3-6 und ihre Bedeutung für den Aufbau der Seligpreisungen bei Mt., Lk. und in Q', *NT* 10 (1968) 148-61.

Mitton, C.L. *The Epistle of James.* London: Marshall, Morgan & Scott, 1966.
Moffat, J. *An Introduction to the Literature of the New Testament.* 3rd rev. edn. Edinburgh: T. & T. Clark, [1918] 1961.
Moo, D.J. *The Letter of James: An Introduction and Commentary.* Grand Rapids: Eerdmans, 1986.
Motyer, J.A. *The Message of James: The Tests of Faith.* Leicester: Inter-varsity Press, 1985.
Mullins, T.Y. 'Jewish Wisdom Literature in the New Testament', *JBL* 68 (1949) 335-39.
Murphy, R.E. 'Ecclesiastes (Qoheleth)', in Brown, Fitzmyer & Murphy, *The Jerome Biblical Commentary*, vol. 1, 534-40.
Mussner, F. *Der Jakobusbrief: Auslegung.* 4th edn. Freiburg: Herder, 1981.
Neirynck, F. 'L'Édition du texte de Q', *EThL* 55 (1979) 373-81.
—*L'Évangile de Luc: Problèmes littéraires et théologiques. Mémorial Lucien Cerfaux.* Gembloux: Duculot, 1973.
—'Q', in Crim, *Interpreter's Dictionary of the Bible, Supplementary Volume*, 715-16.
—'Recent Developments in the Study of Q', in Delobel, *Logia*, 29-75.
—'Studies on Q since 1972', *EThL* 56 (1980) 409-413.
—'The Symbol Q (= Quelle)', *EThL* 54 (1978) 119-25.
Nestle, E. & Aland, K. *Novum Testamentum Graece.* 26th edn, 7th rev. printing. Stuttgart: Deutsche Bibelgesellschaft, 1983.
Oepke, A. 'κένος', *TDNT*, 3 (1965) 659-62.
Ong, W.J. *Orality and Literacy: The Technologizing of the Word.* New York: Methuen, 1982.
Origen. *Commentaire sur Saint Jean. Tome I (Livres I-V). Texte grec, avant-propos, traduction et notes par Cécile Blanc.* Paris: Editions du Cerf, 1966.
Petzer, J.H. & Hartin, P.J. (eds.). *A South African Perspective on the New Testament: Essays by South African New Testament Scholars Presented to Bruce Manning Metzger during his Visit to South Africa in 1985.* Leiden: Brill, 1986.
Polag, A. *Die Christologie der Logienquelle.* Neukirchen-Vluyn: Neukirchener Verlag, 1977.
—*Fragmenta Q: Textheft zur Logienquelle.* Neukirchen-Vluyn: Neukirchener Verlag, 1979.
Price, J.L. *Interpreting the New Testament.* New York: Holt, Rinehart & Winston, 1971.
Rengstorf, K.H. 'κλαίω', *TDNT*, III (1965) 722-26.
Richards, K.H. (ed.). *Society of Biblical Literature 1983 Seminar Papers.* Chico: Scholars, 1983.
Ristow, H. & Matthiae, K. (eds.). *Der historische Jesus und der kerygmatische Christus.* 3rd edn. Berlin: Evangelische Verlagsanstalt, 1964.
Roberts, J.H. 'The Eschatological Transitions to the Pauline Letter Body', *Neotestamentica* 20 (1986) 29-35.
—'Pauline Transitions to the Letter Body', *BEThL* 73 (1986) 93-99.
—'Transitional Techniques to the Letter Body in the Corpus Paulinum', in Petzer & Hartin, *A South African Perspective on the New Testament*, 187-201.

Robinson, J.M. 'Basic Shifts in German Theology', *Interp.* 16 (1962) 76-97.

—'Jesus as Sophos and Sophia: Wisdom Tradition and the Gospels', in Wilken, *Aspects of Wisdom in Judaism and Early Christianity*, 1-16.

—'Logoi Sophon: On the Gattung of Q', in Robinson & Koester, *Trajectories through Early Christianity*, 71-113.

—'The Sermon on the Mount/Plain: Work Sheets for the Reconstruction of Q', in Richards (ed.), *Society of Biblical Literature 1983 Seminar Papers*, 451-54.

Robinson, J.M. & Koester, H. (eds.). *Trajectories through Early Christianity*. Philadelphia: Fortress, 1971.

Ropes, J. *A Critical and Exegetical Commentary on the Epistle of St. James.* Edinburgh: T. & T. Clark, 1916.

Rylaarsdam, J.C. *Revelation in Jewish Wisdom Literature.* Chicago: University of Chicago Press, [1946] 1974.

Schlier, H. 'ἐλεύθερος', *TDNT*, II (1962) 487-502.

—'θλέβω, θλῖψις', *TDNT*, III (1966) 139-48.

Schneider, J. 'ὀμνύιω', *TDNT*, V (1967) 176-85.

Schroeder, D. 'Parenesis', in Crim (ed.), *The Interpreter's Dictionary of the Bible, Supplementary Volume*, 643.

Schubert, P. *Form and Function of the Pauline Thanksgivings.* Berlin: Töpelmann, 1939.

Schürmann, H. *Das Lukasevangelium.* Freiburg: Herder, 1969.

—'Die vorösterlichen Anfänge der Logientradition: Versuch eines formgeschichtlichen Zugangs zum Leben Jesu', in Ristow & Matthiae, *Der historische Jesus und der kerygmatische Christus*, 193-210.

Schulz, S. *Q: Die Spruchquelle der Evangelisten.* Zurich: Theologischer Verlag, 1972.

Schweizer, E. 'ψυχικός', *TDNT*, IX (1974) 661-63.

Scott, R.B.Y. *The Way of Wisdom in the Old Testament.* New York: Macmillan, 1971.

Shepherd, M. 'The Epistle of James and the Gospel of Matthew', *JBL* 75 (1956) 40-51.

Spitta, F. *Der Brief des Jakobus*, in his *Zur Geschichte und Litteratur des Urchristentums.* Göttingen: Vandenhoeck & Ruprecht, 1896, II, 1-239.

Stanton, G.N. 'On the Christology of Q', in Lindars & Smalley, *Christ and Spirit in the New Testament*, 27-42.

—'Salvation Proclaimed: X. Mt 11.28-30: Comfortable Words?', *ET* 94 (1982) 3-9.

Steck, O.H. *Israel und das gewaltsame Geschick der Propheten: Untersuchungen zur Überlieferung des deuteronomistischen Geschichtsbildes im Alten Testament, Spätjudentum und Urchristentum.* Neukirchen-Vluyn: Neukirchener Verlag, 1967.

Strecker, G. 'Die Makarismen der Bergpredigt', *NTS* 17 (1970/71) 255-75.

Suggs, M.J. *Wisdom, Christology, and Law in Matthew's Gospel.* Cambridge, MA: Harvard University Press, 1970.

Taylor, V. 'The Order of Q', *JTS* ns 4 (1953) 27-31.

—'The Original Order of Q', in Higgins, *New Testament Essays*, 1959, 246-69.

—'Some Outstanding New Testament Problems: I. The Elusive Q', *ET* 46 (1934/35) 68-74.

Theissen, G. *Sociology of Early Palestinian Christianity*. Philadelphia: Fortress, 1978.

Thompson, W.T. 'The Epistle of James—A Document of Heavenly Wisdom', *Western Theological Journal* 13 (1978) 7-12.

Thrall, W.F. & Hibbard, A. *A Handbook to Literature*. New York: Odyssey, 1962.

Tödt, H.E. *The Son of Man in the Synoptic Tradition*. Trans. D.M. Barton. Philadelphia: Westminster, 1965.

Tuckett, C.M. 'The Beatitudes: A Source-critical Study with a reply by M.D. Goulder', *NT* 25 (1983) 193-216.

Turner, N. 'Q in Recent Thought', *ET* 80 (1968/69) 324-28.

Vassiliadis, P. 'The Nature and Extent of the Q-Document', *NT* 20 (1978) 49-73.

—'The Original Order of Q: Some Residual Cases', in Delobel, *Logia*, 379-87.

Wenham, D. (ed.). *Gospel Perspectives*, vol. 5: *The Jesus Tradition outside the Gospels*. Sheffield: JSOT, 1985.

Wifstrand, A. 'Stylistic Problems in the Epistles of James and Peter', *ST* 1 (1948) 170-82.

Wilckens, U. 'σοφία', *TDNT*, VIII (1971) 465-526.

Wilken, R.L. (ed.). *Aspects of Wisdom in Judaism and Early Christianity*. Notre Dame: University of Notre Dame Press, 1975.

Worden, R.D. 'The Q Sermon on the Mount/Plain: Variants and Reconstruction', in Richards (ed.), *Society of Biblical Literature 1983 Seminar Papers*, 455-71.

Wrege, H.T. *Die Überlieferungsgeschichte der Bergpredigt*. Tübingen: Mohr (Siebeck), 1968.

Wueller, W.H. 'Der Jakobusbrief im Licht der Rhetorik und Textpragmatik', *Linguistica Biblica* 43 (1978) 5-66.

Zeller, D. *Kommentar zur Logienquelle*. Stuttgart: Katholisches Bibelwerk, 1984.

INDEXES

INDEX OF ANCIENT REFERENCES

OLD TESTAMENT

Genesis
1.2   114
6.9   85
22   82
41.38-39   102
49   16

Exodus
31.3f.   102

Leviticus
19.17   181

Numbers
14.20-24   82

Deuteronomy
18.13   204
26.5-9   91
26.7   91
28.58   170
29.29   170
34.9   102

1 Chronicles
29.4   84

Job
5.11   185
22.29   185
29.12-13   22

Psalms
12.6   108

19.7   93
51.13   181
72.13   91
118.26   67
149.4   185

Proverbs
1.1– 9.18   55
1.7   39
1.8   36
2.6   102
3.34   42, 185
6.12   36
8   38, 116
8.1-6   116
8.4-5   127
8.22ff.   38
8.22-36   114
8.22-31   102
8.27   114
8.34-36   38
9.3   119
10.1–
22.16   55
10.19   37
17.27   42
21.8   108
22.17   55
25.1–
29.27   55
27.1   42
27.21   84
30.1   55
31.1   55

Qoheleth
3.11   41
7.14   41
8.17   41
11.5   41

Isaiah
5.8ff.   71
11.2ff.   103
11.2   102
61.1-3   148, 161
61.1   149

Jeremiah
29   236
29.7   236
31.31-36   107

Ezekiel
3.17-21   181
18.2   37
33.7-9   181

Amos
8.4   91

Zechariah
11.13   84

Malachi
3.5   22

APOCRYPHA

Wisdom of Solomon
2.4   43
2.10-20   43
2.10   91
2.13-18   129
2.17-19   83
4–5   129
6.5-10   209
6.17-20   92, 93
6.18-20   93, 209
7.7   87
7.15   87
7.24-27   102
7.27   118, 120
8.21   87
9.4   87, 102
9.5-10   93
9.5   86, 93
9.6   43, 86,
             88, 102
9.9-18   102
10   116
10.1-4   116
11.1   120

Sirach
1   116
1.1-10   42
1.1-4   102

1.1   87
1.14   39
1.26   87
1.27   42
2.1-6   83
2.17   185
4.10   22
4.17-18   83
6.23-31   92
7.10   87
10.7-18   42
10.10   42
10.23   91
11.16-17   42
13.21-23   90
15.11-20   43
17.3f.   43
17.11   87
17.31   43
18.15   87
19.6-12   42
19.20   170
20.5-8   42
20.14   87
20.18-20   42
22.27   42
24   116, 130
24.1-12   102
24.1-11   127

24.2   87
24.3   39
24.19   39
24.21   39
24.30-34   119
24.33-34   119
27.11   43
28.2-3   181
28.13-26   42
29.9-12   180
35[32].
  7-9   42
39.6   87
41.21   87
42.13   180
44.17   85
51   130
51.26-27   130, 211,
             212

Baruch
4.1-12   127

1–2 Maccabees
2.16   170
10.25ff.   32

NEW TESTAMENT

Matthew
2.1-23   232
3.1-6   123
3.7-12   123
4.1-11   123
5   114
5.1-12   162, 250
5.1   145, 147
5.3ff.   123
5.3-12   145-47,
             165, 247
5.3-6   151, 252

5.3   141, 144,
             148, 149,
             159
5.4   142, 144,
             148, 151
5.5   141, 144,
             148, 150,
             211, 212,
             214
5.6   39, 148,
             157, 159
5.7   110, 141,
             144, 148,

             152, 153,
             214
5.8   142, 144,
             148, 156,
             214, 249
5.9   112, 141,
             144, 148,
             154, 155,
             201, 214
5.10   148, 158,
             159

5.11-12	141, 142, 144, 148, 158, 161	7.3-5	146, 169	11.28-30	130, 134, 211, 212, 254
5.11	159, 201	7.6-14	146	11.28	39
5.13-37	146	7.7-11	173, 174, 176	11.29	211-13
5.12	160, 206			12.33-35	169
5.12c	76	7.7-8	141, 144, 178	12.34b-35	146
5.13-42	164	7.7	141, 144	12.36-37	198
5.16	207	7.11	141, 144, 175	12.38-42	131
5.17-20	207, 247	7.12	146, 169	12.39	142, 166, 183
5.17-19	207, 208	7.15-20	146	12.39b	131
5.17	208	7.16-20	146	12.40	131
5.18-19	141, 144, 182, 208	7.16-18	141, 144, 169	12.41f.	131
5.18	182, 207	7.16	110, 169	12.42	131
5.19	182, 207, 208	7.18	169	13.22	226
5.21-30	141, 165	7.21-27	146	13.24-30	197
5.21-22	144	7.21-23	198	15.14	146, 169
5.21	232	7.21	146, 169, 215	15.24	232
5.22	192, 250	7.24-27	146, 170	16.3	226
5.27-30	166	7.24	141, 144	16.4	183
5.33-37	188	7.26	141, 144	16.28	118
5.34-37	142, 144	7.28	146, 147	17.20	88
5.38-48	146	8.5-13	123	18.4	198
5.39b-41	145	8.19-22	123, 128	18.5	142, 181
5.40-47	164	9.35ff.	123	18.7	70
5.42	145	9.37f.	128	19.21	201, 203
5.43	165	9.37	226	21.5	212
5.44-48	201	10.5-6	232	21.21-22	88
5.44	145, 201	10.7-16	128	21.21	141, 196
5.45-47	145	10.13	226	22.5	226
5.45	201, 203	10.24-25	146, 169	22.8	226
5.48	141, 144, 146, 199, 200, 201, 203	10.40	128	22.34-40	210
		11.2-19	122-24	22.39-40	141
6	146	11.2	124	23.1-36	69
6.9-13	146	11.5	141	23.1-33	118
6.19-21	42, 142, 144, 179	11.16-19	122	23.4-29	163
6.24	142, 144, 183, 184	11.19	51, 122, 124, 134	23.12	142, 185, 198
		11.20	125	23.23	69
7.1-5	146	11.21-23	128	23.25-26	156
7.1-2	142, 144, 146, 167	11.25-30	130, 213	23.25	69
		11.25-27	128, 129, 134, 210	23.27	226
7.1	142, 144, 167, 168	11.25-26	128	23.28	226
		11.27	128	23.29-36	126

23.34-36	116, 121, 125, 127, 131, 132, 134	6.21	152, 157	7.18-35	122, 123
		6.21b	142	7.18-25	128
		6.22-23	141, 145, 158, 162	7.22	141
				7.29	125
23.24	117, 126	6.23	142, 145, 160, 206	7.31-35	122, 133
23.37-39	126			7.34	123
24.33	142, 168, 196	6.23c	76	7.35	51, 120, 122, 125, 128
		6.24-26	69, 146		
25.15	226	6.24-25	142		
25.31-46	191	6.24	163	8.8	193
25.34-35	141, 191	6.25	142, 151, 152, 163, 193	9.27	118
28.18-19	232			9.48	198
				9.57– 10.24	128
Mark		6.26	162		
4	55	6.27-36	146	9.57– 10.22	128
4.21-25	55	6.27-33	164		
4.22	41	6.27-28	145	9.57-60	123, 128
4.26-29	55, 197	6.28	201	9.58	128
4.30-32	55	6.29	145	10.1ff.	123
8.38	183	6.30	145	10.1-12	128
9.1	118	6.31	146, 169	10.1	221
9.42	70	6.32-35	145	10.13-15	128
11.23f.	196, 88	6.36	141, 145, 146, 152-54, 167, 201, 206	10.16	128
11.23	141			10.21-22	128, 133, 134, 210
12.28-34	141				
12.31	164			10.21	128
13.29	142, 168, 196	6.37-42	146	10.22	128
		6.37-38	142, 145, 146	10.27	141
Luke		6.37	142, 145, 167, 168	11.2-4	146, 174
2.40	103			11.9-13	173, 174, 176
3.1-6	123, 128	6.39-40	169		
3.7-9	123	6.39	146	11.9-10	141, 178
3.11	141, 191	6.40	146	11.9	141
3.16f.	123	6.41-42	146, 169	11.13	115, 141, 175
4.1-13	123	6.43-45	146, 169		
4.25	142, 193	6.43-44	141, 145, 146, 169	11.19	88
6.12	145			11.29-32	131
6.17	145	6.45	146	11.29	142
6.20ff.	123	6.46-49	146	11.29b	131
6.20-23	146, 162, 250	6.46-47	141, 145	11.30	131
		6.46	146	11.31f.	131
6.20-22	148	6.47-49	146, 170	11.31	131
6.20	141, 145, 149	6.49	141, 145	11.37-52	69
		7	125	11.37-48	118
6.20a	147	7.1-10	123	11.39	69
6.20b-23	145	7.1	147	11.43-47	163
6.21-25	151	7.1a	146		

11.49-51	116, 121, 127, 131, 132	9.57– 10.24	223	16.17	182, 184, 232	
11.49	117, 120	9.57-62	48	17.1-6	182	
11.51	118	9.57-60	223	17.1	69	
12.33-34	142, 179	10.2-11	48			
12.47	193	10.2	61	*John*		
13.31-33	126	10.3	61	2.19-21	229	
13.34-35	126	10.4	223	4.11	167	
13.34	127	10.12	74	16.24	178	
13.35	127	10.13-15	77	16.26	178	
14.11	142, 185, 198	10.13	69, 70			
16.13	142, 183, 184	10.16	48, 223	*Acts*		
		10.21-22	128, 133	4.1-3	237	
16.17	141, 182, 208	10.23	67	6.1-6	229	
17.1	70	11.2-4	48	6.3	103	
17.3	142, 181	11.4	178	11.2	227	
17.5	88	11.9-13	48	11.19-20	229	
18.3	193, 194	11.9	177	11.22-24	229	
18.14	142, 185	11.11-13	74	15	229	
22.26	198	11.13	74, 174	15.20	228, 231	
		11.24-26	74	15.23	228	
Q		11.29-32	74, 133	18.22	230	
6.20b-49	48	11.31-32	77			
6.20b	66	11.31	74, 77, 132	*Romans*		
6.21	66, 157			3.28	238	
6.22-23	66, 200, 224	11.34-36	74	12–13	165	
		11.39	69, 70	12.9	111	
6.27f.	200	11.42	69, 70	13.9	164, 209	
6.31	61	11.43	69			
6.37	61, 73	11.44	69	*1 Corinthians*		
6.38	61	11.46	69	1.10-13	101	
6.39	74	11.47	69, 70	1.18–		
6.40	61	11.49-51	118, 133	2.16	101	
6.41-42	74	11.52	69, 70	1.26ff.	91	
6.43-44	169	12.2-7	48	1.30	96	
6.45	61	12.11-12	48	2.6-8	96	
6.46	215	12.22b-		2.8	97	
6.47-49	74	31	48	2.10	105	
7.1-10	77	12.33-34	48	2.12	105	
7.18-35	123	12.39	74	2.14	105	
7.23	67	12.43	67	3.18-21	101	
7.28b	124	13.18-19	74	12.8	103	
7.31-35	123, 127	13.20-21	74	16.22	32	
7.33-35	133	13.34	117			
7.35	51, 122	13.35c	67	*2 Corinthians*		
		14.16-24	224	6.6	111	
		14.26	223	10.1	108	
		16.13	184	12.20	101	

Galatians
2.1-10   229
2.11-14   230
2.12   228
2.16   238
5   114
5.20   101
5.22ff.   103
5.22   107, 114
5.23   101
6.1   101, 181
6.18   95

Ephesians
1.1-2   26
1.3-14   26
1.4   91
1.15-17   26
1.17   96
2.4-5   109
3.10-12   96
4.2   101
6.24   95

Philippians
1.10-11   112
3.2   227

1 Thessalonians
5.14   181
5.23   32

1 Timothy
1.5   111

2 Timothy
1.5   111
2.25   101

Titus
1.1   16
3.2   101
3.5   109

Hebrews
10.25   235
13   19
13.17   100

James
1.1-4   88
1.1   15, 25, 26, 30, 77, 82, 245, 246
1.2-27   26, 30, 34, 245, 246
1.2-11   27, 28, 30, 34, 245, 246
1.2-8   81
1.2-4   27, 30, 31, 33, 34, 81, 82, 88, 200, 204, 245, 246
1.2-3   82, 83, 160
1.2   26, 63, 82, 141, 144, 145, 158, 160, 161
1.3-4   82
1.3   82, 85
1.4   63, 82, 85, 86, 141, 144, 199, 200, 204, 205
1.5-8   27, 30, 31, 34, 81, 86, 109, 173, 177, 245, 246
1.5   33, 43, 63, 86, 88, 95, 102, 115, 141, 144, 174, 234
1.6-8   87

1.6   63, 74, 75, 141, 177, 196
1.9-11   27, 29, 30, 34, 89, 236, 245, 246
1.9-10   185, 198
1.10   75
1.11   75
1.12-27   27, 28, 30, 245, 246
1.12-18   27, 30, 31, 33, 88, 206, 245, 246
1.12   32, 68
1.13-15   106
1.13-14   179
1.13   234
1.16   33
1.17-19   106
1.17   102, 106, 111, 141, 144, 174, 175, 204, 234
1.18   78, 106, 111, 115, 176, 213, 236
1.19-27   30, 63, 245, 246
1.19-21   27
1.19   32, 42, 63
1.20-21   30, 246
1.20   29, 101
1.21   101, 106, 111, 193, 212, 213
1.22-25   27, 30, 246
1.22   74, 141, 144, 145, 170, 207
1.23-24   75

1.23	141, 144, 145	2.11	141, 144, 165, 166, 182	3.15	99, 102, 104, 105, 106
1.25	68, 93, 170, 204, 207	2.12-13	89, 92, 93	3.16	62, 98
		2.12	93	3.17-18	97, 98, 101
1.26-27	30, 31, 110, 198, 246	2.13	62, 93, 141, 144, 145, 152, 153, 154	3.17	99, 102, 106, 107, 109, 110, 111, 112, 155, 176, 213, 214
1.27	22, 184				
2.1–5.6	30, 245, 246	2.14-26	30, 198, 245, 246		
2.1-13	29, 30, 81, 89, 134, 245, 246	2.14	63, 215	3.18	62, 99, 108, 112, 141, 144, 154, 155, 213
		2.15-17	75		
		2.15-16	141, 157, 191		
2.1-4	91	2.18-26	110	4.1-10	30, 31, 98, 99, 245, 246
2.1	16, 63, 89, 90, 93, 94, 96, 134, 209, 234, 241	2.18	100		
		2.19	234	4.1-4	99
		2.20	192	4.1	62, 99, 154, 166
		2.21	84, 238		
		2.22	204	4.2-3	141, 144, 176, 177
2.2-13	89	2.24	238		
2.2-6	236	2.26	62	4.2	165, 177
2.2-4	89, 90	3	114, 154	4.3	173, 177
2.2	75, 235	3.1-12	30, 31, 98, 198, 245, 246	4.4	74, 104, 142, 144, 166, 183, 184
2.5-13	89, 90				
2.5-7	90	3.1	63, 98, 234		
2.5-6a	89				
2.5	90, 141, 144, 145, 149, 150, 210	3.2	204	4.6	42, 185
		3.8	98	4.7-10	64, 99
		3.11	98	4.7-8	108
2.6	193, 194, 237	3.12	141, 144, 145, 169	4.8	142, 144, 156
2.6b-7	89, 91	3.13-18	30, 31, 74, 81, 97, 98, 99, 113, 210, 213, 245, 246	4.9	142, 144, 151, 152, 163, 193
2.7	92				
2.8-13	92			4.10	142, 185, 198
2.8-11	89, 92				
2.8	92, 141, 164, 167, 170, 191, 204, 207	3.13	97, 98, 99, 100, 101, 212	4.11-12	30, 31, 245, 246
		3.14-16	97, 98, 101, 106	4.11	142, 144, 145, 166, 167
2.9	209				
2.10	141, 144, 182, 207, 208	3.14	98, 101	4.13-17	30, 71, 245, 246

4.13-16	42	5.9	32, 78,	*1 Peter*	
4.13	71		142, 168,	1.3	109
4.14	43		196	1.7	83, 84
4.17	71, 193	5.10-11	160, 161	2.12	100
5.1-6	29, 30,	5.10	32, 78,	3.2	100
	71, 89,		142, 144,	3.15	101
	163, 236,		145, 158,	5.1	32
	245, 246		160, 161		
5.1	72, 142,	5.11	84, 154,	*2 Peter*	
	163		161, 167	3.12-14	32
5.2-3	141, 144,	5.12	33, 34,		
	179, 180		142, 144,	*1 John*	
5.3	72		188, 245,	5.14-21	33
5.4	234		246	5.14	177
5.5	72, 73,	5.13-20	33	5.15	178
	163	5.13-18	34, 245,	5.16	181
5.6	43, 142,		246		
	144, 145,	5.14	234	*Jude*	
	168	5.16	87	17-25	33
5.7-20	32, 34,	5.17	142, 193	18	32
	245, 246	5.19-20	34, 142,	21	32
5.7-11	31, 32,		181, 245,		
	34, 72,		246		
	88, 245,	5.19	33		
	246	5.20	64		
5.7	197				

QUMRAN

1QS		4.3-11	103
4	114	8.17f.	204

PSEUDEPIGRAPHA

1 Enoch		4.5-6	84	18.1	185
5.6-9	103	27.3-7	84		
42.1-3	127			*Jubilees*	
		Testament of Joseph		19.8	84
		2.7	84	23.10	85
Testament of Job		10.3	185		
1.5	84				

EARLY CHRISTIAN LITERATURE

1 Clement		*Hermas, Vis.*		Ignatius	
38.2	100	3.10.6	177	*Mg.*	
				15.1	110
Didache		*Hermas, Mand.*			
4.7	87	2.4.6	87	*Polycarp*	
		9.4	177	4.2	235
Eusebius		9.11	105		
Hist. Eccl.		11.6.		*Tr.*	
7.9.2	235	11-19	105	1.1	110
7.11.		11.8	103, 107,		
11-12	235		176	Justin	
7.11.17	235	11.9	235	*Dial.*	
		11.13	235	63.5	235
		11.14	235		

INDEX OF AUTHORS

Adamson, J.B. 106, 194

Bammel, E. 212
Bauckham, R. 48, 49, 147, 171, 187, 188
Beardslee, W.A. 45, 60
Bentzen, A. 118
Bertram, G. 210
Betz, H.D. 147
Biggs, H. 46, 47, 57
Black, M. 226
Blass, F. & A. Debrunner 124
Boring, M.E. 222
Brown, R.E. 59, 227, 240
Brown, R.E. & J.P. Meier 227, 228, 240
Brueggemann, W. 40
Büchsel, F. 167
Bultmann, R. 53, 54, 67, 109, 121, 162
Bussby, F. 226

Calvin, J. 15
Carrington, P. 21, 22
Carroll, K.L. 239, 240
Charlesworth, J.H. 83
Christ, F. 45, 119, 126, 130
Crenshaw, J.L. 36, 38
Cullmann, O. 124

Dahood, M. 119
Davids, P.H. 48, 83, 84, 87, 92, 94, 97, 98, 99, 100, 101, 105, 106, 107, 108, 109, 110, 111, 114, 115, 142, 143, 149, 152, 153, 155, 157, 158, 160, 161, 165, 168, 169, 170, 171, 176, 178, 181, 183, 185, 190, 193, 194, 195, 196, 197, 198, 240
Davies, W.D. 45, 53, 142, 200
Delling, G. 203, 204, 205

Deutsch, C. 130
Devisch, M. 56
Dibelius, M. 19, 20, 21, 23, 25, 26, 53, 62, 63, 71, 83, 84, 85, 86, 87, 88, 90, 93, 95, 98, 99, 100, 101, 102, 106, 108, 110, 111, 152, 154, 165, 168, 178, 184, 189, 190, 234, 235
Dillman, C.N. 43
Du Plessis, I.J. 125, 136, 203
du Toit, A.B. 24

Easton, B.S. 17
Edwards, R.A. 45, 51, 53, 60, 61, 66, 69, 70, 72, 79, 121
Exler, F.X.J. 24, 33

Farmer, W.R. 46
Farrar, A.M. 46
Fitzmyer, J.A. 25, 26, 27, 46, 47, 51, 145, 146, 159, 202
Foerster, W. 155
Francis, F. 25, 26, 27, 31, 32, 34
Frankemölle, H. 162
Funk, R.W. 24

Griesbach, J.J. 46
Grundmann, W. 84
Guelich, R.A. 151, 158, 164
Guillaumont, A. et al. 54

Haddas, M. 39
Haenchen, E. 229
Hartin, P.J. 24, 144, 148
Hauck, F. 65, 68, 108, 156
Hauck, F. & S. Schulz 212
Havener, I. 48, 50, 51, 79, 143, 145, 159, 160, 221, 222, 224
Hoffmann, P. 45, 53
Holmberg, B. 230

Hoppe, R. 13, 82, 83, 84, 95, 96, 97,
99, 104, 107, 112, 113, 175, 201,
202, 205, 208, 209

Jacobson, A.D. 45, 46, 48, 52, 69,
70, 74, 76, 120, 122, 123, 128, 130,
131, 146
Jeremias, J. 178
Johnson, M.D. 119, 120, 121

Kee, H.C. 45
Kelber, W. 222, 223, 224, 225
Kirk, J.A. 102, 107, 114, 115
Kittel, G. 140, 142, 150, 153, 165,
166, 168, 178, 216
Kloppenborg, J.S. 45, 48, 49, 51,
56, 58, 183, 186
Koester, H. 222
Kümmel, W.G. 46, 47, 52, 57

Lake, K. 235
Laws, S. 87, 104, 109, 112, 170, 190
Louw, J.P. 24
Lührmann, D. 53, 146
Luther, M. 14, 15
Luz, U. 149, 157

Manson, T.W. 162, 226
Massebieau, L. 15, 16, 17, 235
Mayor, J.B. 16, 42, 142, 237
McEleney, N. 151, 157, 158
McKenzie, J.L. 35, 59
Meier, J.P. 227, 229, 230, 231, 232,
233
Meyer, A. 16, 17, 235
Meyer, P.D. 45, 94
Meyer, R. 156
Michaelis, C. 151
Mitton, C.L. 153
Moffatt, J. 50
Murphy, R.E. 27
Mussner, F. 14, 86, 98, 106, 142,
178, 197, 200, 236

Neirynck, F. 50, 51

Oepke, A. 192
Ong, W.J. 222

Polag, A. 45, 48, 49, 50, 51, 53, 69,
70, 117, 122, 128, 131, 140, 143,
145, 149, 151, 154, 157, 159, 162,
167, 169, 173, 174, 175, 179, 181,
182, 183, 184, 185, 186, 200, 207,
208, 223
Price, J.L. 221

Rengstorf, K.H. 151
Roberts, J.H. 24, 26, 27
Robinson, J.M. 45, 50, 51, 53, 54,
55, 56, 57, 58, 59, 117, 122, 123,
130
Ropes, J.H. 17, 18, 19, 21, 42, 43,
75, 95, 105, 158, 191, 238
Rylaardsdam, J.C. 40, 103

Schneider, J. 189
Schroeder, D. 20
Schubert, P. 24, 25
Schulz, S. 45, 53, 130
Schürmann, H. 151, 162, 220
Schweizer, E. 105
Scott, R.B.Y. 36, 39
Shepherd, M. 23
Spitta, F. 15, 16, 17, 235
Stanton, G.N. 130
Steck, O.H. 45, 77
Strecker, G. 153
Suggs, M.J. 45, 117, 118, 119, 120,
121, 122, 127, 129, 212

Taylor, V. 46, 47, 51, 162
Theissen, G. 222, 223
Thrall, W.F. & A. Hibbard 52
Tödt, H.E. 45, 53
Turner, N. 226

Vassiliadis, P. 51, 226

Wilfstrand, A. 22
Wilckens, U. 60, 121, 124
Wilken, R.L. 60
Worden, R.D. 149, 154, 157

Zeller, D. 79

JOURNAL FOR THE STUDY OF THE NEW TESTAMENT

Supplement Series

1 THE BARREN TEMPLE AND THE WITHERED TREE
  William R. Telford
2 STUDIA BIBLICA 1978
  II. PAPERS ON THE GOSPELS
  Edited by E.A. Livingstone
3 STUDIA BIBLICA 1978
  III. PAPERS ON PAUL AND OTHER NEW TESTAMENT AUTHORS
  Edited by E.A. Livingstone
4 FOLLOWING JESUS
  DISCIPLESHIP IN MARK'S GOSPEL
  Ernest Best
5 THE PEOPLE OF GOD
  Markus Barth
6 PERSECUTION AND MARTYRDOM IN THE THEOLOGY OF PAUL
  John S. Pobee
7 SYNOPTIC STUDIES
  THE AMPLEFORTH CONFERENCE 1982 AND 1983
  Edited by C.M. Tuckett
8 JESUS ON THE MOUNTAIN
  A STUDY IN MATTHEAN THEOLOGY
  Terence L. Donaldson
9 THE HYMNS OF LUKE'S INFANCY NARRATIVES
  THEIR ORIGIN, MEANING AND SIGNIFICANCE
  Stephen Farris
10 CHRIST THE END OF THE LAW
  ROMANS 10.4 IN PAULINE PERSPECTIVE
  Robert Badenas
12 THE LETTERS TO THE SEVEN CHURCHES OF ASIA IN THEIR LOCAL
  SETTING
  Colin J. Hemer
13 JESUS AND THE LAWS OF PURITY
  TRADITION HISTORY AND LEGAL HISTORY IN MARK 7
  Roger P. Booth
14 THE PASSION ACCORDING TO LUKE
  THE SPECIAL MATERIAL OF LUKE 22
  Marion L. Soards
15 HOSTILITY TO WEALTH IN THE SYNOPTIC GOSPELS
  T.E. Schmidt
16 MATTHEW'S COMMUNITY
  THE EVIDENCE OF HIS SPECIAL SAYINGS MATERIAL
  S.H. Brooks

17 THE PARADOX OF THE CROSS IN THE THOUGHT OF ST PAUL
   A.T. Hanson
18 HIDDEN WISDOM AND THE EASY YOKE
   WISDOM, TORAH AND DISCIPLESHIP IN MATTHEW 11.25–30
   C. Deutsch
19 JESUS AND GOD IN PAUL'S ESCHATOLOGY
   L.J. Kreitzer
20 LUKE: A NEW PARADIGM
   M.D. Goulder
21 THE DEPARTURE OF JESUS IN LUKE–ACTS
   THE ASCENSION NARRATIVES IN CONTEXT
   M.C. PARSONS
22 THE DEFEAT OF DEATH
   APOCALYPTIC ESCHATOLOGY IN 1 CORINTHIANS 15 AND ROMANS 5
   M.C. De Boer
23 PAUL THE LETTER-WRITER
   AND THE SECOND LETTER TO TIMOTHY
   M. Prior
24 APOCALYPTIC AND THE NEW TESTAMENT
   ESSAYS IN HONOR OF J. LOUIS MARTYN
   Edited by J. Marcus & M.L. Soards
25 THE UNDERSTANDING SCRIBE
   MATTHEW AND THE APOCALYPTIC IDEAL
   D.E. Orton
26 WATCHWORDS
   MARK 13 IN MARKAN ESCHATOLOGY
   T. Geddert
27 THE DISCIPLES ACCORDING TO MARK
   MARKAN REDACTION IN CURRENT DEBATE
   C.C. Black
28 THE NOBLE DEATH
   GRAECO-ROMAN MARTYROLOGY AND
   PAUL'S CONCEPT OF SALVATION
   D. Seeley
29 ABRAHAM IN GALATIANS
   EPISTOLARY AND RHETORICAL CONTEXTS
   G.W. Hansen
30 EARLY CHRISTIAN RHETORIC AND 2 THESSALONIANS
   F.W. Hughes
31 THE STRUCTURE OF MATTHEW'S GOSPEL
   A STUDY IN LITERARY DESIGN
   D.R. Bauer
32 PETER AND THE BELOVED DISCIPLE
   FIGURES FOR A COMMUNITY IN CRISIS
   K.B. Quast

33 MARK'S AUDIENCE
    THE LITERARY AND SOCIAL SETTING OF MARK 4.11–12
    M.A. Beavis
34 THE GOAL OF OUR INSTRUCTION
    THE STRUCTURE OF THEOLOGY AND ETHICS IN THE PASTORAL
    EPISTLES
    P.H. Towner
35 THE PROVERBS OF JESUS
    ISSUES OF HISTORY AND RHETORIC
    A.P. Winton
36 THE STORY OF CHRIST IN THE ETHICS OF PAUL
    AN ANALYSIS OF THE FUNCTION OF THE HYMNIC MATERIAL
    IN THE PAULINE CORPUS
    S.E. Fowl
37 PAUL AND JESUS
    COLLECTED ESSAYS
    A.J.M. Wedderburn
38 MATTHEW'S MISSIONARY DISCOURSE
    A LITERARY CRITICAL ANALYSIS
    D.J. Weaver
39 FAITH AND OBEDIENCE IN ROMANS
    A STUDY IN ROMANS 1–4
    G.N. Davies
40 IDENTIFYING PAUL'S OPPONENTS
    THE QUESTION OF METHOD IN 2 CORINTHIANS
    J.L. Sumney
41 HUMAN AGENTS OF COSMIC POWER IN HELLENISTIC
    JUDAISM AND THE SYNOPTIC TRADITION
    M.E. Mills
42 MATTHEW'S INCLUSIVE STORY
    A STUDY IN THE NARRATIVE RHETORIC OF THE FIRST GOSPEL
    D.B. Howell
43 JESUS, PAUL AND TORAH
    COLLECTED ESSAYS
    H. Räisänen
44 THE NEW COVENANT IN HEBREWS
    S. Lehne
45 THE RHETORIC OF ROMANS
    ARGUMENTATIVE CONSTRAINT AND STRATEGY AND PAUL'S
    'DIALOGUE WITH JUDAISM'
    N. Elliot
46 THE LAST SHALL BE FIRST
    THE RHETORIC OF REVERSAL IN LUKE
    J.O. York

47 JAMES AND THE 'Q' SAYINGS OF JESUS
    Patrick J. Hartin
48 REFLECTIONS OF GLORY
    THE MOSES–DOXA TRADITION IN 2 CORINTHIANS 3.12-18
    Linda L. Belleville
49 PROLEPTIC PRIESTS
    AN INVESTIGATION OF THE PRIESTHOOD IN HEBREWS
    J.M. Scholer
50 PERSUASIVE ARTISTRY
    STUDIES IN NEW TESTAMENT RHETORIC
    IN HONOR OF GEORGE A. KENNEDY
    Edited by Duane F. Watson